DATE DUE

AP 7 '99			
AP 28 '99			
MY 17 '99			
NO 4 '99			
OC 18 '00			
AP 16 '01			
AP 28 '01			
MY 23 '01			
DE 2 '01			
JE 7 '05			

ELDER ABUSE

ELDER ABUSE
Practice and Policy

Edited by

Rachel Filinson, Ph.D.
Rhode Island College
Providence, Rhode Island

Stanley R. Ingman, Ph.D.
University of Missouri–Columbia
Columbia, Missouri

 *HUMAN SCIENCES PRESS, INC.*

Copyright © 1989 by Human Sciences Press, Inc.
A Subsidiary of Plenum Publishing Corporation
233 Spring Street, New York, N.Y. 10013

Printed in the United States of America

Library of Congress Cataloging in Publication Data

Elder abuse: practice and policy / edited by Rachel Filinson and
    Stanley R. Ingman.
        p.   cm.
    Bibliography: p.
    Includes index.
    ISBN 0-89885-415-6
    1. Aged abuse—United States.   2. Aged abuse—Government policy—
United States.   3. Abused aged—United States.   4. Abused parents—
United States.   I. Filinson, Rachel.   II. Ingman, Stanley R.
HV6626.3.E438   1988
362.6—dc19   87-29709
                                                                         CIP

In memory of H.C. Filinson

Contents

Contributors

Jeffrey M. Anderson, Ph.D.
Texas Department of Human Services

Trudy B. Anderson, Ph.D.
University of North Carolina at Greensboro

Georgia J. Anetzberger, Ph.D.
Case Western Reserve University

L. Rene Bergeron, M.S.W., A.C.S.W.
Community Council of Senior Citizens

James A. Bergman, J.D.
Healthways Foundations, Inc.

Deborah Bookin, M.S.S.A.
Private consultant

Arline Cowell, R.N., P.A.N.
Highland General Hospital

Richard A. Dodder, Ph.D.
Oklahoma State University

Ruth E. Dunkle, Ph.D.
University of Michigan

Rachel Filinson, Ph.D.
Rhode Island College

Terry Fulmer, Ph.D., R.N.
School of Nursing, Columbia University

Michael W. Galbraith, Ed.D.
University of Missouri-Columbia

Bette Hill, Ph.D.
University of Akron

Melanie Hwalek, Ph.D.
SPEC Associates, Inc.

Stanley R. Ingman, Ph.D.
University of Missouri-Columbia

Madelyn Anne Iris, Ph.D.
Metropolitan Chicago Coalition on Aging

Sarah H. Matthews, Ph.D.
Case Western Reserve University

Sharon R. Medved, M.H.S.A.
University of Michigan School of Public Health

Richard B. Miller, Ph.D.
Missouri Southern State College

Linda R. Phillips, Ph.D., M.N.
University of Arizona College of Nursing

Valerie Rinkle, M.P.A.
University of California, San Francisco Medical Center

Sue Ringel Segal, M.A., C.S.W.
Northwest Service Coordination for
the Health Impaired Elderly

Jetse Sprey, Ph.D.
Case Western Reserve University

Caroline Stahl, B.S.
Illinois Department on Aging

Toshio Tatara, Ph.D.
American Public Welfare Association

John T. Theiss, Ph.D.
Texas Department of Human Services

Marshelle Thobaben, R.N., M.S., F.N.P.
Humboldt State University

C. Edwin Vaughan, Ph.D.
University of Missouri-Columbia

Part I

RESEARCH FOUNDATIONS

Chapter 1

INTRODUCTION

Rachel Filinson

The research on elder abuse is sparse, methodologically weak, and theoretically insubstantial—yet elder abuse has been defined and legitimatized as a social problem within a short period of time, and the collective recognition of elder abuse as a matter of public responsibility has been triggered. Because the lack of empirical work is an intrinsically significant feature of the transformation of elder abuse into a social issue, the implications for practice and policy in light of the paucity of sound data are considerable. This chapter introduces the central theme of the book—the relationship between policy development in the area of elder abuse, its implementation, and the research base—and lays the groundwork for the subsequent chapters, which elaborate on this theme.

In considering the construction of social knowledge and the generation of social policy regarding elder abuse, analogies with other forms of domestic violence, namely child abuse and wife battering, are instructive. Like child abuse or wife battering, the discovery of elder abuse and its conceptualization as a social issue were not primarily the result of the emergence or escalation of the problem. Whether we look to Shakespeare's

King Lear or to homicide statistics, the evidence suggests that elder abuse is not a new phenomenon, though the magnitude of the problem is likely to increase as a greater proportion of the population reaches old age. In effect, awareness of abuse was not stimulated by changes in incidence or prevalence, but rather by changes in attitudes. As the women's movement has been credited with fostering recognition of wife abuse, so has the rise of champions for the aged—as well as the snowballing effects of investigations in other areas of abuse—encouraged the transformation of elder abuse into a social problem worthy of state intervention.

The ripeness of the social climate for attention to the problem of elder abuse is manifest when one juxtaposes the exponential growth of legislative and policy responses to the poverty of research studies. Findings from the sparse literature on abuse have been widely disseminated and, it would appear, rapidly translated into law.

In 1980, joint Congressional hearings on abuse concluded with recommendations for the introduction of adult protective service laws and the establishment of a National Center of Adult Abuse. The majority of states have subsequently adopted a number of the proposed elements of the model law, including mandatory reporting, a focus on investigation, a voluntaristic strategy of service delivery for the elderly, a preference given to a least-restrictive type of intervention policy, and mechanisms for court-ordered emergency interventions for mentally incompetent abused elderly. The plea for legal provisions by Congress resulted from hearing anecdotal evidence provided by abused persons and professionals encountering abuse. In retrospect, it is significant to find out that the Congress's estimate of between one-half million and 2½ million abused elder persons in the U.S. was extrapolated from epidemiological studies at a state level, such as the one conducted in Maine and New Hampshire. The study (U.S. House of Representatives, 1980) documented a total of 29 elder abuse citings from the caseloads of 51 community health nurses. Like other epidemiological studies that were to follow, the Maine/New Hampshire study depended on the recall of caseloads by social service staff rather than on a representative sample of elderly persons themselves. The estimate reached by Congress and repeated subsequently seems unreliably high when considered against a unique study based on a probability sample (cited by Hwalek, Sengstock & Lawrence, 1984) that predicted a 1% risk rate. The Congress also concluded from early studies that physical abuse was the most prevalent form of abuse. Although it is probably the form of abuse most memorable to professionals, other studies have failed to confirm that it is the most common form of abuse (cf. Douglass, 1983; Ghent, DaSylva, & Farren, 1985).

In addition, vital parts of the critical testimony have since been refuted by other studies. Claims that women are most-likely perpetrators of abuse and that perpetrators are likely to be old themselves, suggestions that caregivers are themselves former victims of abuse who perpetuate a familial cycle of violence, and the depiction of victims of physical violence as vulnerable, impaired persons dependent on caregivers have not been borne out by more thorough research (cf. Sengstock & Liang, 1982; Wolf, Godkin and Pillemer, 1984). Nevertheless, laws were drafted based upon these and other assumptions about the nature of elder abuse.

Following congressional hearings, the Administration on Aging (AoA) gave priority to elder abuse research, and two projects were launched by Block and Sinnott in Maryland (1979) and by Hickey and Douglass at the University of Michigan Institute of Gerontology (1981a, 1981b). The first study surveyed professionals about their experience of abuse, and followed up a sample of cases. The Michigan study also surveyed professionals, added an overview of available services, and looked at reported crimes against the elderly using statistics of the Detroit Police Department (statistics that are not uniformly collected in states with mandatory reporting laws). These two studies have become the most frequently cited in the literature concerned with the incidence of elder abuse, its definition, and the characteristics of abuse victims. According to Cronin and Allen (1982), who traced the use of AoA-sponsored research on abuse, both projects have served to legitimatize the elder abuse issue and to facilitate intervention. They argue that the research itself did not have direct impact on policy, but rather that the impetus came from policymakers, who used the results to help define the problem or justify the extent of proposed intervention—in this way, explaining the rapid dissemination of findings and their translation into law.

Pedrick-Cornell and Gelles, in 1982, pointed out the serious methodological flaws of these few existing empirical studies, which were used as a basis for implementing new laws. Both AoA studies as well as a Cleveland study (Lau & Kosberg, 1979) that is commonly reviewed, are surveys of practitioners and professionals who were assumed likely to have come into contact with abused adults and who were questioned about their experience with abuse. These studies were obviously skewed because they include only abuse victims who come to the attention of social workers, police, physicians, lawyers, and the like. They were also biased because of the reliance on the memory of professional workers: Only those victims were reported who were remembered by the workers when they filled out the survey. The Maryland study attempted to complete individual case report forms but was unsuccessful. Pedrick-Cornell and Gelles (1982) attribute the failure to confusion over what is meant by the term *case*. The main confusion concerned whether a case means every abused person seen by the professional or simply any event of abuse. In addition, some of the surveyed professionals, particularly ministers, did not use the concept of case in their work. This indicates a limitation of the data, namely that duplicate cases could not be identified. Persons abused more than one time and/or seeking the help of more than one agency would tend to be counted twice by this method of surveying professionals.

Various researchers of elder abuse have also pointed out that the type of abuse documented tends to be related to the type of agency or professional reporting the abuse. Thus health care professionals have focused on physical abuse, and their assessment tools—published in nursing and emergency care journals—center around physical manifestations of abuse. Social service agencies, in contrast, have most often uncovered financial exploitation, psychological abuse, or neglect (Hickey & Douglass, 1981b). Adding to the inconsistency in the type of abuse reported are differences in response rates between different types of agencies. Anderson and colleagues (1984), conducting a mail survey of professionals in Texas, admit to variations in response rate ranging from 12% to 91%, depending on what profession was represented.

Although the above assessment indicates that the bias of agency samples is likely to lead to overestimates of elder abuse, the consensus among field researchers and concerned professionals has been that abuse is grossly underreported (cf. Floyd, 1984; Henton, Cate, & Emery, 1984). The reasons given for this are many: that elderly fear retaliation or are ashamed of family members and do not report abuse; that ageist professionals ignore abuse or mistake abuse for normal aging; that there is little incentive for intervention because there are few solutions that can be offered anyway. Yet in a study by Galbraith and Zdorkowski (1984a), practitioners, who were asked to fill out abuse-assessment forms as they would most typically expect it to occur, assumed the existence of more physical abuse than actually takes place. Figures from New Jersey (Eggers, 1985), which show that only 37% reported abuse cases are found to be valid, may also demonstrate that underreporting may not be the major problem it is believed to be.

The main studies on elderly abuse were based on a very small number of cases. The Cleveland study and the Maryland study have 39 and 26 cases respectively. Moreover, the studies of abuse have suffered from poor response rates. In the Maryland study, for instance, no more than one-fifth of the professionals surveyed responded. The generalizability of the findings is therefore suspect.

The early studies did not use comparison control groups, yet they concluded that the typical victim was 75 or older, white, female, physically impaired, and/or financially dependent on their relatives. Given that the largest subset of the elderly population consists of white females, the results were not helpful in predicting the vulnerability to abuse. Cazenave (1981) has indicated that the greater risk of abuse among whites remains at odds with the risk factors typically related to abuse. It has been widely hypothesized that the correlates of abuse are poverty, social isolation, multigenerational households, substance abuse, and stressful living conditions (cf. Chen, Bell, Dolinsky,

Doyle, & Dunn, 1982; U.S. House of Representatives, 1981c). Cazenave points out that if these are correlates of abuse, and predictive of it, then blacks should be at a greater risk of abuse than whites. If he is correct, we have even greater reason to be wary of the epidemiological data on which we have had so far to rely.

Overarching the methodological problems is the definitional confusion surrounding abuse. Abuse need not mean physical abuse only. Abuse can include verbal abuse, emotional deprivation, financial exploitation, or general neglect. The problem is that we often do not know exactly what kind of abuse is being described in the studies. Violation of rights, for example, may be a major category in one study, whereas in other studies such instances may be divided up and classified under such categories as material abuse, medical abuse, exploitation, sexual abuse, deprivation, or even psychological abuse or neglect. Definitional variation is a problem on two levels. First, we do not know how the professional conceptualized abuse when responding to a questionnaire or recording a case in empirical studies. Phillips and Rempusheski's (1985) study of decision making by professionals in reporting abuse provides a unique insight into the institutional, situational, and personal factors that have an impact on the decision to define a case as abuse. They discovered that commonsense assumptions about abuse were given priority over objective measures by which abuse was to be detected. For example, practitioners were loath to identify as abuse those cases where the abuse was not perceived as intentional, where the victim was seen to be at fault, or where barriers to intervention were regarded as insurmountable. Thus the hidden nature of abuse may not be the result of elderly fear but rather of practitioner perception of the problem.

Secondly, types of abuse have often not been specified in studies. There has been a great deal of ambiguity about the definitions of abuse employed from one study to another, and this makes it difficult to compare one investigation with another.

Definitions of abuse are made further confusing because sometimes the focus has been on adult abuse including incidents to anyone over the age of 21 whereas in other cases, the focus has been on older adults only, starting at ages 60, 65 or even older. Overall, because of the definitional variation, findings on the type of abuse that is most prevalent have varied. The pattern of abuse is made even more complex because many abuse cases have involved multiple forms of abuse.

There has been inconsistency surrounding the distinction made between abuse (acts of commission) and neglect (acts of omission), with not all researchers, practitioners, or policymakers making the distinction or making the distinction in the same way. Even though the injury sustained from an act of neglect may be as serious as one from an act of abuse, and crosscut physical, psychological, and other categories of abuse, the differentiation reflects the different motivation for victimization. Consequently, the appropriate response of practitioners and policymakers will be affected by the categorization of an act as one of abuse versus one of neglect. As stated, although in some instances the distinction between active neglect, passive neglect, and self-neglect has been made, it has not been uniformly applied.

The recent work of the O'Malley research team (O'Malley, O'Malley, Everitt, & Sarson, 1984) concludes that dissimilar phenomena have been subsumed under the concept of elder abuse. Their findings revealed 3 distinct categories of abuse, each requiring a different type of intervention. The first category consists of impaired elderly whose needs have been neglected for a short time due to the weariness of the caregiver (the type that has been emphasized in the earliest literature). The solution for these victims has been deployment of services to buttress the overwhelmed caregiver. The second category consists of impaired individuals who are not dependent on a family caregiver, despite their impairment, who tend to be financially exploited and psychologically abused. The abuse is long term, and successful resolution often requires getting assistance for the impaired person, separating the elderly person from the caregiver, and/or treating the pathologies of the abuser. The third category consists of independent elderly persons who are physically, psychologically, or financially abused by family members who are not caregivers. Again, separation and therapy of the abuser are needed, but not services to the older persons. A study by Wolf, Godkin, and Pillemer (1984) came up with a similar typology.

Although descriptive and exploratory surveys have dominated the research on elder abuse, with few studies aimed at causal-model testing (Hudson, 1986), theory on elder abuse has proliferated. The theoretical richness is owed to the heavy borrowing from the literature on family violence. Theories have been characterized by the diversity found in the family-violence literature, ranging from an emphasis on the pathological traits of the victim and the perpetrator to the societal components of ageism, a culture of violence, and structural problems such as unemployment and poverty. Researchers have particularly stressed the parallels between the dependent elderly adult, one who is mentally and physically impaired, and the child, in supporting the heuristic value of these family-violence models. Steinmetz, for example, in congressional hearings, depicted victims of physical violence as vulnerable impaired persons dependent on caregivers (U.S. House of Representatives, 1981b). The underlying premise of her model is a conflict perspective on the family in which individual needs and assertiveness must be delicately balanced against family stability. The difference between a normal and pathological family is therefore only a matter of degree, crossing a threshold when individual needs or desires impair family equilibrium. This theme pervades the literature on the family and the aged. Brody's (1981) characterization of the woman "caught in the middle," the middle-aged woman torn between competing obligations to herself, to her nuclear family, and to an older relative suggests similarly that crisis is always imminent, and tensions are always just beneath the surface of smooth family relations.

In determining the adequacy of this theoretical model for elder abuse, we can first consider its adequacy within the domain for which it was initially developed. Wardell, Gillespie, and Leffler (1983) have maintained that the domestic-violence model espouses a misogynist view of the abuse incident by focusing on the shortcomings of the victim in her familial role and on her complicity in perpetuating and hiding the event. When the model is applied to elder abuse, we find the same emphasis on the characteristics of the victim being used to explain the violent event and its invisibility. The characterization is an ageist and stereotypical one, and one that does not square with the most rigorous studies using control groups. The study of three model projects in New York, Massachusetts, and Rhode Island (Wolf et al., 1984) found that abuse victims were less cognitively and functionally impaired than the control group. Similarly, O'Malley, O'Malley, Everitt, and Sarson (1984), examining cases of the Health Care Center of Massachusetts General Hospital, found that abuse was rare among those elderly persons who were impaired and received extensive caregiving from relatives. Both the Wolf and the O'Malley teams found physical abuse to be related to the pathology of the perpetrator and correlated with the younger family member's dependence, including financial dependence on the older person—not the reverse. The view of elder abuse as involving primarily frail, dependent elderly has serious implications for policy, and if this view is invalid, it promotes inappropriate policy responses. This view advances an argument that existing assault laws are insufficient because frail, dependent, elderly persons cannot avail themselves of the benefits of legal protection from their family persecutors, and that professionals require increased statutory power to act in their interests.

Stark and Flitcraft (1983) among others have further criticized the family-violence model for its faulty operationalization. It has been devised, they assert, in order to confirm an image of the family as a cradle of violence while simultaneously leveling the institutionalized gender differences that exist in the use of violence. By lumping together threats and arguments with physical violence, and ignoring the different consequences of these acts, the leading exponents of the family-violence model have claimed that violence perpetrated by females is equivalent to that perpetrated by males. When the model is applied to elder abuse, we find the same tendency to reject the systematic bases for subordination in the family as well as the gender-based differences in power and the use of violence. The testimony in Congressional hearings, for example, posited that females are likely perpetrators of violence against relatives. When abuse is disaggregated according to type, however, as Sengstock and Liang (1982) and Giordano (1982) did in their respective studies, it is found that physical abuse is correlated with a male perpetrator as is multiple abuse.

The lack of congruence between the theoretical model and recent data is significant because it suggests that the model may be of limited utility when applied to a concept that is as elusive, ambiguous, and multidimensional as elder abuse. The complexity of the elder abuse phenomenon and the various motivations and circumstances for abuse suggest that a multifaceted approach to dealing with the problem is needed. Where abuse is intentional, punitive measures may be indicated. Where abuse is more a matter of neglect, including self-neglect, services rather than punishment or separation of the elder from the caregiver are indicated. Unfortunately, state laws have not always recognized the diversity of the elder abuse concept when framing laws in response to the problem, nor has the family-violence model guided policy uniformly. A 1984 Kentucky law, for example, does not seek to prosecute abusers (Tamme, 1985), although in the experience of dealing with spouse abuse, it has been shown that punishment through arrest and imprisonment has lowered recidivism and may be necessary in those cases where abusers are not responsive to therapy. Indiana, by contrast, considers the county prosecutor to be integral in implementation of the abuse law, which is not likely to be warranted when abuse arises from caregiver stress.

The inadequacy of the laws reflects not only the paucity of data on which laws were spawned but also the lack of funding for increased services to accompany the new statutes. In a study of the Rhode Island agency implementing a mandatory abuse law, for example, Wolf, Godkin, and Pillemer (1984) found that the investigation of cases, rather than directly or indirectly providing any of the interventions necessary, monopolized most of agency time. In other words, the passage of elder abuse laws has not guaranteed improvement in service delivery to abuse victims.

We are at a critical juncture in the elder abuse field. While Callahan (1986) has referred to elder abuse as a dying nonissue that is no longer saleable to politicians, we nevertheless find that an apparatus for responding to abuse has been established in a vast majority of states, and practitioners have been mandated to detect abuse and implement the law. Moreover, although this band-aid approach to dealing with elder abuse has been soundly criticized, there is little reason to believe that policy will move toward dealing with the larger issue underlying it, namely, a lack of formal services that could reduce caregiver stress and enable the elderly to continue to live independently. With cost-containment policies (e.g., Diagnostic Related Groups) providing incentives for hospitals to discharge patients one or two days earlier, there is evidence that informalization of care is occurring: that the formal home care, hospice, adult day care, and other health and social services are not expanding to meet the challenge of deinstitutionalization of the elderly to the community. Just as the deinstitutionalization of mental health care did not result in an adequate community care response, we may expect that the informalization of care of the aged will only exacerbate caregiver burden and insufficient service to frail elderly at risk (Estes, 1987; Newcomer, Wood, & Sanker, 1985).

Our purpose here will be to examine the practice tools and policy initiatives that have been formulated in response to what are now universally regarded as faulty theoretical premises and poor research. In examining the data currently being generated by practitioners and through the data collection systems instituted by state law, we will illustrate that the evidence further calls into question the original research findings that stimulated the practice and policy in the first place. We will also consider how the issue of elder abuse may be more soundly reformulated and the response to it more appropriately redesigned in light of the accumulating evidence.

The book is organized into three parts. Part I provides an overview of the early research studies that were instrumental in crystallizing a programmatic response to elder abuse, a critique of the shortcomings of the research, an exploration of the theoretical foundations of the policy that eventually evolved, and the findings of recent studies that contradict the earliest research.

In Chapter 2, Galbraith reviews comprehensively the definitional, methodological, and theoretical shortcomings of elder abuse research. He point outs that definitional confusion has prevented the comparison and integration of studies; unrepresentative and localized sampling has prevented their generalizability; and the lack of empirical verification of theories of abuse through research has prevented further theoretical advancement. The consequences for practitioners and policymakers is that they are obliged to act and speak at cross-purposes because the disparate definitions of the phenomenon hinder consensus. The legislation that was hurriedly passed as a result of the meager research efforts gives an illusory sense of progress, Galbraith maintains, while it overlooks the larger problems that contribute to abuse.

Anetzberger (Chapter 3), using data from a unique study of perpetrators of elder abuse, questions the fundamental premises about abuse that have circulated widely and influenced practice and policy. Her study's findings suggest that perpetrator pathology and perceived social isolation, rather than caregiver stress, victim dependency, and a history of family violence are the correlates of abuse. She concludes that the abused elderly would be better served by intervention strategies organized through multiple-service systems (not just the protective-service system) that detect and treat the pathology of the perpetrator.

Sprey and Matthews, in Chapter 4, contend that elder abuse arose as a "folk category" of limited conceptual utility because age per se is inadequate to explain causally the variety of phenomena subsumed under it. The domestic violence approach, which has dominated the field, is useful for only a few of the faces of elderly mistreatment, because it is unable to explain the modal type of abuse, self-neglect. There is a tendency to concentrate on developing scientific files of the individuals involved in abuse cases rather than on understanding the destructive relationships that cause them. Given the lack of sound empirical basis and a sense of causality, as well as the dangers of applying the pseudo-scientific profiles, Sprey and Matthews suggest augmenting the meager social science input with a generous dose of common sense from professionals. The remaining parts of the book attempt to do just that.

In Part II, perspectives from the nursing, legal and social

work professions on the difficulties encountered by practitioners in recognizing and responding to abuse are presented. In Chapter 5, Bookin and Dunkle assert that assessment of abuse cases is complicated by the effects of practitioners' personal views of the appropriate use of force within the family, ageist attitudes, varied professional standards, perceptions of the situation that are at odds with those of the older adult, and misinterpretations of the situation by persons reporting abuse to the authorities. Although the passage of legislation has improved the visibility of and access to elder abuse cases, uncertain guidelines, inadequate funds for services, and a lack of understanding of the protective-service worker's role by professionals and the community hinder the uncovering and processing of cases.

Fulmer (Chapter 6) in a similar vein, describes the dilemma of practitioners who are mandated to implement laws that vary substantially from state to state, yet must make critical decisions without the guidance of effective protocols for the assessment of elder abuse. She explains that the effects of normal aging and of chronic health conditions associated with aging may be indistinguishable from those of abuse or neglect. As a result, a thorough history, provided by the elder—which is not always available—and a consideration of all potential causes of an injury are essential parts of the assessment procedure.

Phillips, in Chapter 7, elaborates further on the ambiguities of case detection and intervention, suggesting that practitioners have been misled by the invalid parallels that have been drawn between elder abuse and child abuse. Unlike child abuse, elder abuse does not typically involve a clear-cut perpetrator:victim dyad. Once abuse has been identified, the practitioner, with a scarcity of alternatives to offer the elder, must choose from an uneasy mixture of legal and therapeutic interventions. Phillips encourages practitioners to recognize the limitations of the law and their own biases in interpreting it.

In Chapter 8, Bergman, one of the pioneering researchers of abuse, acknowledges that interventions must be designed so that they are able to accommodate the diversity of abuse cases that confront the practitioner. He explains that abuse cases differ greatly in terms of the competence of the victim, the extent to which crisis or chronicity *characterizes* the abuse, the willingness of the victim to allow intervention, and the seriousness of the abuse. In the model for intervention he has designed, the nature of the appropriate response is contingent upon which combination of these four factors applies.

Segal and Iris (Chapter 9) focus on the challenge to practitioners of simultaneously protecting the vulnerable abuse victim's individual rights while keeping the family unit intact whenever possible. Developed from a demonstration project tested in the state of Illinois, their strategy calls for combining a family systems approach with a range of legal interventions.

Anderson, in Chapter 10, examines the practitioner's role from the outside rather than from the inside, and explores interprofessional differences in recognizing and tackling elder abuse. In a comparative study of physicians, nurses, social workers, clergy, police officers, and lawyers, she found differences between occupational groups in their exposures to elder abuse and in their perceptions of its prevalence.

Part III addresses policy—both its process and effects—at the federal, state, and to a lesser extent, local level. In Chapter 11, Rinkle traces the recent trend in federal initiatives in elder abuse over 10 years. She highlights the ongoing debate over whether legal devices should be fashioned after the domestic violence model or the child abuse model, which presumes an incompetent victim who is dependent on a stressed, abusive caregiver for survival. Most recent policy has moved away from the child abuse model and has favored a concentration on the overarching causes of abuse, namely, a lack of resources to sustain older adults independently in the community.

Thobaben (Chapter 12) presents an overview of state elder abuse law, with respect to eleven basic components. She outlines the features of a model law, originally formulated in early Congressional reports on elder abuse but which are not currently embodied in any single state law, and discusses those features about which there is the greatest controversy.

The diversity described in Thobaben's overview is in Chapter 13 reflected in Tatara's investigation of the national incidence of abuse through the assembly of data collected by states with elder abuse laws. Because definitions of abuse in state laws ranged from those including self-abuse/neglect and institutional abuse/neglect to those including only reports of abuse/ neglect by informal caregivers in domestic settings, it was not possible to calculate a single estimate of incidence. Instead, it was necessary to categorize states into 4 groups according to definitions of abuse in the law, and to examine each such group separately. The rates of incidence obtained in this manner vary, depending on how broadly or narrowly abuse is defined within each state, and, according to Tatara, are likely to be underestimates.

In Chapter 14, Miller and Dodder, relying on data collected in a single state, Florida, discover a pattern of abuse discrepant from the pattern that had been documented in earlier studies and rapidly disseminated. In their analysis of a state-wide data set from a period of 4½ years, they distinguish between abuse, which is intentional and involves a perpetrator, and neglect, which need not be intentional nor involve a perpetrator. Applying the distinction, they found that neglect, particularly self-neglect, was more prevalent than abuse; that male relatives were more likely the perpetrators of physical abuse than were female relatives; and that women were more at risk of abuse and neglect, particularly abuse, than were men. These findings indicate that, contrary to the views held in the field, a large proportion of elder abuse does not implicate perpetrators, and physical abuse tends to be a crime committed by male relatives against females.

The salience of self-neglect in the Miller and Dodder study of elder abuse illustrates that elder abuse is a phenomenon created by the very programs and data-collection systems meant to identify and enumerate it. This is substantiated by Vaughan's comparison of Iowa and Missouri (Chapter 15), in which he documents elder-abuse incidence rates in Iowa that are one-tenth of those in Missouri. This enormous disparity is attributed to the Iowa elder abuse program's incorporation into adult protective services under the aegis of a human services department—whereas Missouri developed a unit of 200 + staff to focus exclusively on elder mistreatment, administered by an autonomous Division of Aging and funded by discretionary Block Grant assistance. Vaughan's analysis documents that although states may borrow from one another the content of their elder abuse programs or legislation, the ultimate form introduced into a state depends on how the programs and legislation are grafted onto an existing aging network and human-service delivery system.

Hwalek, Hill and Stahl, in Chapter 16, examine the evolution of state elder abuse law in Illinois. The Illinois experience is unique on three counts. First, four demonstration projects were launched and evaluated before any legislation on abuse was passed. Second, the focus of the law, devised subsequent to evaluation, shifts away from simply investigating and documenting abuse by featuring voluntary rather than mandatory reporting; treatment of the family, not the victim alone; and the availability of supplemental services to be deployed in emergency cases, or where community services are insufficient. Third, self-neglect cases are not dealt with directly by the protective-service system but are instead referred to designated agencies.

Medved's analysis (Chapter 17) of the process by which Michigan responded to increased awareness of elder abuse may serve as a microcosm for what happened elsewhere in the country. She attributes both the rapidity with which the law was passed and its subsequent weakness to the concern with elder abuse being widely shared, but only as a peripheral interest to a number of groups. Thus, even though there was general support for the transition of elder abuse from a vague problem to an urgent one worthy of attention, the continuing stimulus that would give an elder abuse statute teeth and direction after enactment failed to materialize.

Chapter 18, by Bergeron, on the elder abuse law in New Hampshire, also considers the limitations of a state law, but from a different angle than Medved's. Bergeron contends that there are unrealistic expectations about the capacity of the law to empower practitioners to intervene successfully in abuse cases in a meaningful way. She argues that the law cannot actually achieve what is typically expected of it because its effective operation depends on the coordination of a network of service providers over whom the protective-service system has no direct control. Bergeron describes a locally based task force of service providers cooperating to improve and expand service delivery to abused elders while remaining within the confines of the law.

Anderson and Theiss's review (Chapter 19) of the 1985 legislative response in Texas to sensationalized accounts of elder abuse highlights the oversimplification of the proposed solution that emphasized a criminal justice approach and enactment of a filial responsibility statute. A key informant survey, which collected information from over 1,000 professionals representing 10 professional groups, was able to alter the ultimate policy decision so that funding for services was increased, in the face of overall budget cuts, rather than punitive measures augmented. Anderson and Theiss underline the vital role played by the Gray Panthers in encouraging that research be carried out before the initial policy decision was implemented. In the area of elder abuse, the wariness with which grassroots senior advocates such as the American Association of Retired Persons (AARP) (Lee Pearson, personal communication, March, 1986) have scrutinized the flourishing legislative activity is notable.

In Chapter 20, Cowell summarizes the efforts of a state commission in California (to which she presented testimony) to formulate and enact recommendations that would eradicate abuse of the aged in institutions. Within the 5-year time period she covers, we find that, like a many-headed hydra, new obstacles to the eradication of abuse appear as soon as others are removed. Cowell accounts for the endless barriers as indications that legislation alone cannot bring about change. She proposes that legislation must be coupled with volunteer initiatives consisting of laypersons and professionals, nursing home industry representatives and regulators, residents and staff, working jointly to identify and to attempt to solve the problems of elder abuse.

ACKNOWLEDGMENTS

Support for this chapter, and for the development of ideas for this volume, was provided by a 1986 Summer Faculty

Award to Rachel Filinson, funded through the Chancellor's Council of Purdue University Calumet, Hammond, Indiana.

Dr. Ingman would like to extend his appreciation to the Institute for Health and Aging, University of California-San Francisco, and the PEW Mid-Career Health Policy Fellowship Program at the University of California-San Francisco, for their support of this volume in 1986 and 1987.

Chapter 2

A CRITICAL EXAMINATION OF THE DEFINITIONAL, METHODOLOGICAL, AND THEORETICAL PROBLEMS OF ELDER ABUSE

Michael W. Galbraith

Since the first elder abuse studies appeared in the literature in the 1970s, the investigations and interest of researchers, policymakers, and practitioners concerning the issue has grown steadily. Individuals from various disciplines such as social service (Callahan, 1982; Langley, 1981), health care (Ferguson & Beck, 1983; Galbraith & Zdorkowski, 1984a), law (Katz, 1980; Kapp & Bigot, 1985), and adult education (Galbraith & Zdorkowski, 1984b) have publicly acknowledged and formally accepted elder abuse as a matter of social concern. In addition to the voluminous accounts of elder abuse in the professional journals, state and agency reports, and conference proceedings, a number of books on the topic from various perspectives have appeared as well (Costa, 1984; Galbraith, 1986a; Johnson, O'Brien, & Hudson, 1985; Kosberg, 1983; Pillemer & Wolf, 1986; Quinn & Tomita, 1986). With the increasing investigation of elder abuse comes various definitional, methodological, and theoretical problems. This chapter examines briefly some of these components confronting the issue of elder abuse and their implications for practice and policy.

DEFINITIONAL DILEMMA

A critical review of the literature concerning elder abuse reveals that a common definitional frame of reference is absent. The problem of definitions utilized in the elder abuse research has been addressed (Douglass & Hickey, 1983; Galbraith, 1986b; Galbraith & Zdorkowski, 1985; Johnson, 1986; Pedrick-Cornell & Gelles, 1982; Zdorkowski & Galbraith, 1985). Since the early studies on elder abuse (Block & Sinnott, 1979; Crouse, Cobbs, Harris, Kopecky & Poertner, 1981; Hickey & Douglass, 1981a, 1981b; Lau & Kosberg, 1979; O'Malley, Segars, Perez, Mitchell, & Knuepfel, 1979; Steinmetz, 1978) to the most recent studies (Phillips & Rempusheski, 1985; Pillemer, 1986), definitions within the research studies, policy statements, and legislative acts have been inconsistent. In examining this definitional dilemma, Pedrick-Cornell and Gelles (1982) state:

> Perhaps the most significant impediment in the development of the adequate knowledge base on intrafamily violence and abuse has been the problem of developing a satisfactory and acceptable definition of violence and abuse. (p. 458)

Most elder abuse studies have included categories of physical abuse, psychological abuse, and violation of rights (this may include unreasonable confinement, financial exploitation, infringement of personal rights, economic abuse) to explain elder abuse behavioral manifestations (Block & Sinnott, 1979; Galbraith, 1984; Lau & Kosberg, 1979). Others have differentiated between the terms *abuse* and *neglect*, which has resulted in categories such as *active neglect, passive neglect, physical neglect*, and *psychological neglect* (Crouse, Cobbs, Harris, Kopecky, & Poertner, 1981; Douglass, Hickey, & Noel, 1980; Hickey & Douglass, 1981a, 1981b; Hwalek & Sengstock, 1986; Sengstock, Hwalek, & Moshier, 1986). Douglass and Hickey (1983, p.124) believed "the actions or inactions of the caregivers formed the basis of the definitions" and the consequences of abuse and neglect were "equally damaging to a victim." They viewed their definitional distinctions as means of deciding how support services could have aided in the prevention of abuse and neglect.

Unfortunately, what is classified as abuse in one study may be classified as neglect in another study. At best, the differences in definitions, terminology, and meaning of elder abuse make it impossible to compare research findings and to increase collaboration of colleagues in the development of assessment instruments, as well as to move toward a standard definition that would be acceptable to public policymakers and researchers on a national basis. In addition to these limitations, Johnson (1986, p.168) suggests that without a "standard definition of elder abuse, causal theory cannot be explored."

Johnson (1986) contends that a tautological problem exists in that researchers have used the term *elder abuse* to define itself. She suggests that the focus should be on the development of a conceptual framework in which "abuse is free to take its place as a form of mistreatment" (p.177). As a result, the concept of elder mistreatment should be used. Johnson has provided a framework and parameters for conceptualizing elder mistreatment that would allow researchers, policymakers, and practitioners to conceptualize the variable, to specify behavioral manifestations, to measure observable events, and to distinguish the act from the cause. Implementing this suggested framework would move the investigation of elder mistreatment toward a more scientific orientation.

The terms *neglect* and *abuse* as utilized in many studies continue to create a problematic situation in explaining the elder abuse phenomenon. Although it is important to examine and understand this concern from a broad perspective, the victimization of the elder individual must be the ultimate concern. If we continue to use the term *neglect* (acts of omission) and the term *abuse* (acts of commission), the definitional dilemma will be perpetuated. *Neglect* is a term that seems to be related to the characteristics of the abuser whereas *abuse* is a term that refers to the abused. Although the intentionality of the situation is important to understand, the end result of a neglectful act still may be categorized as abuse, whether physical, psychological, or infringement of rights. It is the end result of the acts of omission and commission on the elderly individual that should be the ultimate concern and guiding consideration as an adequate definition of elder abuse is developed. The term *neglect* as a separate and distinct categorization should be omitted from the elder abuse dialogue and should be considered as another form of abuse. This may further the development and understanding of an adequate definition.

METHODOLOGICAL PROBLEMS

Elder abuse research suffers not only from the definitional dilemma discussed above but also from a plethora of methodological problems. Data have been derived from health and social service professionals providing retrospective case material, agency records, and, least frequently, elderly abused individuals and abusers themselves. Hudson (1986) provides an excellent overview of the various elder abuse research studies and their findings. Three types of research dominate the literature: descriptive survey, exploratory survey, and causal-model testing. Most studies have not employed comparison control-group techniques that would allow for some generalization to the larger population. Instead, small nonrepresentative samples have been used that have yielded particular information rather than generalizable information. Because of the differences in sampling and data-collection techniques, the different research findings of elder abuse cannot be compared systematically. Galbraith and Zdorkowski (1986, p.168) have suggested that in elder abuse research, "generalizations are suspect because of the limited amount and uncertain quality of the empirical information each [researcher] has gathered and . . . raw data are suspect because of the informal, localized language that has guided its [sic] collection and classification."

As mentioned above, elder abuse research has yielded studies that lack control group techniques and are characterized by case duplication and uninformed opinion. This not only limits any comparability but also adds confusion to the definition, meaning, and understanding of the phenomenon of elder abuse. Although the findings in the various studies have revealed a consistent image of the individual most likely to be abused, and to a lesser extent of the abuser, the difficulty is not with the methodology employed as much as with the interpretation of the data. As a result, the research studies have added to the definitional dilemma of elder abuse, as well as hindered the basic understanding of the incidence and prevalence of the problem.

THEORETICAL PERSPECTIVES

No single theory provides the entire explanation of why elder abuse occurs. Phillips (1986, p.197) states, "currently many theoretical explanations for elder abuse have been suggested and accepted, few have been subjected to the rigor of empirical testing." The theories that attempt to explain elder abuse are drawn heavily from other family violence research (Pedrick-Cornell & Gelles, 1982). None has proven effective in predicting abuse. The purpose of this section will be to describe briefly four competing theories that attempt to explain elder abuse but have not been empirically substantiated.

The first theoretical framework is the *psychopathological*, which holds as a basic premise that abusers have personality problems and disorders that cause them to be abusive (Hickey & Douglass, 1981b). Characteristics of psychopathological individuals include inadequate self-control, compulsiveness, sadism, undifferentiated types of mental illness, or displaced aggression. Because of the inherent problems and the close proximity to the abusers, family members become the objects of the abusive behavior. Abusers may be unable to discriminate between their own feelings and the behaviors they exhibit. The combination of the psychopathological individual and a family-structure factor of a dependent elderly person could produce abusive behavior.

One of the most widely accepted theoretical explanations is that of a *situational model*. The basic premise of the situational model is that "as the stress associated with certain situational and/or structural factors increase for the abuser, the likelihood increases of abuse acts directed at a vulnerable individual who is seen as being associated with the stress (Phillips, 1986, p.198). Situational variables that can be associated with abuse of the elderly have included economic, physical, social-psychological, and environmental conditions, isolation, and life crisis (Galbraith & Davison, 1985).

The *social exchange* theory is another conceptual model that has attempted to explain elder abuse. Homans (1961) suggests that this theory is premised on the idea that social interaction involves the exchange of rewards and punishments between at least two people and that all individuals seek to maximize rewards and minimize punishments in their interaction with others. If the resources or access to resources are not equal between two persons in an interaction, then an imbalance in social exchange exists that results in a power advantage for one of the persons involved in the social exchange. This theoretical construct can be used to explain elder abuse if the assumptions are correct and it is accepted that elderly people are more powerless, dependent, and vulnerable than those who provide the caregiving function. As the more powerless, the elderly have fewer alternatives to continuing the interaction and thus become the victims of a more powerful and controlling caregiver.

A fourth theoretical explanation of elder abuse is that of *symbolic interactionism*. This theory is predicated on the assumption that social interaction is a process between at least two individuals that occurs over time; consists of identifiable phases that are recurring, interrelated, and loosely sequenced; and requires constant negotiation and renegotiation to establish a working consensus about the symbolic meaning of the encounter (McCall & Simmons, 1966). The major premise underlying this theory is that of role and image identification. If perceptions of the interaction change over time, then the reactions to the situation are influenced as well as the consequences of that relationship between the elderly person and the caregiver. An abusive act may be the result of the interaction.

IMPLICATIONS FOR PRACTICE AND POLICY

The definitional, methodological, and theoretical problems confronting the issue of elder abuse have critical implications for practice and policy. As the perceptions of elder abuse have increased, so has the effort to do something about the problem by practitioners, researchers, policymakers, and governors. This effort has been undermined by the confusion in the definitional construct of elder abuse. Even though distinctions have been made by researchers investigating elder abuse, the various distinctions have not been made or accurately applied by practitioners or policymakers. The plethora of definitions has resulted largely because of the localized and informal language that has guided data collection and classification, as well as the type of professionals reporting the incidences. As a result, practitioners and policymakers are confronted with numerous definitions and little consensus on the meaning of what constitutes each type of abuse and neglect.

The methodology utilized in gathering elder abuse data has resulted in a misinterpretation and overestimation of the magnitude of the problem by practitioners and policymakers. To espouse that 2½ million elderly individuals are being abused and neglected is somewhat meaningless when such estimates are based on small, nonrandom research samples, and, in many instances, upon rather uninformed respondents. Although definitionally and methodologically flawed, the attempts to attack and solve the problem have outpaced the research efforts that would result in meaningful, accurate, and useful information from which to build a solid foundation for practice and for the development of policy.

Perhaps the most significant implication that stems from the definitional, methodological, and theoretical concerns of elder abuse has been the development of state legislation that deals with the protection and mandatory reporting of suspected abuse. Such legislation seems to have been enacted in a rather hurried manner, without careful consideration for its implications for the practitioner and the individuals whom it is to protect. Utilizing research data that are flawed by definitional, methodological, and theoretical problems, policymakers have passed legislation in a majority of states concerned with adult-abuse reporting statutes or comprehensive adult protective services (Traxler, 1986). The majority of these statutes focus on the purpose of case finding, and have enforcement-oriented approaches, which are demanding if not impossible for practitioners to maintain.

The mandatory-reporting laws seem to suggest an inappropriate intrusion and violation of the individual's privacy and autonomy, which they are meant to protect. Mandating professionals (i.e., physicians, social workers, clergy, counselors) to report suspected abuse and neglect also negates the confidentiality privilege between themselves and the client. The laws assume on the basis of age alone that aging individuals are incompetent to make life decisions on their own behalf. They are not focused on the need to help the elderly make appropriate decisions, but rather are directed at allowing practitioners to assume such a responsibility.

Policymakers have concentrated on the importance of elder abuse far more than addressing some of the other typical problems confronting the dependent and frail elderly individual. As a result, social policymakers have established two separate social service systems: one for certain types of adult service needs, and one specifically for the elderly. In most cases, states lack the appropriations for the specific activities mandated in the statutes as well as the basis for financing ancillary services needed to adequately address the service plans connected with the investigation of reported elder abuse cases. The result of such a social policy has been to create an illusory sense of progress toward solution of a complex problem; whereas the situation is that practitioners are not adequately prepared to meet the policy's prescribed mandates, and that the policy is one that the elderly, at whom it is directed, may not find in their best interests.

Chapter 3

IMPLICATIONS OF RESEARCH ON ELDER ABUSE PERPETRATORS
Rethinking Current Social Policy and Programming

Georgia J. Anetzberger

Research on elder abuse has gone through an evolutionary process similar to research on other abused populations. Beginning with attempts to demonstrate the existence of the problem as well as describe its dimensions (Block & Sinnott, 1979; Chen, Bell, Dolinsky, Doyle, & Dunn, 1982; Douglass, Hickey, & Noel, 1980; Lau & Kosberg, 1979; O'Malley, Segars, Perez, Mitchell, & Knuepfel, 1979; Rathbone-McCuan, 1980), investigations proceeded to explore causation by testing hypotheses and assumptions generated in earlier studies (Phillips, 1983a; Sengstock & Liang, 1982; Steinmetz & Amsden, 1983; Wolf, Godkin, & Pillemer, 1984).

Until recently no researcher had interviewed the perpetrators of elder abuse. Existing studies depended on second- or third-hand perceptions of abuse dimensions, or etiology through interview with the victims or with the related service providers, respectively. Although these perceptions are important for understanding elder abuse, they have their limitations. Most importantly, they cannot offer information on the motivations and feelings surrounding abuse occurrence, which are subjective factors known only to the perpetrators but are essential to any explanation of abuse and therefore are critical to formulating appropriate problem-specific intervention strategies.

This chapter summarizes recent research on elder-abuse perpetrators (Anetzberger, 1987) and discusses its implications for current social policy and programming.

RESEARCH ON ADULT OFFSPRING WHO PHYSICALLY ABUSE

Methodology

Toward explaining the physical abuse of elderly parents by their adult offspring, research was conducted in the six-county region of Northeast Ohio. Using purposive comparison as the research design, meaningful explanatory variables were systematically identified and examined, and their interrelationships were explored through two in-depth and focused interviews with abusing adult offspring. Existing theoretical perspectives set within a conceptual framework provided the initial basis for inquiry. Examined in particular as explanations for the occurrence of abuse were the salience of abuse socialization, pathology, stress, and social isolation for the perpetrator, and vulnerability for the victim.

Interview schedules were specially developed for the study, combining closed- and open-ended questions, and including indices to measure such constructs as social isolation and burden of elder caregiving. Coding generally followed standard formats, and Likert-type scaling was used to measure certain concepts. Data analysis was descriptive in form. Responses to open-ended questions and extraneous remarks were content-analyzed.

Twenty-one participating hospitals and human service agencies examined their case records and identified 40 adult offspring who qualified for inclusion in the study by virtue of having physically abused an elder parent within the previous 18 months. To be included in the sample, the abuse additionally had to be verified according to established criteria. Fifteen qualifying adult offspring were interviewed, although background information was obtained from referral-source case-workers on the total research sample, and used in demonstrating the interviewed sample to be representative of the whole. An average of almost 2 months separated the first interview from the second. Together the interviews averaged about 4 hours in length. For each, the respondent was paid $10.

Findings

From responses and remarks of the interviewed sample during the two interviews, a profile of the abusing adult offspring emerged. Accordingly, the abusing adult offspring could be characterized as a white, middle-aged man, who is Catholic, unmarried, high-school educated, and working as an operator or laborer to earn a moderate annual income. The elder parent whom he abuses is his natural mother with whom he has lived for several years, and who is very old with both physical and mental impairments.

The abusing adult offspring typically has inflicted three different forms of violence on his elder parent during recent years, usually pushing, grabbing, shoving, or shaking, as well as throwing something at the elder parent and slapping her. Reasoning, however, is the most common means by which he handles conflict with the elder parent, and verbal or symbolic aggression is the elder's conflict tactic of choice. The abusing adult offspring did not grow up in a violent home. Although he was slapped or spanked as a child, this is considered acceptable discipline in American society (Straus, Gelles, & Steinmetz, 1980). Moreover, his parents usually handled disagreements with each other by arguing and yelling rather than through violence.

The typical abusing adult offspring has a characteristic pathology, most commonly emotional distress, mental illness, or alcoholism. Although he has not been stressed by recent life-crisis events, he has been burdened by close contact with the elder parent, particularly by her disturbing behaviors, such as being demanding or critical, and by his lack of available personal time because of caregiving responsibilities. What makes the situation more unbearable for him is a perceived lack of support from family members, especially siblings or aunts and uncles, who either do not exist or are unwilling to help. On this basis, the adult offspring is left to provide care to the elder parent in seeming isolation. Actually, he often does provide considerable care, but it is ordinarily provided within a network of informal contact and support from particular household members and friends.

Besides profiling the abusing adult offspring, research findings suggested a typology. The three distinct groups that emerged from data analysis are labeled the *hostiles*, *authoritarians*, and *dependents*—after each one's most dominant feature.

The hostiles were found to be the most abused as children and the most abusive as adults. They provided the least amount of caregiving, but were the most burdened by it. Their relationship problems with the elder parent were many and long term. The hostiles provided care out of felt responsibility or family pressure, were the least likely to coreside with the elder parent, and the most likely to blame the elder parent when things went wrong.

In contrast, the authoritarians were the only subjects with no characteristic pathology. They did, however, have rigid expectations regarding the elder parents and a tendency to punish the elder parents for failing to comply with established norms. The authoritarians provided the most elder care, but found it less burdensome than did the hostiles. They more frequently lived with the elder parent and enjoyed it. The authoritarians infantilized the elder parent, became unhappy when the elder parent seemed to prefer anyone else, and resentful when she made private matters public. They were the only married subjects, less educated than the hostiles but just as likely to be employed and of at least moderate income.

Finally, the dependents had lived extensively with and were financially dependent on the elder parent. Unmarried, poorly educated, unemployed, and low-income, they had the fewest social contacts, engaged in the fewest activities, and experienced the fewest stressor events. They were ambivalent about relations with the elder parent, the least likely to admit abuse infliction, and the least likely to have committed serious abuse.

The results of the research on abusing adult offspring have obvious limitations. The lack of comparison group, small sample sizes, and the types of referral sources potentially bias and reduce the generalizability of findings. Moreover, the restricted definition of elder abuse offers little, if any, understanding of other maltreatment forms of other perpetrator categories.

Rethinking Current Social Policy and Programming

Recognizing the above limitations, the research on filial caregivers who abuse still provides useful information to policymakers and program planners. It does this by challenging current perceptions of the family's role in elder care, enlarging the range of practitioners responsible for problem prevention and resolution, offering an alternative etiological model for policy or program design, and suggesting the need for various intervention strategies depending on the particular configuration of abuser characteristics.

The Role of Family

Prevailing social policy emphasizes the importance of family, especially adult sons and daughters, in assuming greater responsibility for the care of elderly persons. The rationale for this is both philosophically and fiscally based. Family is seen as providing better elder care than formal sources, due to more interpersonal understanding and commitment, and as providing such care at little public cost. Findings from research, however, suggest that not all adult offspring have the capability for assuming such responsibility. For example, pathologies such as mental illness and alcoholism render some adult offspring unable to tolerate the stresses of caregiving or unable to control aggression. In this regard, it should be emphasized that the costs of caregiving that result from abuse infliction are very great and include expenditures for health care of abused elders, therapy for distraught adult offspring, as well as the physical and emotional damage to both parties, which cannot be measured monetarily.

Just as social policy supports families that assume the caregiving role, it must support those that decline this role. It can do this in part by providing viable caregiving alternatives, including as a minimum the availability of sound, low-cost residential facilities ranging from adult family homes and congregate care, through nursing homes. Housing alternatives such as these may decrease the need for the abusing adult offspring and elder parent to live together, and so decrease the negatively charged intimacy that can foster abuse occurrence.

Broadening Responsibility

The findings from the research on the abusing adult offspring also suggest multiple service system involvement in preventing and treating elder abuse. More specifically, because a major factor explaining physical abuse is perpetrator pathology, the various service systems most concerned with pathologies such as mental illness and alcoholism should assume roles in helping adult offspring who are so afflicted to make appropriate decisions in caring for an elder parent, in addition to providing the treatment for emotional damage caused by caregiving that is inappropriately assumed. Other programs compatible with these services systems that may benefit abusing offspring include support groups for adult offspring with "difficult" elder parents, or for those declining the caregiver role but burdened by guilt as a result. It is important that the language used to describe these programs does not suggest wrongdoing by the adult offspring, or adult offspring are unlikely to become involved—elder abuse being more tabooed than child abuse or spouse abuse (Wolf, Godkin, & Pillemer, 1984). To date, few such service systems have become interested in elder abuse, and few prevention or treatment models have emerged from such systems.

The results of this research further indicate that a variety of support services are required to prevent elder abuse by filial caregivers. Because most adult offspring in the study lacked available or willing family to assist with caregiving, for those who do assume the task, substitutes must be made available from formal sources. Substitutes should include respite care and homemaker services, which although present in most communities, are usually too costly or difficult to arrange for many of the adult offspring with the characteristics identified through this research.

Alternative Etiological Models

To date, many of the policies and programs developed to prevent and treat elder abuse have been modeled after those used in child abuse. For example, adult protective services are similar to child protective services in general methodology and design. The findings from this research suggest that the etiology of elder abuse may differ from that of child abuse in important respects (Gelles & Straus, 1979; Gil, 1974; Straus, Gelles, & Steinmetz, 1980). For instance, in elder abuse there seems to be greater influence from pathology and less from external stress and a history of family violence. The implication of this for policy and programming is that existing elder abuse laws and services should be reevaluated for their appropriateness to the targeted population. For example, adult protective-service laws that provide a penalty for abuse infliction might more appropriately require therapy for the pathological perpetrator who can benefit or special mediation services when long-term conflict between perpetrator and victim is identified.

Besides being modeled after child abuse and so often inappropriate because of divergent etiologies, adult protective-service laws and programs also have been developed on the assumption that the major causes of elder abuse were those emphasized in the early literature on the subject, for example, stress and a history of family violence (Langley, 1981). Although these factors may be important in explaining other abuse forms, because they are less important in explaining physical abuse, existing laws and services need to be reevaluated based on this new understanding of the problem. For instance, risk-assessment tools emphasizing caregiver stress over other indicators of elder abuse should be modified to reflect the contribution of factors such as perpetrator pathology and perceived social isolation.

Varied Intervention Strategies

The typology of abuse perpetrators that is emerging from this research suggests a need to differentiate intervention strategy by the configuration of abuser characteristics. For example, financial support and employment counseling may be useful for dependents in reducing their economic dependency and need to live with the elder parent. Nonetheless, these interventions would prove less useful for authoritarians than would caregiver support groups offering constructive peer interaction (and sometimes pressure), as well as help for developing more appropriate expectations regarding an impaired elder's behavior.

In conclusion, compared with other abused populations, research on elder abuse remains in its infancy stage. It is important for policymakers and program planners to realize this as they develop strategies to prevent and treat the problem. Certainly it is premature in our understanding of elder abuse as a complex phenomenon to become locked into systems that ultimately prove ineffective—because they were designed before actual abuse etiology and dimensions were known. We must remain flexible, willing to modify or even radically change direction as discoveries emerge and traditional thinking is challenged.

Chapter 4

THE PERILS OF DRAWING POLICY IMPLICATIONS FROM RESEARCH
The Case of Elder Mistreatment

Jetse Sprey
and Sarah H. Matthews

This chapter focuses on the relationship between social policy and the current clinical and research literature on the mistreatment of elderly persons. The relatively small base of research literature has been reviewed comprehensively by a number of scholars. They have concluded that the findings are difficult to catalogue because of noncomparable research designs (Hudson, 1986) that render it impossible to make definitive assessments of the incidence and prevalence of elder mistreatment or of the typical victims and perpetrators involved (Pedrick-Cornell & Gelles, 1982). Except for a recent study based on a probability sample in Boston (Pillemer & Finkelhor, 1986), in which elderly respondents were asked about forms of domestic violence perpetrated against them (but *not* about acts they themselves had committed), research to date has focused on persons who have come to the attention of social service agencies and/or hospitals. In light of this, it is not our intention to present another thorough survey of the literature, but rather to discuss the processes of definition and conceptualization within the field, two issues that are basic to its contribution to social policy.

To organize our discussion, three additional issues will be addressed. First, the status of research and description in the field is evaluated. Second, issues stemming from conceptualization and explanation of elder mistreatment and neglect are examined. Finally, the difficulty of formulating and implementing social policy from the current research findings is addressed.

RESEARCH AND DESCRIPTION

The study of the phenomena of elder mistreatment still is in its infancy. It is thus not surprising to see researchers groping for a set of descriptive categories that ultimately will provide a coherent inventory of its social content. Kuhn (1970) suggested that the exploration of a "new" scientific territory does not start from scratch, but rather charts its course within the confines of preexisting analytic frames of reference. As indicated by the almost universal use of the term *abuse*, attempts to describe and conceptualize the mistreatment of older people almost without exception occur within the framework of domestic violence (cf. O'Malley, O'Malley, Everitt, & Sarson, 1984; Pedrick-Cornell & Gelles, 1982; Rathbone-McCuan, 1980; Steinmetz, 1981, 1983). Gelles and Cornell (1985, p. 100), for example, see "abuse of the elderly" as a form of "hidden" family violence and consequently devote most of their brief treatment to the question of why caregivers occasionally abuse or neglect their "dependent" elderly parents. Apart from the fact that recent research does not support this premise (Phillips, 1983a; Pillemer, 1985; Pillemer & Finkelhor, 1986), it does not allow for any explanation for the findings that at least some elder "abuse" occurs between older spouses and that most neglect seems to be self-inflicted.

The constraining influence of a domestic-violence orientation on the interpretation of evidence is apparent in a report by Salend, Kane, Satz, and Pynoos (1984) on interviews with 16 "administrators of state agencies charged with implementing [elder abuse reporting] statutes" and, in each state, "one or more supervisors of adult protective-service workers within large urban social service departments" (p. 61).

> In all states, the highest percentage of reported cases was classified as neglect; physical abuse was less frequently reported, and the smallest proportion of reports involved exploitation. Respondents believed that the typical case of elder maltreatment involved financial or emotional stress experienced by the older person's caretaker. (p. 64)

Because most of the neglect cases involve self-neglect, the emotionally "stressed" caregivers seem pertinent only to the explanation of the less frequent abusive cases. A focus on the "typical" caregivers, however is a better fit with the preexisting domestic-violence perspective and, as such, takes precedence over other, more relevant ideas. Additional evidence regarding the effect of this perspective is found in the fact that the targets of recent studies are "caregivers" and/or "victims" (cf. Anetzberger, 1986; Korbin, Eckert, Anetzberger, Whittemore, Mitchell, & Vargo, 1987; Phillips, 1983a; Steinmetz, 1983). Pillemer and Finkelhor (1986), for example, designed their recent study "to oversample elderly individuals living with others, and particularly to oversample for those living with persons of a younger generation." Self-neglect, the modal category of those requiring adult protective services (Salend, Kane, Satz & Pynoos, 1984), then, is given short shrift in such research, the implicit assumption being that old age itself is an adequate explanation and, therefore, theoretically uninteresting.

Almost without exception, those writing about elder mistreatment begin with a discussion of the changing demographic structure of the population (Gelles & Cornell, 1985; Pedrick-Cornell & Gelles, 1982; Quinn & Tomita, 1986; Salend, Kane, Satz, & Pynoos, 1984; Steinmetz, 1981, 1983). Without doubt, more individuals are surviving to old age, and the most rapidly increasing portion of the population consists of individuals over the age of 85. It is also true that advanced age carries increased risks of physical, mental, and financial dependency (Katz, Branch, Papsidero, Beck, & Green, 1983). There is no clear evidence, however, that the incidence of being mistreated is higher among the very old. In fact, women over 75 are more likely to live alone, thereby reducing their risk of being physically abused by spouses or younger housemates (Pillemer & Finkelhor, 1986). Suggesting, then, that elder mistreatment or neglect is a very real possibility for anyone who lives long enough (Quinn & Tomita, 1986; Steinmetz, 1981), in addition to being ageist (Faulkner, 1982), is unnecessarily pessimistic.

The research literature consistently does indicate that when the perpetrator and the victim live together, one (or both) of them is physically, mentally, or economically dependent. Households comprising adults who are not married (either legally or common law) are unusual, except among the young. This living arrangement occurs in American society almost exclusively when one, or both, of the adults is, for whatever reason, incapable of or unwilling to live independently. It is a mistake to assume without evidence that those who live with someone other than a spouse are a representative sample of the older population; of its physically, mentally, or financially dependent segment; or even of those aged 85 + who are dependent. By the same token, it is equally erroneous to assume that those with whom these elders live represent an unbiased sample of either relatives or other individuals. A careful reading of the literature indicates that, unless the researcher deliberately chooses spouse or adult daughter caregivers, most of the examples are of elderly women who are living with unmarried sons, nephews, more distant relatives, or paid attendants (cf. Anetzberger, 1986; Quinn & Tomita, 1986; Rathbone-Mc-Cuan, 1980). The description of the genesis and course of such special reciprocal arrangements and their potential linkages with exploitative or coercive tactics demands a wider perspective than that offered by the study of domestic violence.

In summary, the conceptually narrow and often normative approach characteristic of the domestic-violence field is useful for the study of only a few of the many faces of elderly mistreatment. At best, it may be appropriate for the analysis of verbal and physical violence between older spouses and between members of different age categories in families and kin groups. The danger of overuse of this approach is that it deflects attention from the most commonly reported type of problem, self-neglect.

Concepts and Explanations

Obviously one cannot describe something without at least some idea of what to look for, so that a decision can be made about what to incorporate and what to exclude from a definition. As stated above, even the description of an unexplored part of the real world typically develops within some established analytical framework. This is even more pertinent to conceptualization, especially the selection of one's "primitives," that is, those independent concepts that are not defined in terms already occurring in the theory (Rudner, 1966, p. 19). Concepts, as analytical tools, are formulated as vehicles for thought and measurement. As a vocabulary, then, their content and mutual coherence are of prime importance. Many definitional schemes, regardless of the quality of their terms, do not lend themselves to conceptualization. The category labeled *elderly mistreatment* is a case in point. It is a folk category—that is, one named by those directly involved with its manifest reality, and considered to be important and/or problematic enough to warrant classification (Hammel, 1984, p. 29). Such labels are rarely conceptual or designed for the purpose of research. To ignore this may lead to the accumulation of analytically irrelevant information—or noise—and a subject matter that appears virtually inaccessible to anything but vacuous explanations (cf. Phillips, 1986).

The author of a recent and thorough treatment of the defining procedures in the domain of elder mistreatment considers it "surprising and a matter of concern that there is no comprehensive definition of the term 'elder abuse'" (Johnson, 1986, p. 168). Given that elder mistreatment is a folk category, however, we would be surprised if there were such an all-encompassing definition at this time. That the category includes phenomena such as neglect by others, self-neglect, physical and verbal coercion, and exploitation, supports this contention. Despite the fact that all these cases do involve old individuals, a meaningful common denominator is absent. It is conceivable, but unlikely, that at a future time, most researchers could agree on shared definitions for all observable forms of maltreatment, but to translate these into one coherent conceptual frame of reference seems impossible.

In order to clarify this point, replace the term *elder abuse* with *abuse of persons who wear glasses*. Such individuals make up a sizeable proportion of the population, and a number of them doubtlessly are exploited, neglected, or abused, Why not study them? One answer is that there is no reason to believe that any of these people are singled out for maltreatment *because* they wear glasses, and except for incidental cases, this assumption appears to be correct. Is there, however, a good reason to assume that the elderly *as a category* are more mistreatment-prone than eyeglass wearers? Do elderly spouses abuse or neglect each other *because* of their age? Do older individuals neglect themselves *because* they are old? Old age per se is not synonymous with being helpless, without resources, dependent, or easily victimized, and, therefore, is ipso facto a poor basis for conceptual thought.

The foregoing aims to accentuate the distinction between the descriptive process and conceptual reasoning. Definitions or definitional schemes, unless undertaken with concept formation in mind, remain instrumental. One defines because of a desire to report, classify, or enumerate specific events. One selects those definitions that serve one's purpose. In view of this, unless cooperative work or conceptualization becomes a factor, it is understandable that most investigators will be loath to modify their favorite definitions—which often are no more than folk categories.

In the research literature, most manifestations of elder mistreatment are described on the individual rather than relational level. For some types of questioning—psychological or physiological—this is appropriate, but not necessarily for others, such as sociological and anthropological ones. To move beyond a conception of the use of force or neglect as something someone does to someone else is to introduce the notion of reciprocity, which is more than the mere summation of the psychological profiles of abusers and victims. It is analytically interesting, for example, to hypothesize that certain relationships—such as asymmetrical ones—are potentially prone to abuse or neglect. Who does what to whom and why is then a related but separate issue, and as such might be better pursued within a different theoretical context. Such explanations need not be competitive, but can be viewed rather as characteristic of questioning within a folk category that has no real conceptual core.

Some research on abuse does, indeed, fall into the relational category, but halts its interpretation without fully exploring the implications of the structural aspects of the data. Both Pillemer (1985) and Phillips (1983a), for example, report that "dependency" of their old subjects is not statistically associated with the likelihood of abuse. Could this mean that symmetrical relationships are likely to be associated with the use of coercive strategies such as intimidation and the use of force? And where does neglect fit in? Does it imply dependency by definition? And, if so, does it make sense to hypothesize a quest for independence or autonomy as a "cause" of self-neglect? These are abstract questions. They therefore require careful conceptualization and lines of reasoning that extend beyond the immediate confines of elderly mistreatment and require data about persons or social categories who are *not old* as well as not mistreated.

Valid definitions are a necessary but not a sufficient step toward conceptual thought and explanation. Those "surface" phenomena that together appear to comprise the category of elder mistreatment reflect, even at first glance, a complex and multilayered causal structure. Needless to say, substantive areas—in this case, elder mistreatment—are not to be equated with theoretical perspectives. A social-exchange approach, as proposed by Gelles and Cornell (1985), for example, seems suitable for the analysis of the social-psychological aspects of interspousal violence, regardless of age. The same may hold for symbolic interactionist theory (cf. Phillips, 1986). Various levels of structural analysis, the life course approach, and functionalism, each in its own way, may offer explanations of specific phenomena within the category of elderly mistreatment. We disagree with the assumption that such different perspectives are necessarily "competing" (Phillips, 1986, p. 197). The usefulness of each explanatory approach depends on exactly what is being explained. Lines of questioning become of decisive importance in making theoretical sense of a set of events that on a surface level seem to defy meaningful categorical conceptualization. To ask why given individuals turn into abusers or exploiters, for instance, is essentially a psychological issue. To query under what conditions such persons actually abuse quite specific others requires social-psychological analysis. And to ask which attributes of familial structures may induce relations that are violent or neglect-prone is for sociologists and anthropologists to explain.

Finally, it is a mistake to view the current plethora of inconsistent research findings on elderly mistreatment purely as a result of inadequate research and/or technical procedures. Phillips (1986, p. 201) explains the "inconsistent fit between the situation model [of elder abuse] and the available empirical data" as being due to the "many methodological problems that have plagued the studies." We would argue that what is lacking cannot be remedied by improved research techniques alone, but also requires questioning designed to discover the causality that underlies each of the many separate events that constitute the contemporary mistreatment of older people. The description of the folk category of elderly mistreatment remains incomplete, so that conceptual thought is constrained because of the overly narrow focus on violence and abuse.

RESEARCH AND SOCIAL POLICY

Within the limited scope of this brief presentation, some points warrant reiterating. First, the actual content of the behavioral category of elderly mistreatment remains incompletely described. Due to problems with sampling, access to populations, and the relative newness of the field, many elementary facts about the distribution and magnitude of existing coercion, neglect, and exploitation still must be discovered. A second and interdependent problem is the poor conceptualization of the various forms—especially, the actual processes of the potentially destructive *relationships* that exist among older persons themselves, and between them and members of their households, families, neighborhoods, or institutional settings. What is needed, then, is inventive and unbiased conceptual thought designed to make theoretical sense of a set of phenomena characterized by great diversity both empirically and with respect to the norms and values that structure its sociocultural setting.

Finally, on the explanatory level, we argue that no single theoretical approach is suitable to account for events as diverse as physical and verbal coercion, exploitation, neglect, or self-neglect. The quest for *the* causal explanation of the phenomenon of elderly mistreatment merely reflects the mistaken assumption that because all events have causes, there must be *one* cause for everything. Regrettably, things are not that simple.

It is thus not realistic to consider the realm of elderly mistreatment as an integrated field of study. Instead, it is a classificatory catchall that brings together the concerns of clinicians, researchers, and others about a set of behaviors that touch the lives of a number of older persons in tragic and destructive ways. In view of this, we do not believe that social scientists are in a position to propose policies to deal with the prevention and management of the mistreatment of elderly persons. This does not mean, however, that all efforts to formulate effective measures are unrealistic or that a policy of noninvolvement is appropriate.

A much-ignored but crucial aspect of all social problems is the specific societal context in which, in this case, abusers and victims, but also those who wish to intervene or legislate, are jointly enmeshed. Public definition of a phenomenon as socially harmful reflects shared values. The mistreatment of old people, however, is embedded in a multitude of controversial and often conflicting values. It involves issues of familial responsibility and of autonomy as well as ones of loyalty and of privacy in close relationships. It invokes the interdependence between such values and the nature of our current industrial society and capitalist economy. Policy formulation raises questions about the use of power, that is, the conditions under which coercion and physical force are appropriate and socially acceptable, especially in the case of persons who choose to "neglect" themselves (Faulkner, 1982). Finally, fundamental disagreements exist between individuals and groups about the role of government in the prevention and control of cases of neglect, exploitation, or coercion of older persons. In the meantime, policy enactment, for lack of a sound foundation in substantive and theoretical knowledge, must be directed toward controlling poorly understood problems and alleviating the consequences—rather than the causes—of a range of mistreatments.

Social policies should strike a balance between the state of knowledge about the phenomena in question and common sense. The latter must serve as a reminder of possible limitations under varying conditions and allow for realistic application and further improvements. A given policy, then, requires a sound empirical basis and a sense of causality so as to foresee its consequences. As we argued earlier, the field of elderly mistreatment lacks both, which places a great deal of weight on the second component, common sense. Because we really do not know what "causes" individuals to neglect or mistreat elderly persons, or elders to neglect themselves, effective prevention is not possible. One might argue that if all elders who require help with activities of daily living had sufficient funds to pay qualified and motivated caregivers good salaries, the rate of neglect would significantly decrease. On the other hand, increasing the incomes of elders might make them more attractive targets for exploitation by financially strapped relatives and friends. In that case, providing adequate incomes for middle-aged adults might prove more effective. Policies that are based on a mix of descriptive knowledge and normative considerations may lead through a process of trial-and-error to some sound policy decisions. Due to the absence of theoretical understanding, however, it is likely that at least some policy decisions will result in scapegoating and discriminatory actions against those who—for whatever reason—appear to fit the "scientific" profile of the abuser or the victim (Faulkner, 1982). For example, just about *any* younger caregiver living with a dependent elder is likely to be seen as a potential abuser, or any frail elder living alone as a candidate for self-neglect.

We suggest, therefore, that inputs from social science

must be generously augmented with the "common sense" that has been acquired by those professionals, who, as part of their work, must deal with the consequences of elder mistreatment, whether other- or self-inflicted. We also see a need for a willingness on their parts to evaluate the wisdom of existing policies as new conceptualizations lead to different interpretations of the various kinds of harmful and destructive behaviors.

It does not really matter exactly how many old persons are mistreated; even *one* case is socially unacceptable. Whether 3% or 6% or 10% of all persons over 65 are abused is largely irrelevant. What must be known is who and where they are, and equally important, which forms of elder-elder and elder-other relationships are most likely to be associated with *what* types of mistreatment or neglect. Our conceptual and theoretical approaches toward the phenomena that comprise the social category of elderly mistreatment, thus, should be fragmented. As such, they will derive much or, perhaps, most of their real causal understanding from comparisons with or analogies to the study of other social phenomena. This, we believe, eventually will make the "field" of elderly mistreatment one in which scholars representing different research traditions and value orientations continue to meet and, occasionally, confront one another, and, at the same time, provide practitioners with knowledge that will eventually make possible prevention, rather than only the management of consequences.

Part II

PRACTICE ISSUES

Chapter 5

ASSESSMENT PROBLEMS IN CASES OF ELDER ABUSE

Deborah Bookin and Ruth E. Dunkle

In the decade since elder abuse was first publicly recognized, additional research and practice experience have revealed an impressive constellation of issues and problems that confront those who are called upon to serve elderly victims of abuse, neglect, and exploitation. The present challenges facing human service practitioners who work with abused elderly reflect an eclectic combination of problems intrinsic to the nature of elder abuse, as well as those posed by the current state of knowledge, legislative initiatives, funding, and community services. Nowhere are these challenges more critical than in the assessment of suspected cases of abuse, during which time practitioners must gather the information that will guide their work with elderly victims.

Ideally, the assessment process in cases of elder abuse should be a protracted and systematic one. Because the needs and problems of the abused elder and his or her family are generally extensive and multifaceted, considerable time must be spent in obtaining an accurate perception of facts relevant to the elder's situation. Professionals from a number of disciplines, including medicine, nursing, social work, and psychology, are likely to be called upon to participate in the comprehensive assessment of the elder's needs. Resistance from a variety of sources, including both laymen and professionals, is likely to be encountered. Resources available to facilitate the assessment may be limited, and expectations of what can be accomplished may vary greatly.

Despite the expansion of the knowledge base on elder abuse and the introduction of much-needed assessment tools, practitioners who carry primary responsibility for the assessment of elder abuse continue to express frustration at the many obstacles and problems that can hinder their efforts to assist elderly victims. This chapter examines selected issues in three areas related to the assessment of elder abuse: the practitioner's perspective, the nature of the problem, and the present state of legislation and services for elderly victims.

THE PRACTITIONER'S PERSPECTIVE

Some protective-service practitioners have likened their role in the assessment process to that of a *detective*, ferreting out important facts despite their relative obscurity. Yet, the process may be even more complicated than even practitioners realize. Unrecognized factors may alter perceptions of what they and others observe, relative to the abuse situation.

Attitudes About Violence and Aging

All those involved in the assessment process—the practitioner, the elder, the elder's family, concerned individuals in the community, and other professionals—bring a unique set of values and attitudes to the assessment process. Most importantly, they bring their individual views concerning what constitutes domestic violence, formed during their own socialization within the family (Straus, Gelles, & Steinmetz, 1980). There are significant differences in the manners and degrees to which families embrace the use of violence or force, and such differences affect how individuals subsequently view various acts and behaviors (Bookin & Dunkle, 1985).

Similarly, attitudes about the elderly and the aging process are also brought into the assessment process. A lack of accurate knowledge concerning the aging process and what constitutes "normal aging" may contribute to the perpetuation of negative stereotypes and perceptions that skew how individuals view the behavior or condition of the elder. An elder's difficult behavior may be perceived as being the result of obstinacy or sheer hostility, when in fact it is the result of illness, disability, or the caregiver's lack of knowledge or skills related to appropriate caregiving techniques.

Impact of Professional Standards and Biases

Practitioners may also find themselves and other professionals influenced by standards established by the various human service professions. Participants at the Research Conference on Elder Abuse and Neglect (Family Research Laboratory, 1986, p. 2) determined that "the definition, and therefore basic conceptions of abuse itself, varied with professional perspective and that even within the same profession different parameters are used." Therefore, it is highly advantageous for practitioners assuming primary responsibility for the assessment process to familiarize themselves with relevant differences between the standards of the various professions with whom they must work, and how they may affect how other professionals view the elder's situation.

Influence of Other Factors

Research conducted by Phillips (1983b) suggests that even when individuals have relatively concrete guidelines upon which to base their perceptions, situational factors may alter their perceptions of whether a situation is one of abuse. A number of nurses participating in the study were reluctant to label a case as being one of abuse if they found the elder to have "some less than desirable characteristic" that might precipitate her or his maltreatment, or if the elder's caregiver/abuser was elderly, infirm, and perceived as "doing the best he can." In still another study, Phillips and Rempusheski (1986b) found that health care providers were reluctant to label a situation as being abusive if they had a good relationship with the caregiver/abuser and the abuser was perceived as being "cooperative."

Finding Common Ground

The values and attitudes of many of the individuals the practitioner is likely to encounter in the assessment process go largely unrecognized or unacknowledged. Identifying the various attitudes and values operant in the elder's situation is not a simple task and can add considerable time to the length of the assessment process. However, little meaningful work can be accomplished until those involved are able to begin dialogue from a common point of reference. Thus, the practitioner must recognize that each case of elder abuse presents a situation in which perceptions by all those involved may vary significantly. Part of his or her work during this stage of intervention will be to help bridge such gaps in perception and help all relevant parties to reach common ground (Bookin & Dunkle, 1985).

The Nature of the Problem

Simply knowing what elder abuse is does not guarantee that the practitioner will succeed in identifying the elderly victim of abuse and in making an adequate assessment of the situation. Despite the fact that many victims of elder abuse share common characteristics, there is no definitive profile of the "typical" victim at the present time that can be applied to all situations. Elder abuse is known to cross racial, religious, and socioeconomic strata and can take a number of different forms in a given situation. For this reason, Quinn and Tomita (1986, p. 33) caution practitioners to "maintain a high index of suspicion for elder abuse when working in any situation where older people are involved."

Elder abuse is most typically a family problem that occurs within an intricate system of family relationships and issues (Wolf & Pillemer, 1984). Quinn and Tomita (1986) note that a number of situations involving family caregivers can put the elder at increased risk of abuse: the caregiver's unrealistic expectations of the elder (especially if the elder is ill); the care-giver's incompetency in that role due to his or her own prob-lems or pathological characteristics (e.g., mental illness, alcohol-ism, or drug abuse); the elder's care needs being in excess of the caregiver's ability to meet them; or the caregiver's feeling obliged to care for the elder, despite the fact that the caregiver may not wish to do so.

Lack of Visibility and Access

Wolf and Pillemer (1984) describe the abused elder as being "particularly cut off from the rest of the world." They note that elderly victims of abuse may have few or no regular contacts with professionals who might be able to assist them, unlike abused children who daily come into contact with those in helping roles. In addition, the frailty and ill health of many elderly victims further curtail outside contacts that might lead to the identification of the abuse.

Those professionals with whom the elderly victim does come into contact may not be able to recognize the abuse be-cause it is in its early stages, when symptoms are most often subtle and difficult to detect, or because they are unaware that such forms of maltreatment exist. Although elder abuse is re-ported to be within the "typical experience" of most workers in the human-service professions, the type and stage of abuse with which each worker regularly comes into contact can vary from setting to setting (Douglass, Hickey, & Noel, 1980; Hickey & Douglass, 1981b). Over time, professionals may adopt their own "personal profiles" of abuse victims, which may cause them to look for certain indicators of abuse and overlook others, thereby contributing to the possibility that they may not recognize the elderly victim (Bookin & Dunkle, 1985).

Even when alleged abuse does come to the attention of practitioners, they are likely to get little help from elderly vic-tims, who may be afraid to admit what is happening for a num-ber of reasons: fear of reprisal or nursing home placement; mistrust of practitioners or their agencies; belief that the situa-tion is not likely to change; or denial that such a terrible thing could be occurring at the hands of a loved one (Bookin &

Dunkle, 1985; Quinn & Tomita, 1986). The entire family is likely to hide the maltreatment out of fear that the abuser will be punished or that the family will be disrupted. In order to gain access to the situation, the practitioner must be able to win the trust, or at least tolerance, of both the elder and his family. Wolf and Pillemer (1984) report that workers find it helpful to assume the role of a "friendly helper" or "salesman" trying to "sell" services to the elder in such situations.

Referrals and Expectations of Practitioner

Although practitioners are likely to receive referrals from a variety of sources, family members and neighbors have been found to make the largest number of reports (Wolf & Pillemer, 1984). According to the Elder Abuse Project (American Public Welfare Association and National Association of State Units on Aging, 1986a, 1986b, 1986c), the substantiation rate for reports of suspected abuse ranges from 70.8% to 79.2% in states that maintain data on abuse and neglect involving only the elderly. States that collect data on adults of all ages report the substantiation rate for abuse and neglect of all adults to be between 60.2% and 62.8%.

Despite the relatively high substantiation rate for reports of elder abuse, cases stemming from false reports exist. Inaccurate referrals are likely to be made as the result of malevolent intentions, lack of knowledge, or the presence of other conditions whose symptoms mimic those of elder abuse. Individuals who are angry with an elder or the elder's family may use a referral as a means of retaliation or revenge. In other cases, a referrer may not understand that an elder's vocalness about not receiving adequate care may be due to serious illness or dementia, rather than due to actual inadequacies of care. The referrer may be unaware that certain medications can cause an elder to bruise easily and exhibit an array of wounds that are not the results of physical abuse. An elder who repeatedly visits a hospital emergency room suffering injuries from numerous falls may not after all be the victim of an abuser, but rather the victim of a profusion of scatter rugs or other physical obstacles in the home that can cause the elder to fall.

Elder abuse is such a serious condition that no report, however trivial, should be discounted. Yet, making an accurate assessment of the elder's situation can take considerable time and yield only limited results. Because elder abuse is a family problem, the practitioner must assess not only the comprehensive needs of the elder, but also of the family. Wolf and Pillemer (1984) observe:

> Assessing elder abuse and neglect is rarely simple. Cases do not fit into neat little categories; instead each has its own individual peculiarities. Often there are two victims and no one is at fault. Rather, the abused and often the family are in need of help, no matter what label is attached to the situation. (p. 34)

In observing the assessment process, the referrer and other concerned individuals in the community may not understand the importance of an extended, thorough assessment, and put considerable pressure on the practitioner to intervene immediately (Quinn & Tomita, 1986; Wolf & Pillemer, 1984). Wolf and Pillemer (1984) report that most cases of elder abuse are not emergency situations, but are the result of chronic problems that have evolved over time. Although elders in such situations may require immediate attention, Wolf and Pillemer note that it is not always clear just how to go about evaluating the validity of a perceived threat to the elder's safety, nor what should be done in the elder's behalf. Even though emergency situations do occur, Wolf and Pillemer relate that workers often find that what first presents itself as an emergency is in actuality a "regular occurrence."

In the case of bona fide emergencies, a variety of tasks must be compressed into a relatively brief time (Collins & LaFrance, 1982). Wolf and Pillemer (1984) suggest that preplanned protocols for dealing with emergency situations, as well as ready access to medical, legal, and law enforcement personnel and facilities can facilitate the swift handling of such cases.

The Present State of Legislation and Services

The introduction of laws designed to address the problem of elder abuse was welcomed by practitioners as a much-needed solution to a troubling problem. Most states now have some form of legislation to address the problem of elder abuse, as well as regulations or policies for implementation (American Public Welfare Association and National Association of State Units on Aging, 1986a, 1986b, 1986c). Yet, despite the fact that these laws were enacted with good intentions, their impact is now viewed with some ambivalence by practitioners. Many positive results can be cited, but additional questions have been raised about new problems that have resulted from weaknesses in the legislation or a lack of commitment to implementation of the laws.

Serving the Needs of Elderly Victims

It is generally recognized that the enactment of elder abuse legislation has led to greater public recognition of the problem, as well as a growing influx of new cases (Quinn & Tomita, 1986; Wolf & Pillemer, 1984). The creation of a system for the mandatory reporting of known or suspected cases in most states with abuse legislation has created a mechanism for identifying cases. However, practitioners express concern that simply bringing new cases to their attention is not enough. Funding for new and existing services needs to be mandated to meet the growing demand. In particular, they cite the need for greater access to legal, medical, and psychiatric consultation— important dimensions of the assessment process. The availability of in-home medical and psychiatric services and emergency-housing options for cases involving both medical and nonmedical emergencies are also cited as major needs that are yet to be adequately addressed (Bookin & Dunkle, 1987).

Despite the continuing influx of cases, less than one-quarter of the states having elder abuse legislation allocate specific funds for services to abused elders (American Public Welfare Association and National Association of State Units on Aging,

1986a, 1986b, 1986c). One practitioner described the situation as one of being asked to do more and more with less and less money, resources, and staff (Bookin & Dunkle, 1987). Such a situation raises the issue of whether it is indeed ethical to focus so much energy on identifying new cases, when there is insufficient attention given to funding the services required by elderly victims of abuse.

Guidelines for Identifying Abuse

Practitioners report that legal definitions of elder abuse established by these laws do not always provide them with the kind of concrete guidelines they need in order to help them make a determination in a particular case. In some cases, such definitions are too broad to be of assistance to the practitioner who must decide whether a "borderline" case is actually one of abuse. Although some practitioners report no hesitation concerning the use of guidelines set forth by these definitions, others express frustration and uncertainty as to how they may be applied in actual case situations.

In such circumstances, the practitioner and his or her colleagues may find themselves in the uncomfortable position of having to make a determination, believing that they are using their best judgment, but feeling little support from others in the community (Bookin & Dunkle, 1987). Such a situation is not entirely the fault of legislation or those who draft it, but is rather a reflection of the general ambivalence of society, the state of knowledge, and the fact that elder abuse is fraught with gray areas. Until this can be resolved more satisfactorily, many practitioners have turned to their colleagues. Consulting informally with other practitioners, working in teams, or establishing professional networks for consultation and support are resources cited as most helpful (Bookin & Dunkle, 1987; Wolf & Pillemer, 1984).

Access to the Elder

There appears to be little disagreement that legislation has provided assistance to practitioners in gaining entry to alleged abuse situations where access to the elder is barred by a family member or other individual, or in cases in which someone attempts to obstruct or interfere with the investigation. As one practitioner pointed out, informing the elder and others of the practitioner's legal right to investigate can be an effective mechanism to encourage voluntary actions on the part of the elder and her or his family, and to mobilize resources more effectively (Bookin & Dunkle, 1987).

However, others note that having to notify the elder and the family of the practitioner's legal mandate to investigate can also have a negative effect—particularly in cases of neglect and self-neglect. Because client and family can quickly become alienated or defensive when informed that a report of abuse has been made, such notification can quickly put a damper on the practitioner's efforts to assume a "friendly helper" role. The additional barriers raised can prevent the practitioner from being able to establish a trusting relationship with the elder or from obtaining the information necessary to accurately assess the elder's situation (Bookin & Dunkle, 1987).

This dilemma has no easy answer. Because the rights of elders and their families must be protected, greater consideration should be given to developing legal and administrative procedures.

Assisting Practitioners with Their Work

Changes in legislation and funding of services for abused elders are only two issues that practitioners report as being necessary to work more effectively with elderly victims of abuse. An exploratory survey of practitioners at two urban protective-service agencies, conducted by Bookin and Dunkle (1987), suggests that practitioners view greater cooperation from the community (neighbors, friends, and relatives of the elder) and from other professionals and service providers as the two factors they believe most important for them to do their jobs more effectively. Over half of those surveyed said that caseloads should be reduced, but an almost equal number stated that "greater appreciation and respect for the role of protective service workers by others" was of comparable importance to their ability to carry out their effort. Some practitioners express frustration that their work does not seem to be well understood or appreciated. Practitioners complain that both the general public and other human-service professionals have a poor understanding of what elder abuse legislation can accomplish and have unrealistic expectations of what practitioners are legally allowed to do.

It is unlikely that such attitudes, misconceptions, or lack of support will change without vigorous public and professional education. In the meantime, peer support continues to be an important mainstay for practitioners who shoulder the greatest responsibility in working with victims of elder abuse.

CONCLUSION

This chapter focuses on three areas in which practitioners experience problems during the assessment of elder abuse: the practitioner's perspective, the nature of this problem, and legislative and service issues. Each of these areas encompasses dimensions whose influence extend far beyond the assessment process, but this chapter limits discussion of these issues solely to the assessment process.

From the practitioner's perspective, attitudes about violence and aging, as well as the impact of professional standards and biases, are all significant to the assessment process. In reviewing the nature of the problem, it is clear that there is no definitive profile of the "typical" victim that can be used to facilitate the identification of abuse. Lack of visibility of the elderly victim due to problems of access, referral, and practitioner expectations also contribute to the confusion. The recent development of legislation to aid practitioners to meet the needs of these elderly victims has created additional problems that they must also address.

This chapter demonstrates the complex nature of assessment, highlighting the need for additional research and evaluation in the area of abuse of the elderly. Such research and evaluation must focus concretely on ways to facilitate the work of practitioners who are called upon to assist elderly victims of abuse. Of equal importance, practitioners must receive increased cooperation and support from both other professionals and the general public. Greater commitment must be given to strengthening elder abuse legislation by allocating sufficient funds to ensure effective implementation as well as the provision of much-needed services to elderly victims of abuse.

ACKNOWLEDGMENTS

The authors gratefully acknowledge the contribution of the staffs of the Chronic Illness Center and the Cuyahoga County Department of Health and Human Services Division— Adult Services Department, Cleveland, Ohio, in the preparation of this chapter.

Chapter 6

CLINICAL ASSESSMENT
OF ELDER ABUSE

Terry Fulmer

In clinical assessment, the term *elder abuse* can encompass a broad array of signs, symptoms, and behaviors. The literature cited throughout the chapters of this volume abounds with discussion of the difficulty regarding the nomenclature surrounding abuse, neglect, and mistreatment. Currently it seems that definitions for elder abuse utilized in the clinical setting derive from the legislation that controls the mandated-reporter laws in each state. Because there is no federal legislation, each state necessarily relies on its own definition of elder abuse, and therefore clinical-assessment skills evolve from the framework inherent in the state laws. For example, some states, such as Ohio, include the concept of self-abuse in the appropriate reporting law, whereas others, such as Massachusetts, exclude this concept. In a like manner, some statutes address the issue of financial exploitation but others do not. Salend, Kane, Satz, and Pynoos (1984) provide an excellent summary of the similarities and differences in reporting law.

Given that statutes have failed to provide a mechanism for the collection of consistent information, and because current definitions are far from precise, clinicians are left in the uncomfortable position of being mandated reporters without having clear guidelines about what to report. At the same time, clinicians are acutely aware that bad things can and do happen to old people, and that such occurrences should be reported to appropriate agencies in order to ensure the health and well-being of the elderly. The purpose of this chapter is to provide guidelines for the clinical assessment of suspected elder abuse victims within the context of state reporting laws that are imperfect due to the lack of empirically tested definitions of elder abuse.

The format and headings utilized for the purpose of discussing clinical assessments of elder abuse have been taken from guidelines provided by the Department of Health and Human Services (1980, Table 6-1). Even though these headings are far from perfect, they provide an approach to assessment that encompasses the majority of categorical areas described in the elder abuse literature.

Table 6-1   Physical Indicators of Abuse and Neglect

Type of abuse/neglect	*Possible physical indicators*
Physical abuse	Unexplained bruises and welts:
	— on face, lips, mouth
	— on torso, back, buttocks, thighs
	— in various stages of healing
	— clustered, forming regular patterns
	— reflecting shape of article used to inflict (electric cord, belt buckle)
	— on several different surface areas
	— regularly appear after absence, weekend, or vacation
	Unexplained burns:
	— cigar, cigarette burns, especially on soles, palms, back, or buttocks
	— immersion burns (socklike, glovelike, doughnut shaped, on buttocks or genitalia)
	— patterned like electric burner, iron, etc.

Table 6-1 (*continued*)

Type of abuse/neglect	*Possible physical indicators*
	— rope burns on arms, legs, neck, or torso
	Unexplained fractures:
	— to skull, nose, facial structure
	— in various stages of healing
	— multiple or spiral fractures
	Unexplained lacerations or abrasions:
	— to mouth, lips, gums, eyes
	— to external genitalia
Physical neglect	Consistent hunger, poor hygiene, inappropriate dress
	Consistent lack of supervision, especially in dangerous activities or long periods
	Constant fatigue or listlessness
	Unattended physical problems or medical needs
	Abandonment
Sexual abuse	Difficulty in walking or sitting
	Torn, stained, or bloody underclothing
	Pain or itching in genital area
	Bruises or bleeding in external genitalia, vaginal, or anal areas
Emotional maltreatment	Habit disorder (sucking, biting, rocking, etc.)
	Conduct disorders (antisocial, destructive, etc.)
	Neurotic traits (sleep disorders, speech disorders, inhibition of play)
	Psychoneurotic reaction (hysteria, obsession, compulsion, phobias, hypochondria)

From the United States Department of Health and Human Services, 1980.

Physical Abuse

The clinical assessment of physical abuse signs and symptoms is guided by an understanding of the physical indicators that may be caused by an action that harms the person. For the purpose of this discussion, physical abuse actions that are addressed include only those that are intentional. The debate regarding intentional versus unintentional actions is not addressed in this chapter, but has been discussed elsewhere (Fulmer & O'Malley, 1987). Physical indicators that may be the result of physical abuse include unexplained bruises, welts, burns, fractures, lacerations, or abrasions. These signs may be apparent on hidden areas of the body, such as the torso, back, buttocks, or thighs, where they are unlikely to be detected while the elder is clothed. The shape of the instruments with which injuries were inflicted, such as belt buckles or cords, may also be detectable.

Fractures or bruises that show various stages of healing at the same time should always arouse suspicion of possible elder abuse. When fractures or bruises present in this way, the history of the event rarely seems plausible. It is well known that there is an expected and predictable resolution of a bruise that can be recognized by its color (Quinn & Tomita, 1986). For example, it is known that bruises can be dated in the following way:

0–2 days	Swollen tender
2–5 days	Red-blue
5–7 days	Green
7–10 days	Yellow
10–14 days	Brown
2–4 weeks	Clear

If the history stated that trauma only occurred once, yet the clinical signs and symptoms suggest multiple bruising, abuse should be suspected. In the absence of an appropriate explanation, bruises or fractures in multiple stages of healing should be considered possible consequences of elder abuse.

When the health care professional is conducting a clinical

assessment of an elderly person who is suspected to have sustained abuse, it is important that there be excellent documentation of any history that is inconsistent with the alleged trauma or with the various stages of healing of a bruise, laceration, or abrasion—and any bruise that appears to take on the shape of an object must be followed up carefully. In addition, there should be a high degree of suspicion when there are bruises, burns, lacerations, or abrasions on several different surfaces of the body.

PHYSICAL NEGLECT

Clinical assessment of physical neglect is much more difficult than the same assessment for physical abuse. Physical neglect signs and symptoms are frequently the very signs and symptoms that may occur with normal events of aging, or with usual signs and symptoms of chronic diseases that are prevalent in the elderly. It is known that in elderly individuals over the age of 65, there is an average of 3 to 5 chronic conditions per person. Certainly these conditions affect the presentation of the elderly as they come to the attention of the clinician, and may overlap with the signs and symptoms of neglect. It may be that there is a possible cumulative effect of age in conjunction with disease signs and symptoms that overlap with those of neglect. The problem is that there is no way to weigh these factors, and it is difficult to state emphatically which changes are from aging versus those that are the result of neglect.

In relation to the category of neglect, it is also important to be clear regarding whether one is talking about self-neglect or neglect that has occurred due to an intervention or lack of intervention on the part of a care provider. This latter category is further delineated when one considers whether the neglect arose out of an intentional omission of an activity that would have sustained the elder's health and well-being versus an error in judgment or a lack of knowledge. Clearly, the area of elder neglect is the most difficult to assess, and it may take a number of experts in the field of geriatrics as well as extensive interviews with the care providers and the elder in order to discern

Table 6-2   Evaluation of Neglect

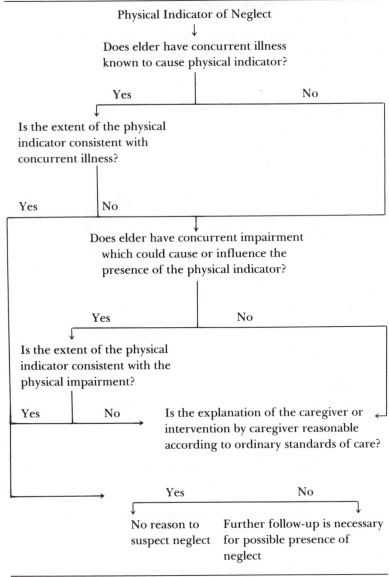

Physical Indicator of Neglect
↓
Does elder have concurrent illness
known to cause physical indicator?

Yes   No

Is the extent of the physical
indicator consistent with
concurrent illness?

Yes   No

Does elder have concurrent impairment
which could cause or influence the
presence of the physical indicator?

Yes   No

Is the extent of the physical
indicator consistent with the
physical impairment?

Yes   No   Is the explanation of the caregiver or
intervention by caregiver reasonable
according to ordinary standards of care?

Yes   No

No reason to   Further follow-up is necessary
suspect neglect   for possible presence of
neglect

From Fulmer, T. and Ashley, J. "Neglect: What Part of Abuse?," *Pride Institute Journal*, 5(4), 18–24, Fall, 1986.

neglect from inadequate care that result from the convergence of a number of bad situations. Table 6-2 presents a decision tree for evaluation of neglect.

For example, if one were to focus on the indicator of "persistent hunger" as a possible symptom of elder neglect (Table 6-3), it would be important to consider what medications the elderly person was taking in order to determine whether or not the medications were a part of that symptom, as is the case with drugs such as Ritalin, which may be used in order to counteract depression in the elderly. Persistent hunger could also be a symptom of diabetes mellitus, which in and of itself would constitute a disease state and would therefore not be an indicator of physical neglect. Finally, persistent hunger could result from an elder's inability to get to a store to buy food. The category

Table 6-3   Evaluation of Indicator: Persistent Hunger

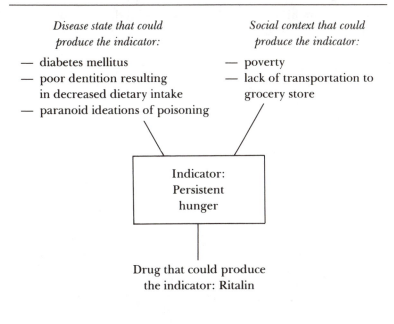

Disease state that could produce the indicator:

— diabetes mellitus
— poor dentition resulting in decreased dietary intake
— paranoid ideations of poisoning

Social context that could produce the indicator:

— poverty
— lack of transportation to grocery store

Indicator: Persistent hunger

Drug that could produce the indicator: Ritalin

Possible causes of the indicator: Persistent hunger

of physical neglect is one that will need a great deal of attention in the research arenas in the near future.

SEXUAL ABUSE

Indicators of sexual abuse in the elderly are rarely documented and, perhaps even worse, are even more rarely considered. An elderly person may be the victim of sexual abuse and yet be extremely reluctant to mention it due to the taboo nature of the subject. Our culture considers the elderly to be relatively sexless or asexual (Butler & Lewis, 1976). If one were to examine a random sample of clinical records in patients over the age of 75, it would not be unusual to find that the genital/reproductive examination has been deferred and that no history has been elicited. Sexual abuse indicators for an older person might include difficulty in walking or sitting as well as pain or itching in the genital area. Venereal disease would also be an indicator, and clinical assessment might necessarily include appropriate blood tests. Due to the extreme sensitivity of the issue of sexual abuse, it is important to elicit any expert help available for the purpose of providing the best possible assessment with the least amount of psychological distress to the elderly person.

EMOTIONAL MALTREATMENT

Clinical assessment of emotional maltreatment as a part of elder abuse is also a difficult area. Emotional maltreatment is sometimes labeled *psychological abuse*, and common definitions usually include the concepts of mental anguish, intimidation, threats, and isolation (Wolf, 1986). Possible indicators of these events might include conduct disorders, such as antisocial or destructive behavior. Habit disorders may also evolve in the form of sucking, biting, rocking, or other behaviors of that nature. Neurotic traits such as sleep disorders, speech disorders, or psychoneurotic interactions in the form of hysteria, compulsion, phobias, or hypochondriasis may also be considered under this category. Clearly, this is an area that requires expert assessment and is highly likely to be referred to psychiatrists and psychologists with special training.

CONCLUSION

For all forms of suspected abuse, a history elicited from the elderly person is essential for successful understanding of the nature of events that may or may not be elder abuse. Theories that suggest that elderly persons who are extremely dependent, isolated, or abnormal from the standpoint of an alcoholic problem, a mental retardation problem, or a psychiatric impairment, provide further areas that must be explored when one is conducting an assessment for elder abuse. A psychosocial assessment that elicits information pertaining to the elderly person's financial situation, living arrangement, and support system is extremely important in order to put the situation in a context that provides the total picture about the event in question. The observed relationship with the care providers should also be evaluated, as well as any interactions that can be documented, along with a notation about the elderly person's ability to express needs.

The crux of the successful clinical assessment lies in rigorous documentation. In light of the legislative mandate for reporting, the clinician's diagnosis of suspected abuse should always be recorded. Given the lack of clear or uniform guidelines for detecting abuse, it is important for clinicians to utilize terminology that is standardized and therefore understood among peers in the field. Likert-scale ratings have been found to be extremely useful in determining intensity, degree, and extent of the problem. By recognizing the issues that confound assessment, and developing a common framework in which to organize assessment, clinicians can maximize their ability to detect and intervene in abuse cases.

Chapter 7

ISSUES INVOLVED IN IDENTIFYING AND INTERVENING IN ELDER ABUSE

Linda R. Phillips

Despite increasing public awareness, a growing amount of legislative activity, and an accumulating body of professional geriatric literature on the topic, clinicians continue to find family-mediated elder abuse in the community setting to be a complex and perplexing phenomenon. Although most states have reporting laws that provide legal definitions of elder abuse and guidelines for case detection, operational definitions of elder abuse that provide clear direction for identifying an individual elder as a victim continue to elude health professionals. In most communities, agencies exist that are designated with the legal responsibility of protecting the welfare of disabled adults, but the range of interventions available for elder abuse remains limited, and health professionals continue to express dissatisfaction with the efficacy of available treatment strategies and resources. In short, despite 10 years of public and professional attention to the problem, controversy continues to exist regarding what constitutes elder abuse, how to recognize an abused elder, and what courses of action are most likely to be effective for ameliorating the problem. This chapter explores the roots of these problems and identifies some of the issues involved in developing sensitive, effective clinical programs for detecting and intervening in cases of elder abuse.

THE ROOTS OF CASE-IDENTIFICATION PROBLEMS

If all cases of family-mediated elder abuse involved broken bones and a perpetrator with demonic qualities and evil intent, there would be no problem with identifying each and every case. Unfortunately for the purposes of identification such clear signs are rarely present. Most legislation and much of the literature on elder abuse focuses on evident signs of damage as defining characteristics of the phenomenon, and on situations in which the elder admits to the problem; clinically, however, such cases are more the exception than the rule. More typically, clinicians struggle with situations in which it is difficult to identify clear signs of damage, where the intentions of the perpetrators are neither demonic nor evil, where the identification of a responsible party is difficult, and where the elder is unable or unwilling to participate in the identification process. The roots of the problems with case identification, then, lie in the nature of the assumptions that currently underlie our understanding of family violence, in the unresolved issues our society has about the care and treatment of elders, and in the unresolved role conflicts among health professionals.

After its "discovery" in the late 1970s, elder abuse was immediately claimed by the family-violence experts. The reasons for ownership were quite logical. Elder abuse, after all, has certain characteristics in common with other forms of abuse and, in its most virulent form, elder abuse is violent. In addition, because elders are frequently accorded childlike status in our society, the situations of vulnerable children and vulnerable elders were equated, and the child abuse model was adopted to guide case identification and intervention in situations involving elder abuse. As a result, elder abuse immediately inherited all of the problems that have not been resolved in identifying and helping abused children. For example, despite over 30 years of experience, clinicians have not yet resolved the issues involved in identifying and handling cases of child neglect. A second set of problems arose as a result of applying what is actually a poorly fitting model (the child abuse model) to elder abuse. For example, the situations of children and elders are actually quite different, as Finkelhor and Pillemer (1984) have indicated, with elders having much more economic, legal, and emotional independence than is possible for children. In addition to inherited problems and the problems of applying a poorly fitting model to elder abuse, a third set of problems with case identification has arisen that is directly attributable to the adoption of elder abuse by the family-violence community.

The notion of family violence raises certain clear expectations about the nature of the relationships between the abused and the abuser. First, it is expected that the behaviors of the perpetrators cause visible and irreparable damage, and that if the damage is not visible, then the situation is tolerable. Second, it is expected that victims and perpetrators are identifiable. Third, it is expected that victims are uninvolved (innocent) in arousing the behavior being displayed. If the victims are not innocent, then it is expected that they deserve what they are getting. Fourth, it is expected that the perpetrator's actions are motivated by malevolent intent. The realities of elder abuse challenge each of these expectations.

With regard to the first expectation, although cases in which the elderly person is maimed or mutilated are not unheard of, such cases do not constitute the majority of those encountered by clinicians. It is much more common for clinicians to encounter situations where, for example, the elder's needs for food, hygiene, medication, or medical care are not being met, or where the elder is belittled and denigrated. Consequently, in a majority of cases of elder abuse, the clinician is faced with the problem of determining the point at which irreparable harm is likely to occur, rather than whether or not irreparable harm has already occurred. This is a problem for which the family-violence model has few guidelines.

With regard to the second expectation, many of the cases of elder abuse seen by clinicians do not involve a clear victim or a clear perpetrator. Because most elderly adults are legally (and actually) autonomous human beings, it is often difficult to determine who exactly is responsible for the situation being observed. For example, is it the responsibility of an adult child to enforce rules of cleanliness on a legally competent elder when the elder does not want to be clean? What is the effect of geographic distance or filial distance on legal and moral responsibilities? Who is the victim and who is the perpetrator in situations where a legally competent elder refuses to act in his or her own best interests? And perhaps even more basic than any of these is the question of how responsibility can be assigned in a society that has yet to establish clear criteria regarding the minimum material and emotional rights to which every individual in the society is entitled?

The third expectation associated with the adoption of elder abuse by the family-violence community is that victims, by definition, are supposed to be innocent, and if they are not, they probably deserve what they get. Elder abuse is a phenomenon that is embedded in complex intimate interactions that have extended over decades. As a result, identifying who "fired the first shot" can be extremely difficult. In addition, elders come in all varieties. Some are sweet and easy to care for and some are not. The intention here is not to suggest that victim blaming is appropriate, but rather to acknowledge that the reality of the interactional nature of elder abuse can greatly complicate case identification for clinicians. As long as elder abuse is viewed from the perspective of family violence, clinicians will continue to struggle with whether total innocence is necessary before it is possible to state unequivocally that elder abuse is present.

The fourth expectation is that abuse is motivated by malevolent intent. In reality, probably very few individuals who are responsible for the kinds of situations that perplex clinicians are actually motivated by evil intentions. In most of the situations in which clinicians are involved, the abuser is providing some sort of care to the elderly person. Reports from clinicians (Phillips & Rempusheski, 1985) reveal that in such situations, a sizable portion of responsible individuals lacks the knowledge and skills necessary for meeting the needs of an elder. Another portion is made up of individuals who lack the personal resources required for caregiving because they themselves are ill, old, or disabled. Another portion consists of individuals who are operating in good faith guided by punitive, dogmatic personal belief systems that influence their interpretations regarding the appropriate ways of enacting the caregiving role (Phillips & Rempusheski, 1986a). Although it is true that regardless of the motivation, abusive acts should stand for themselves, in practice, these factors influence the likelihood of an individual's being perceived as an abuser or not.

In summary, clinicians' problems with identifying elder abuse are related, in part, to the fit between the models and expectations associated with family violence and the realities of family-mediated elder abuse. Equipped with stereotypes and assumptions about child abuse and with very little research-based information available that modifies or challenges the accuracy of these assumptions, clinicians are left with little help in sorting out the complexities and making the difficult decisions required for accurate case detection.

ROOTS OF INTERVENTION PROBLEMS

Although case identification is difficult for clinicians, in some ways determining appropriate interventions is even more so. Three major factors account for these difficulties. First, elders, regardless of popular stereotypes, are autonomous and have the right to self-determination. Therefore, as long as the elderly individuals are not considered legally incompetent, their decisions about appropriate intervention are final. As a result, clinicians can work extensively to identify what they consider to be the appropriate intervention alternatives, but in the end, the elder has the right to say no (and frequently does). Second, in reality, there are few alternatives available to help abused elders. Despite emotional media appeals, the situation has changed little in the past 10 years. For most situations there are no good answers, and little money has been allocated to improve or expand treatment options. Third, intervention for elder abuse is an uneasy mixture of legal and therapeutic strategies. On the one hand, there are legal imperatives involved, in that, in most states, reporting is mandatory, and life-threatening situations that are clearly the fault of some individuals are eligible for prosecution within the criminal justice system. On the other hand, whereas reporting is often mandatory, accepting treatment is not. Elders have the right to refuse intervention, caregivers have the right to refuse intervention, and eliciting the prerogatives of the legal system, particularly if the situation is not clearly identifiable by law as abuse, can make situations worse than they already are. In addition, clinicians are educated to cure and not to punish, and blending elements of the cure model with elements of the retribution model is very difficult for most clinicians.

Phillips and Rempusheski (1986b) found that clinicians perceive that there are basically three kinds of interventions available to them: legal interventions, therapeutic interventions, and self-protective interventions. Legal interventions, which involve enlisting the assistance of the criminal-justice system for protection of the elder and prosecution of the abuser, are rarely used by health professionals unless there is irrefutable, documented evidence. Even in states with mandatory-reporting laws, health professionals should be cautious, because often what they consider to be irrefutable evidence is not so considered by protective-service and criminal-justice agencies.

Therapeutic strategies include interventions such as educating the abuser, increasing services to support the abuser, and providing counseling to defuse the situation. Clinicians indicate that they tend to view therapeutic strategies as graded from those that are least disruptive to those that are maximally disruptive. An intervention such as caregiver education has minimal disruptive power, and an intervention such as confronting the caregiver has maximal disruptive power. Clinicians tend to begin initial treatment attempts with interventions that are minimally disruptive, reserving those with maximum disruptive power for use as last resorts. As a result of this practice, it is possible for an intervention strategy chosen in a particular situation not to match the intensity of intervention needed to protect the elder (for example, the clinician chooses to intervene by teaching the caregiver about nutrition when the elder is starving and in need of more aggressive treatment).

Self-protective strategies include activities designed to protect the health care professional from the caregiver's retribu-

tion, from professional embarrassment, and from postdecisional regret. All three of these matters are of primary concern
to clinicians. Clinicians fear that caregivers will take legal action
against them if they are unable to prove accusations of elder
abuse. This fear is especially pronounced when particular elders are seen as potentially unreliable and likely to change
their stories in the end. Because of the controversy surrounding elder abuse and the political turmoil associated with interagency relations, losing face because of an inappropriate referral or report is another fear of clinicians. Last, because there
are no good interventions available, clinicians fear that their
choosing among the equally bad alternatives available will result in their making the elder's situation worse and hence cause
postdecisional regret. The types of activities associated with
self-protection include closing the case, eliciting the support of
superiors or coworkers, and compiling extensive documentation for prolonged periods of time. The need for clinicians to
employ self-protective strategies is testimony to the difficulty
involved in designing interventions for use in situations where
there are abused elders.

DEVELOPING PROGRAMS FOR DETECTION AND INTERVENTION

There is little doubt that accurate identification and effective treatment for family-mediated elder abuse is dependent on
the clinicians' abilities to resist being immobilized by the difficulties and to focus clearly on the issues. There are some
guidelines that may help with this task.

First, it is essential that clinicians be acquainted with the
controversies surrounding elder abuse, and to have the realiza-
tion that they are not the only ones struggling with these hard
decisions. There are currently no definitive criteria for identifying abused elders and no good interventions that are totally
acceptable to all parties involved. It is important that clinicians
know that not only do they not know the answers but that no-
body does.

Second, shared decision making is essential. The decision-
making literature clearly identifies decisions such as the ones

surrounding case identification and intervention for elder abuse as "hot" decisions, or ones that involve highly emotionally charged content, a high degree of ego involvement, and a high likelihood of postdecisional regret (Janis & Mann, 1973). One method for reducing the emotional charge of such decisions is team involvement, so that the alternatives chosen are the best possible under the circumstances, and the responsibilities for undesirable consequences are shared among a group.

Third, it is important for clinicians to realize that factors other than the evidence can influence their decisions about whether or not abuse is present and how to intervene. Elder abuse can exist even when the caregiver is old and ill or when the elder is difficult and provocative. Although issues such as previous lifestyle and cultural patterns have an effect on decisions about elder abuse, they should not be the determining factors in such decisions.

Fourth, it is equally important for clinicians to realize that not all of the situations that they associate with the word *abuse* are so defined by law. Currently some of the interagency difficulties encountered in reporting and intervening for elder abuse and the frustrations of clinicians are related to the narrow range of behaviors that are actually covered by the law. Key to improving communications among professionals and overall efficacy of the system is knowledge of the various conceptualizations of elder abuse being used and their relationship to decisions regarding the presence and absence of abuse.

In summary, the guidelines offered in various publications about identifying and intervening in cases of elder abuse in no way match the complexities of the situations clinicians encounter in practice. To date, our knowledge base for the phenomenon of elder abuse is actually very scant, yet clinicians can hardly wait for new knowledge to be generated before attempting to ameliorate the situations encountered in practice. Until there is a knowledge base sufficient to meet the need, the only alternative is to use the available knowledge along with a sensitivity to underlying issues.

Chapter 8

RESPONDING TO ABUSE AND NEGLECT CASES
Protective Services Versus Crisis Intervention

James A. Bergman

In recent years, elder abuse, particularly physical abuse of vulnerable, physically or mentally disabled elders, has received increased attention from researchers, the Congress and the media (Bergman, 1981; U.S. House of Representatives, 1979, 1980, 1981a, 1981b). In reality, elder abuse cases are just a segment of what the social work profession has long referred to as protective-service cases. Protective-service cases include neglect, financial exploitation, emotional harassment, and abandonment, as well as physical abuse. The majority of these cases involve people whose current problems have existed for years, but some are of recent origin or are emergency situations. In addition, protective services may be necessary for not only the mentally incompetent elder, but for the mentally competent elder as well.

Given the variability of client types, kinds of abuse encountered, and degree of immediate risk involved in different cases, the challenge of creating a protective-service system is to create a system that can respond to the heterogeneity of problems. In this chapter, the factors that must be taken into account in dealing with the variety of elder abuse cases are outlined, and the components of a system that can deal with the multitude of issues that are subsumed under the classification of elder abuse are presented.

I. Four Client Types in Elder Abuse and Neglect Cases

Individual victims of elder abuse and neglect are not susceptible to easy classification. The uniqueness and variety of the cases does not mean that there are no common characteristics. Legal Research and Services for the Elderly, of Boston, in 1979 created four categories of elder abuse and neglect cases that have proved useful in understanding, assessing, and planning for victims of elder abuse and neglect. These four client categories then served as a basis for developing case protocols (Bergman, 1984; Villmoare & Bergman, 1981).

These four basic client categories of elder abuse and neglect are:

1. *Competent, consenting client*: the client who appears to be mentally competent and who consents to assessment and assistance.
2. *Competent, nonconsenting client*: the client who appears to be mentally competent, who may refuse assessment, and who does refuse assistance.
3. *Incompetent client*: the client who (regardless of the degree of cooperation) appears to lack sufficient mental capacity to make informed decisions concerning his or her own care.
4. *Emergency client*: the client who is in immediate danger of death or serious physical or mental harm, and who may not consent to help, and may or may not be mentally competent.

These four categories have as their point of reference the client's *right* and *ability* to determine the system's response to her or his problems. The client's rights and wishes will bring the protective-service system to a halt, time and time again, unless preplanned responses are available for each client type.

Workers with the elderly have often spoken of their feelings of helplessness when confronted with suspected victims of abuse who refused assessment and services. Concerns over protecting clients' rights in potential guardianship situations and questions about the proper use of legal representation for agency staff and clients in such situations have often been expressed by workers (Bergman, 1982; Collins & LaFrance, 1982). These problems can be lessened and in many cases solved if agencies have a list of steps and time frames that should be followed when workers are confronted with such situations.

II. CHARACTERISTICS OF ELDER ABUSE AND NEGLECT RESPONSE SYSTEMS

Elder abuse and neglect cases are forms of protective-service cases, and as such normally require the interdisciplinary approach of a protective-service system to resolve. Such a protective-service system is set up to handle long-term problem cases, not to provide quick-fix solutions. However, included within such a system needs to be a crisis-intervention capacity.

An effective protective-service or elder-abuse-and-neglect response system has the capacity to identify, assess, and treat both victims and their families. This is a system created to handle the most difficult cases that social service, health care, mental health, and legal service organizations encounter. As such, it is not surprising that few comprehensive protective-service systems exist anywhere in the country.

The goal should be to attempt, step by step, to create a comprehensive protective-service system that serves the elderly and their families. The following is a brief description of the characteristics that most authorities agree should be a part of such a system.

A. General Systems Characteristics

The three essential elements of any effective protective services system are:

1. A coordinated, interdisciplinary serv respond to both chronic and emergen
2. A set of core services (social, health, l health and legal services) available to cases.
3. A set of preplanned individual case responses oᵣ ₚ tocols to guide service providers in responding to emergency and chronic cases.

As basic and logical as this sounds, creating such a system is difficult because it requires cooperation between many service providers and long-term commitment of time and resources. Impediments to creating such a system include lack of resources, agency turf battles, personality and historical differences, staff turnover, and disagreements about who is currently doing what and who ought to do what in the future. In spite of such impediments, effective protective-service systems can be and are created.

One of the most effective vehicles for creating and maintaining a well-functioning protective-service system is the establishment of an interagency protective-service committee composed of frontline and supervisory staff of the social service, health care, mental health, housing and legal service agencies in the area. Such a committee should:

Establish informal and, later, formal linkages between the agencies that will lead to the development of responses or protocols to respond to individual protective-service cases.

Provide regular, monthly meetings to review how the current system is responding to known protective-service cases.

Provide a vehicle for identifying problems or gaps in the existing response system and planning ways of overcoming these problems.

Provide an educational forum for having special presentations or speakers on topics of interest to the members.

Provide a place for frontline workers to get to know each other and provide mutual peer support, which is important for workers who handle protective-service cases.

B. *Core Services in a Protective-Service System*

Even though few protective-service clients require all the services an area has to offer, a comprehensive protective-service system needs certain basic, core services if the system is going to be capable of responding effectively to the myriad of cases that present themselves. Few agencies, if any, are capable of providing or even coordinating all these services. Thus, a protective-service system depends upon cooperation between organizations.

The core services include the following:

1. Protective-service workers: The protective-service worker is normally a social worker or caseworker experienced in handling difficult cases. The worker should have an ongoing case load of 10 to 20 protective-service cases, but certainly no more than 25. She or he is the pivotal worker on most protective-service cases, with primary responsibility for doing the casework during the time a client is considered a protective-service client, and coordinating services for and with the client.

2. Case-assessment capacity: The case-assessment capacity is not one service, but is instead a formal or informal agreement among organizations in the area on how to conduct assessments of protective-service clients, and agreements that various professionals will do their best to be available, as needed, to assist in assessing clients.

3. Core social services: These services need to be available on a priority basis. They include caseworkers, homemaker services, meals, chore services, friendly visitors, and transportation.

4. Core health services: These services include inpatient and outpatient care, physicians, visiting nurses, home health services, physical and speech therapists, and ambulance services.

5. Core mental health services: These services also include inpatient, outpatient, and community care, in addition to inpatient and outpatient psychiatric care and assessment services, mental health counseling, and psychiatric social workers.
6. Guardianship services: These services include the capacity to assist in assessing clients, providing case-consultation advice to other service providers, petitioning for and appearing in court on guardianship and conservatorship cases, and serving as guardian or conservator for persons when appointed by the court to handle their personal and/or financial affairs.
7. Legal services: Services of lawyers and paralegals are needed to provide advice and/or representation to elders faced with problems that require legal intervention.
8. Emergency cash assistance: One or more organizations in the area need to have a small amount of cash available to give or loan to clients who are faced with emergency food, clothing, housing, medical, or other personal needs and who lack the financial resources to meet these needs.
9. Police services: Every city or town has police, and in some protective-service cases, their presence can be very helpful.
10. Emergency services: A 24-hour/7-day-per-week response capacity needs to be available for emergency cases.
11. Emergency housing services: Emergency housing or shelter is essential in some protective-service cases.
12. Crisis-intervention capacity: Like the case-assessment capacity, the crisis-intervention capacity is not one service, but is instead an agreed-upon system of cooperation among area organizations to enable them to respond to emergency protective-service cases. These cases involve clients who are in imminent danger of severe, possibly life-threatening harm, who have not yet been judged by a court to be mentally incompetent, and who initially may refuse to consent to be helped. For these cases, a crisis-intervention capacity

may be needed. Such a capacity requires the 24-hour on-call availability of: a protective service worker; a guardianship-services worker; a doctor; a psychiatrist; a lawyer; the police; and hospital and mental hospital facilities. All these personnel are not likely to be needed in each case, but they do need to be available if needed.

C. Casework Goals and Responses in Elder Abuse and Neglect Cases

As stated above, protective-service cases, including elder abuse and neglect cases, normally involve people who have been at risk for months or, more likely, years. Therefore to remove the person from risk permanently normally means making lifestyle changes. Wrenching someone out of his current lifestyle and depositing him in a new setting in which he is expected to adopt a new lifestyle has all the makings of a disaster. Yet the rush-in-and-save approach is frequently encountered in elder abuse and neglect cases. Above all else, the casework goal in elder abuse and neglect cases should be: Whatever you do, do not make it worse.

When elder abuse and neglect cases—or other protective-service cases—are being assessed, the following questions need to be asked at the outset, and the case should be handled in accordance with the answers obtained.

1. Risk: Is the person at some significant risk of physical, emotional, or financial harm as a result of their own actions or omissions to act? If so, the person is a likely candidate for protective service and/or crisis intervention.

2. Emergency or chronic condition: Is the person in an emergency condition, that is, one that is imminently life threatening, or likely to result in severe physical, emotional, or financial harm within the next 24 to 48 hours? Or is the condition chronic, that is, has the person been in this condition or situation for some time and survived, and does the person seem to be continuing to survive in spite of the risk?

If the person is in an emergency condition, then crisis intervention appears appropriate. Once the emergency is resolved, the worker should determine whether further protective-service work is needed, whether concrete services are required, or whether nursing home placement might be the best solution.

If the person's condition is not life threatening, albeit shocking or repugnant, and appears to be a chronic condition in which the person is continuing to live, then the person is likely to be a potential protective-service case, for which crisis intervention would be inappropriate. There would be a clear need to obtain as much history as possible about the person— lifestyle, medical history and so forth—so that an accurate assessment could be made about how the person came to be at risk. The history would provide many clues as to what solutions are feasible, and how easy or difficult it will be to get the person to accept these changes.

3. Mental competency: Is the person mentally capable of making informed decisions about his or her life? For both crisis-intervention and protective-service strategies, the steps taken by the worker will depend on the degree of mental competency of the alleged abuse victim.

If the person appears to be mentally competent, then he has a right to decide what to do about his situation, no matter how serious it is. However, if the worker is quite certain the person does not understand what he is doing, and it is a medical or psychiatric emergency, the worker should call the police or ambulance service to attempt to get them to rush the person to the hospital or mental health facility. Once at the hospital or mental health facility, life-saving treatment may be provided and, if it is a mental health facility, a decision can be made whether to attempt to move for an emergency admission.

The police or ambulance service normally will not transport a person who is actively refusing to go, even one who appears to be mentally incompetent. In that situation, the worker should seek an immediate assessment from a guardianship-services specialist to determine if an emergency guardianship might be obtained. If it is, then treatment may proceed. Emergency guardianship may be obtained in a few hours, but normally only with extraordinary efforts by lawyers, doctors, psychiatrists, caseworkers, and the courts.

In those cases where the client appears to be mentally incompetent, but an emergency has not arisen, the worker should nevertheless explore whether she is capable of making informed decisions about her current situation, and whether a court-appointed guardian or conservator may be needed.

4. Assistance wanted: Does the person consent to be helped? The overall casework goal is to develop a relationship of mutual trust and respect, so that together you may develop and implement a case plan to which the client will consent, and which will reduce or eliminate the risk the client faces.

If the person is mentally competent, but will not consent to be helped, she has the right to refuse, even in an emergency. The worker is then left only with "creative-casework" techniques to try to convince the person to consent to services. If that fails, the worker has no recourse but to allow the person to implement her decision to be left alone. The worker may, of course, try to talk further with the person later, or try to find someone else who might be successful in getting the person to change her mind.

If the person who does not consent to intervention appears mentally incompetent, an assessment by a guardianship services specialist and/or a psychiatrist should be obtained to determine if the objections are made by a mentally competent adult. If the person appears mentally incompetent based on an assessment, a petition should be filed with the court for the appointment of a guardian or conservator. If appointed, the guardian or conservator may make decisions on the person's behalf, and the protective-service worker may coordinate service provision with the guardian or conservator.

Although there is considerable variation in the specific crisis-intervention and protective-service strategies locally available to deal with abuse cases, and though there are differences in the legal mechanisms for handling mental incompetency, the protocol outlined above should serve as an algorithm applicable to a wide variety of settings. Protective-service workers must be aware of their obligations to those most difficult and stressful clients—the nonconsenting and/or incompetent clients—as well as the limits of their mandate to intervene. With a systematic approach, and caution, the protective-service worker can avoid trampling the rights of the victim in the rush to save.

Chapter 9

STRATEGIES FOR SERVICE PROVISION

The Use of Legal Interventions in a Systems Approach to Casework

Sue Ringel Segal and Madelyn Anne Iris

Noninstitutional elder abuse occurs within the social framework of the family or household and is influenced by surrounding systems. Victims include those who are physically maltreated, as well as those who are subjected to verbal and emotional abuse, financial exploitation, and intentional and nonintentional neglect. Frequently, several types of abuse occur simultaneously, leading to complex levels of problem solving and necessitating input from multiple systems. Such cases often project criminal aspects as well as counseling issues, thus warranting intervention from both the social work and legal systems.

The North Suburban Cook County Elder Abuse Project tested the application of legal interventions to cases of elder abuse within the framework of a systems approach to casework. This chapter describes the application of a systems approach to casework in elder abuse, and through examples illustrates the application of legal interventions as tools in the prevention and alleviation of victimization of the elderly.

BACKGROUND

In 1985, a 2-year model elder abuse project began in a three-township area of north suburban Chicago; in 1986 the project expanded to include six other townships. Complete descriptions of all project findings, including data collection strategies and methodology, can be found in the final research report (see Iris, 1987). Findings described in this chapter are based on an analysis of data collected through December, 1986.

The project grew out of a grass-roots effort by a group of local professionals. Funding was provided by grants from a private foundation, the local area agency on aging, and the State of Illinois Elder Abuse Demonstration Project. Intake, investigation, and service access were provided by four social service agencies designated as State of Illinois Case Coordination Units. A telephone hotline provided 24-hour-response capabilities for investigation of voluntary reports of elder abuse.

A major goal of the project was to develop a community-wide network of cooperating agencies to address the problem of elder abuse. To achieve this goal, two elder abuse consortia were organized, comprised of representatives from social and health service agencies, hospitals, law-enforcement programs, legal services, municipal and township governments, and other organizations serving the elderly.

Each consortium met on a monthly basis to develop local intervention strategies and to promote collaborative problem solving. Meetings focused on review of project cases, as well as the sharing of information, education, and research programs, and the development of speakers' bureaus. The monthly meetings facilitated greater communication among separate organizational systems, served as sources of professional education about elder abuse, and provided support to caseworkers working with elder abuse clients. Professional and public educational efforts led to better identification of victims and enhanced the ability of existing systems to intervene in cases of abuse and neglect.

Description of Legal Interventions

Four types of legal interventions have potential usefulness in resolving cases of elder abuse. Orders of protection (or restraining orders), as authorized under the Illinois Domestic Violence Act, provide a mechanism for removing the abuser from the home and for preventing further abuse or harassment.

In a few cases, guardianship of the person and/or estate has proven to be the most appropriate intervention. Because guardianship is used when a person suffers from a diagnosed mental impairment, guardianships are usually viewed as an intervention of last resort (see Regan, 1981).

Representative payeeships offer a less restrictive alternative to guardianships of the estate. However, they can be used only for particular types of incomes, such as social security or government pensions. Further, an individual or agency must be willing to serve as the representative payee. In addition, monitoring of the payee's activities is minimal, and protection from abuse is not guaranteed.

Finally, involuntary commitments for psychiatric evaluation and treatment can also be used to resolve cases of elder abuse, particularly if the abuser suffers from a chronic mental disorder that precludes the possibility of successful intervention through any means other than medical and/or psychiatric intervention. However, involuntary commitments can only be obtained when the immediate safety and well-being of the victim or abuser is directly threatened.

Summary of Project Findings

By June, 1987 the North Suburban Cook County Elder Abuse Project had served approximately 237 clients. Most clients were women (75%), ranging from 55 to 98 years of age. Although 50% of these women were widowed, 39.2% were married. In contrast, 63.8% of male clients were married, and only 27.7% were widowed.

Most victims lived with either a spouse (43%) or a child or children (26.2%), whereas 15.2% of the clients lived alone.

Eighty-five percent of the clients lived in their own homes or apartments. Thus, when a client did live with a child, it was usually the child who lived in the home of the elderly person. A wide range of income levels is found: from less than $12,000 a year (54.9%) to over $20,000 (45%).

Although most clients had at least one health problem, the population was not characterized by high levels of impairments or inability to perform activities of daily living. Seventy percent of the clients were considered oriented to time, place, and person.

Familial relationships between victims and abusers were the most common: 33.5% of the abusers were spouses and 26.8% were children, 15.6% were categorized as relatives other than spouse or child, and less than 10% were nonrelatives. Of the abusers, 57.1% were women and 42.9% were men.

Eight general types of abuse were indicated on the report forms:

Type of abuse	*Frequency of occurrence*
Psychological, emotional and verbal abuse	46.3%
Physical abuse	40.6%
Financial exploitation	32.5%
Passive neglect	23.8%
Deprivation (of food, medicine, services)	23.1%
Confinement	9.4%
Self-neglect	16.3%
Sexual abuse	one case reported

Multiple abuse was indicated for a large number of clients; out of 158 cases, a single type of abuse was listed in only 65 cases. At times, two, three, and even four types of abuse were listed for a single case. Substantiation rates ranged from 73.8% in cases of physical abuse to 30.7% for cases of financial exploitation.

The findings show three types of abuse situations that predominated: (1) chronic abuse within the family (i.e., domestic violence grown old); (2) chronic abuse within the family requiring immediate intervention; and (3) abuse within a family due to a change in the living situation or status of the victim. The research distinguished chronic abuse cases that required immediate intervention from those in which participants were resistant to efforts to alleviate the abuse. Change in the victim's status was often due to the onset of a disease, or loss of a support, such as a spouse.

Resolution of the abuse involved dealing with a variety of issues, including mutual interdependence between the victim and the abuser; the willingness of both parties to change the situation; and the likelihood of a successful separation of victim from abuser. The victim's mental capacities were also thought to be of potential significance.

SYSTEMS THEORY AND THE FAMILY

For many years, traditional intervention techniques used in the helping professions focused on the psychodynamic (intrapsychic) approach, in which the person is viewed as an entity separate from the environment. Only recently has the social environment played a role in intervention with the individual. The *systems theory* is based on the premise, as expressed by Minuchin (1974), that "man is not an isolate." Within social gerontology, attention to the importance of the family in intervention with the elderly is even more recent (Rathbone-McCuan, Travis, & Voyles, 1983).

The family system becomes increasingly important to older persons as other social supports break down and disappear. When some part of the domestic system becomes dysfunctional, abuse and neglect can occur either from within the family itself or from nonrelated household members. Because of the growing dependence of older persons on family members for social and functional survival, family history and patterns of family dynamics as well as interpersonal relationships must be accounted for when assessing alleged elder abuse situations. Interventions must be family oriented and focus on the role and position of each member within the family or household system, and not just on the older person as victim (see Bookin & Dunkle, 1985).

In a systems approach to elder abuse, the systems concept is expanded to include formal and informal community service networks, as well as institutions such as police and the health department. The intervening caseworker must coordinate the various systems which might provide services in cases of elder abuse. Attention must be given to a "cross interpretation" of their different methods and theories (Douglass & Hickey, 1983).

For example, elder abuse often occurs within the context of the household, which usually includes family members such as spouses, children, and in-laws. Yet the household system is influenced by the larger family system outside the domicile, and may be affected by a system of community supports dependent on state and federal dictates. In Illinois, these larger systems are coordinated by the local Case Coordination Units. Figure 9-1 illustrates this concept of interrelated and hierarchical systems.

In this model, the primary focus is on balancing the need to protect the victim against the desire to maintain the family or domestic unit. Thus, in the Elder Abuse Project, casework interventions were aimed at stopping abuse or neglect by involving both victims and their families, including the abuser, in the investigation, planning, and service-delivery phases. When necessary, a gamut of social, health, and other supportive services were offered to supplement or supplant those provided by the alleged abusive caretaker or family member. Legal services and options were usually discussed at the initial interview, and a description of such interventions was left with the alleged victim.

The Elder Abuse Consortia fostered integration of services across agencies and institutions in various ways: (1) by bringing together representatives from various types of agencies, such as municipal departments, police, and health care institutions; (2) through case presentations; and (3) through discussions of emerging issues illustrating the complex nature of family and interpersonal relations within the social system where abuse occurs.

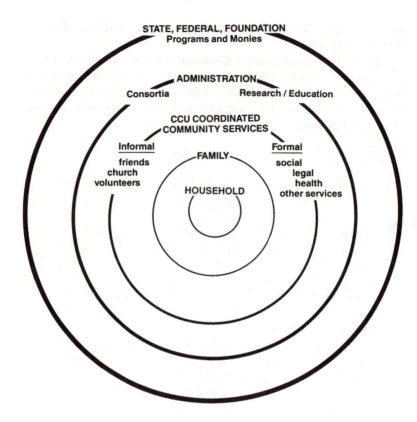

Figure 9-1.   Coordinated case-service system.

The Use of Legal Interventions in a Systems Approach

A number of legal interventions were used to alleviate abuse during the 2-year project. For example, orders of protection and guardianships were used in a number of cases, or were presented to the client as appropriate options. However, it is clear that although actual use of these interventions was deemed an important measure of the effectiveness of legal interventions in resolving cases of elder abuse, knowledge of legal options and access to legal counsel were equally important. For example, caseworkers consulted regularly with the attorney from the legal-assistance agency in order to plan an intervention strategy.

Several composite cases illustrate the ways in which a systems theory in elder abuse intervention was blended with the legal-intervention model, with the goal of maintaining the family system as well as the independence and well-being of both victim and abuser.

Case Example 1

Mrs. W. was referred to the Project through the Elder Abuse Hotline. She complained of years of verbal and emotional abuse, as well as financial exploitation and confinement, all allegedly perpetrated by her husband. These accusations had been previously lodged with a local agency that tried to work with her around her frequent complaints and to help her move out of the house. The agency worked only with Mrs. W. and did not attempt to discuss the accusations with her husband, or involve him in intervention or planning.

The Elder Abuse Project caseworker, on a suspicion, had Mrs. W. evaluated by a geriatric physician, who diagnosed her various physical problems as well as a form of senile dementia. The caseworker found indications of verbal abuse by both parties, compounded by Mrs. W.'s decline in functional abilities and her husband's increased, stressful role in caretaking.

Planned interventions included adult day care for Mrs. W., as well as housekeeping and supportive counseling to her husband to help alleviate his stress. Financial-planning services were also offered to help Mr. W. prepare for his wife's long-term medical and protective needs.

A second example illustrates the use of legal interventions in the family system.

Case Example 2

Following the amputation of one of his legs, Mr. D.'s daughter called the local social service agency, requesting assistance in providing personal care for her father. At the initial assessment the caseworker noted bruises on Mr. D.'s arms and face. He stated that his wife, Mrs. D., was an impatient person and sometimes became angry because of his infirmity. Mrs. D. denied these charges and refused further contact with the caseworker.

The case was referred to the Elder Abuse Project caseworker for investigation. After repeated visits by the Elder Abuse Project worker, Mr. D. confessed that his wife had been an alcoholic for many years. Previously, Mr. D. had been able to withstand his wife's physical violence and verbal harangues, but changes in his health status limited his ability to tolerate his wife's abuse.

Mr. D.'s daughter corroborated this and provided further insights into the situation. She voiced her own frustration, and stated she had no control over her mother's behavior. However, she wanted very much to continue to support her father and provide care for him.

After repeated incidents of physical violence, Mr. D. realized he could no longer protect himself from his wife's abuse, and with the assistance of the Project Caseworker and legal services attorney he filed for an Order of Protection.

Following Mrs. D.'s removal from the home, increased supportive services were provided to Mr. D. and development of the care plan included consultation with both Mr. D. and his daugther. During follow-up visits, the caseworker supported Mr. D. in his decision to separate from his wife.

The Project caseworker maintained contact with Mrs. D., who was offered assistance in relocation. A range of social and health services were subsequently provided.

The use of other types of legal interventions are illustrated in a third example, involving an elderly mother and her mentally ill daughter.

Case Example 3

Mrs. B., housebound due to a chronic, debilitating physical illness, lived in her own apartment while her daughter, Mrs. T., lived nearby with her husband and child. Several years earlier, Mrs. T. had been appointed a representative payee for her mother.

Mrs. B. was referred to the Elder Abuse caseworker by the local Victim Witness Program. The referral was prompted by her calls to the police, complaining her daughter was threatening and harassing her with phone calls and visits, and had misappropriated her social security checks.

During the investigation, the elder abuse worker ascertained that Mrs. T. was suffering from a longstanding personality disorder. Discussions with Mrs. B. and other family members indicated Mrs. T. would not cooperate in the investigation. The caseworker's attempts to speak with Mrs. T. were rebuffed. Inquiries to the Social Security Administration indicated Mrs. T. had been filing false reports as a representative payee.

The legal-services attorney assisted Mrs. B. in having her daughter removed as representative payee, and designated a sister instead. Mrs. B. chose not to pursue charges against her daughter, but did seek services from a home-health agency to help support her in her home. Mrs. T. was outraged by this action, but under threat of an order of protection maintained a distance from her mother and ceased her harassing behavior.

Mrs. T.'s husband considered using a civil commitment to obtain psychiatric services for his wife, but was able to persuade her to admit herself to a psychiatric hospital where she was placed on medication. However, after discharge she stopped her medications, left her husband and child, and at present her whereabouts are unknown.

DISCUSSION

These cases demonstrate the various types of abusive situations dealt with by Elder Abuse Project staff, as well as the different uses of legal interventions within a family-systems approach. In the first example, no specific legal intervention was used. However, due to Mrs. W.'s decreasing mental competency, a guardianship may be necessary to protect Mrs. W., and guarantee her financial support and conservation of the family's resources.

In the second example we find a blend of ongoing domestic violence compounded by substance abuse. When linked to a situation in which one partner suffers from increasing physical disability, such chronic abuse becomes a turning point for ending the relationship. Orders of protection provide an immediate remedy for such physical violence without endangering the victim with loss of residence or forfeiture of assets. In addition, a divorce or legal separation can be implemented to guarantee individual rights and to establish a plan for long-term financial stability.

The third case illustrates how the threat of legal intervention can be used to alleviate abuse, even when family members are involved. For example, Mrs. B. was empowered with the knowledge that legal interventions were available to protect her from her daughter's harassment and exploitation. Mr. T. was motivated to consider an involuntary commitment for his wife when support for this action was provided by the elder abuse caseworker. In addition, this case demonstrates that all agencies, not just those directly involved in dealing with elder abuse, must be mindful of the potential for abuse when implementing legal supports such as representative payees or guardianships.

This discussion illustrates the important role a systems approach plays in intervention in cases of elder abuse. Project caseworkers utilized a variety of legal interventions, including guardianships, orders of protection, and divorce, as a means of alleviating abuse and protecting elderly victims from continued exploitation and harm. Most importantly, knowledge of legal options was judged a valuable tool for enabling victims to bring about change in their own situations.

However, a number of issues emerged that demonstrate a continual tension between the family-systems approach and the legal-intervention model. For example, social workers practice the tenet of the "least restrictive alternative" in service provision (see Langley, 1981) and are committed to working within the family system. In contrast, attorneys serve in the best interests of the individual client, utilizing the courts as a primary means of intervention, dispute resolution, and remedy.

In addition, it was often difficult for the elderly victim to even consider taking legal action against a family member. Such clients were unaware that such actions were possible, and the majority were hesitant to become involved with the court system. Many clients were unwilling to sacrifice familial relationships, even when their own safety and well-being were threatened. These clients often needed many hours of counseling before acknowledging such steps were advisable. Clients who pursued legal interventions, such as orders of protection, frequently needed ongoing support for their decision.

CONCLUSION

The Elder Abuse Project provides substantial evidence of the various ways in which legal interventions can be used to alleviate elder abuse. However, existing laws and statutes do not fully address the needs of all abused elderly. Increased professional training and familiarity with the law is needed to assure appropriate and timely use of available legal interventions. Getting the courts, local police, physicians, and hospitals to acknowledge the existence of elder abuse in the community and to recognize its significance is a continual problem. The legal-intervention model served to increase client awareness of individual rights under the law and to educate social service personnel about the law. When blended with a systems approach to casework, this model proved to be an excellent strategy for aiding victims of elder abuse while recognizing the strength and importance of familial relationships and long-standing networks of support.

Acknowledgments

Various agencies played an important role in the development and successful outcome of this project. The Northwest Suburban Council for Community Services provided a major impetus for the concept of an elder abuse project. Northwest Service Coordination for the Health Impaired Elderly served as the administrative agency for the project and was instrumental in developing the model. The Metropolitan Chicago Coalition on Aging also participated in the development of the project, and was responsible for qualitative research activities as well as public-education efforts. The Suburban Cook County Area Agency on Aging assisted in the development of the model and provided staff support and expertise throughout the 27-month project, as well as financial support. Finally, legal counsel was provided by the Cook County Legal Assistance Foundation. The Retirement Research Foundation generously provided financial support for expansion of services into township areas not served by the state-funded demonstration project. The Case Coordination Units serving the project areas deserve mention. Thanks go to Family Counseling Service of Evanston/Skokie, Parkside Human Services, Northshore Senior Center, Northwest Community Service, and Elk Grove-Schaumberg Counseling Program.

The authors wish to thank Ms. Beth Haywood of the Suburban Cook County Area Agency on Aging for her careful review of this work, and Ms. Rosa Hano, M.S.W., for her comments.

Chapter 10

COMMUNITY PROFESSIONALS AND THEIR PERSPECTIVES ON ELDER ABUSE

Trudy B. Anderson

Community professionals may view older persons who have been mistreated by caregivers from the medical perspective, the social services perspective, or the legal perspective; even within each perspective, there are subviews. Within the medical perspective, for example, physicians and nurses are likely to have distinctive views about elder abuse because of differences in their formal training, experiences with older persons, and the stage at which each professional becomes involved in the detection process.

Because practitioners working in the community are the persons who are in a position to detect and report abnormal injuries and conditions, their perspectives on elder abuse are important for improving intervention strategies. Yet, little is known about the views of community professionals on this social issue. This chapter adds to the body of research by examining whether occupational perspective influences: (1) exposure to the elder abuse problem, (2) perception of the prevalence of this phenomenon in their community, and (3) perception of the seriousness of various abusive acts.

PROFESSIONAL ORIENTATION

Several researchers and practitioners (Bookin & Dunkle, 1985; Douglass, 1983; Douglass & Hickey, 1983; Hickey & Douglass, 1981a, 1981b; Hudson, 1986; Quinn & Tomita, 1986) have commented on the impact of professional orientatation on perceptions of elder abuse. Douglass and Hickey (Douglass, 1983; Douglass & Hickey, 1983; Hickey & Douglass, 1981a, 1981b) have found that the perspective of professionals influenced the type of abuse with which they have contact. Police officers, lawyers, and mental health workers regularly deal with elders who have been verbally and emotionally abused and less frequently assist those who have been physically mistreated. These researchers (Hickey & Douglass, 1981b) also have reported that in explaining the causes of elder mistreatment, practitioners working with older adults were found to be influenced by the occupational perspective. Lawyers and social workers perceive dependency on the caregiver as the main cause, whereas police officers and nurses view a lifecycle of violence as the critical element. Practitioners (Quinn & Tomita, 1986) additionally have noted that various human service professionals have different approaches to intervention. For example, social workers will try to change the situation or the behavior that led to the elderly person's being mistreated, whereas police officers will attempt to determine if the abuser has broken any laws or if the abused elder's rights have been violated, and nurses will endeavor to restore the elderly person's health.

METHOD

Sample

Data were obtained from a variety of professionals working in a south central metropolitan area with a high proportion of elderly residents (U.S. Bureau of the Census, 1980a). A list of physicians who limit their practice to family medicine, lawyers who advertise as specialists in family law, and ministers who sponsor special programs for the elderly law was obtained from the Yellow Pages of the city's telephone directory. Because nurses, social workers, and police officers do not advertise their services, hospital emergency rooms, social service agencies, and police departments were contacted for the names of persons who might have dealt with cases of elder abuse. These professionals then were asked to provide names of other professionals, as were subsequent respondents. A majority of the respondents (68%) provided names of at least one other practitioner; in a number of instances, more than one respondent suggested the same individual as a potential interviewee. Thus, a purposive procedure was used to obtain a nonprobability sample of community professionals likely to have had some experience with abused elderly persons.

Sixty-three community professionals, or 73% of those contacted, were surveyed. In 56 cases (89%), the interviews were conducted in the respondents' offices; but when after three callbacks respondents' schedules prevented a personal interview, the survey was completed over the telephone. Telephone interviews were only necessary in 7 cases (11%).

The sample included physicians (n = 14), nurses (n = 8), social workers (n = 11), clergy (n = 9), police officers (n = 7), and lawyers (n = 14), and thereby encompassed a wide range of professionals who were likely to have come in contact with abused older persons. The sample was predominantly white (94%) and male (71%); it also was rather young with three-fourths of the respondents being between the ages of 25 and 44. Social workers were the youngest professional groups, with all under the age of 45. Not surprisingly, most respondents were highly educated, with four-fifths (84%) having completed at least four years of college. Police officers were the least educated, with the majority (57%) completing only 1 to 3 years of college.

Measures

1. Exposure. Exposure to elder abuse as a problem was measured in terms of each community professional's having read an article in a professional publication in the past year or having attended a seminar, workshop, or conference on this topic. Responses were dichotomized: 0 "no," and 1 "yes."

2. Perceived Prevalence. Perception of the commonness of the elder abuse problem was assessed by having each practitioner consider how prevalent elder abuse is in their community, compared will spouse and child abuse. Responses were coded: 1 "rather rare"; 2 "prevalent, but not as prevalent as either spouse or child abuse"; 3 "as prevalent as spouse and child abuse"; and 4 "more prevalent than either or both spouse and child abuse."

3. Perceived Seriousness. After being informed that acts of abuse toward elderly persons vary in terms of their degree of seriousness, each practitioner was asked to rate the seriousness of 18 different caregiver acts of mistreatment of an elder. The acts were coded: 1 "not at all serious," 2 "slightly (somewhat) serious," 3 "very serious," and 4 "extremely serious." Nonphysical acts as well as physical ones were included in the list of caregiver acts of elder abuse. There is some disagreement regarding the classification of withholding food and medicine. Some gerontologists (e.g., Lau & Kosberg, 1979) have considered these acts as forms of physical abuse, whereas others (Hickey & Douglass, 1981a) have placed them in the category of active neglect. In this paper, withholding food and withholding medicine are categorized as nonphysical acts because they do not involve bodily force. Other nonphysical acts included in the items presented to the community professionals covered material abuse (e.g., taking the elder's social security checks or selling the elder's home) and violation of constitutional rights (e.g., forcing the elder into a nursing home) (Hickey & Douglass, 1981a; Lau & Kosberg, 1979).

RESULTS

Exposure to the Elder Abuse Problem

Knowledge about the problem is important if practitioners are to detect elder abuse and intervene (Bookin & Dunkle,

1985; Hudson, 1986). About 54% of the practitioners had been exposed to the elder abuse problems either through articles in professional publications or through attendance at seminars or in-service training sessions. Most of the community professionals, therefore, were informed about the mistreatment of older persons by caregivers. Occupational perspective had a significant impact on exposure to the problem of elder abuse (M = .5397; t = 2.267, p < .0006). Compared with the other practitioners, a greater proportion (over 54%) of the nurses, social workers, and clergy were informed about this issue. It is apparent that the orientation of the professionals affects familiarity with the dynamics of caregivers who mistreat elderly persons.

Perceived Prevalence of Elder Abuse

The literature is inconsistent regarding the frequency of elder abuse as compared with the frequency of other forms of family mistreatment. Some gerontologists (see Hudson, 1986) estimate that elder abuse is less common than spouse abuse but is at least as common as child abuse, whereas others (see Bookin & Dunkle, 1985) figure that it is only slightly less frequent than child abuse.

Some professional groups working in the community have more contact with abused elderly persons than do others (Hickey & Douglass, 1981a, 1981b); the practitioners' experiences with mistreated older persons may be reflected in their views of the regularity with which this problem occurs. Table 10-1 summarizes the community professionals' perceptions of the prevalence of elder abuse. About two-thirds (65%) of these practitioners viewed elder abuse as prevalent in their community, but not as common as either spouse or child abuse. Despite this considerable amount of consensus, there were significant differences. Police officers were the practitioners most likely to hold the view that elder abuse is less prevalent, followed by clergy, lawyers, and physicians. In contrast, nurses and, to a lesser extent, social workers were apt to consider elder abuse at least as common as spouse or child abuse. Occupational perspective, therefore, appears to have some influence on perceptions of the magnitude of the problem of the elderly being mistreated.

Table 10-1   Perceived Prevalence of Elder Abuse by Community Professionals[a][b]

	Community professionals					
Perceived Prevalence	Physicians (n = 14) %	Nurses (n = 8) %	Social workers (n = 11) %	Clergy (n = 9) %	Police officers (n = 7) %	Lawyers (n = 14) %
Rather rare	7			11	14	7
Prevalent but less so than spouse or child abuse	71	38	45	78	86	71
As prevalent as spouse and child abuse	14	62	27			14
More prevalent than either or both spouse or child abuse	7		27	11		7
Total	99	100	100	100	100	99

Note: Perceived prevalence was coded: 1 = rather rare; 2 = prevalent, but not as prevalent as either spouse or child abuse; 3 = as prevalent as spouse and child abuse; 4 = more prevalent than either or both spouse and child abuse.
[a] Figures may not total 100 because of rounding error.
[b] $M = 2.3175$, df = 5, t = 1.521, p = .0554.

Perceived Seriousness of Elder Abuse

The community professionals' perceptions of the seriousness of abusive acts is likely to have an impact on intervention. When practitioners encounter an elder abuse case with an injury or condition that they do not consider very serious, they in all probability will fail to report it.

The perceived seriousness of the various abusive acts was dichotomized into "not very serious" and "very serious." "Very serious" was selected as the cutting point because it represented the median response for the item with the least amount of consensus: namely, "shook by the shoulders."

Surprisingly, nonphysical acts were not perceived as less serious than were physical acts. Some nonphysical acts, in fact, were viewed as just as grave as physical ones: The same proportion of community professionals perceived as equally harmful, "caregiver sold elder's home without consent" and "caregiver kicked elder" (94%) as well as "caregiver withheld food

**Table 10-2   Proportion Perceiving Elder Abuse Acts
as Very Serious by Community Professionals**

Elder abuse act	Community professionals					
	Physicians (n = 14) %	Nurses (n = 8) %	Social workers (n = 11) %	Clergy (n = 9) %	Police officers (n = 7) %	Lawyers (n = 14) %
Physical act by caregiver:						
Shook elder by the shoulders	43	62	73	44	57	79
Threw an object at elder	71	88	82	89	71	86
Tied elder in a chair	77[a]	100	82	78	86	100
Pushed elder	86	100	82	78	100	79
Slapped elder in the face with hand	86	100	91	89	57	93
Kicked elder	100	88	91	100	86	93
Threatened to use knife or gun on elder	92	88	91	100	100	100
Slapped elder on the face with an object	100	88	100	100	86	93
Burned elder with a cigarette	93	88	100	100	100	100
Banged elder against the wall	93	100	100	100	86	100
Hit elder with an object	100	88	100	100	100	100
Hit elder with fist	100	100	100	100	86	100
Beat elder	100	100	100	100	100	100
Nonphysical act by caregiver:						
Placed elder in nursing home when not necessary	75[a]	86[a]	64	89	71	86
Forced elder to sign over social security check or insurance benefits	86	75	82	100	100	100[a]
Sold elder's home without consent	93	88	82	100	100	100
Withheld food from elder	93	88	100	100	86	100
Withheld from or gave too much prescribed medication to elder	100	100	100	100	100	100

Note: Perceived seriousness coded: 0 = not very serious; 1 = very serious.
[a] Missing cases.

from elder" and "caregiver threatened to use knife or gun on elder" (95%). Some nonphysical acts were even viewed as more injurious than those that inflicted bodily harm. "Caregiver forced elder to sign over social security check or insurance benefits" (90%), for example, was generally viewed by the practitioners as more serious than "caregiver slapped elder in the face with hand" (87%).

Table 10-2 examines the practitioners' perceptions of the seriousness of acts of elder abuse. Professional orientation was not found to influence significantly the perceived seriousness of any of these acts. Rather, there was considerable agreement among professionals that almost any act is as serious as any other abusive act; over 70% of the respondents within each professional group viewed all but two acts as very serious. The two acts on which there is some disagreement are "shook elder by the shoulders" and "placed elder in nursing home when not needing such care." Physicians and clergy were the practitioners most likely to consider the former abusive act as not very serious, whereas some social workers viewed the latter as not harmful.

DISCUSSION

This chapter examines whether occupational perspective influences professionals' exposure to and views about mistreated older persons. The literature suggests that knowledge about elder abuse and its signs increases the practitioners' ability to detect mistreated older persons. Most of the professionals in this study had been informed about abused elders during the year prior to the study; still, occupational perspective had a significant impact on exposure. Nurses, social workers, and clergy with aging congregations were more likely to be knowledgeable about this problem. Some professionals, therefore, are more expert about the conditions that lead to, as well as the signs of, elderly persons being abused. This finding is important because practitioners' awareness of elder abuse facilitates intervention, at least in the early stages of the detection process.

These findings have been consistent with the research that suggests that elder abuse is prevalent but less common than either spouse or child abuse. Although the majority of these practitioners held this view, nurses and social workers generally considered elder abuse to be at least as common as other forms of family mistreatment. Differential knowledge and experience probably account for differential perceptions of the commonness of elder abuse.

Although occupational perspective was found to influence exposure and perceived prevalence, it had no effect on perceived seriousness of abusive acts. There was, in fact, considerable consensus among practitioners that almost any abusive act toward an elderly person is a very serious act. There were only two acts that fewer than 70% of the respondents within each professional group considered very serious: shaking an elder by the shoulder and placing an elder in nursing home when the elder does not need such care. The data suggest that these practitioners consider the consequences of the abusive acts without regard for the caregiver's intent and are generally in agreement about unacceptable ways of treating older persons. This finding does not support the Michigan study (Hickey & Douglass, 1981a, p. 506), which reported that professionals perceived elder abuse "as a somewhat 'normal' phenomenon in our society" and do not consider as abuse the consequences of nonphysical acts, such as withholding food. These contradictory findings may reflect differential attitudes about aging and violence; such attitudes may be more critical than occupational perspective in explaining professionals' views of the seriousness of elder mistreatment.

IMPLICATIONS

Education

Successful intervention requires that all community professionals from clergy to lawyers be knowledgeable about the dynamics of elder abuse as well as the differences between this form of maltreatment and child and spouse abuse. Practitioner groups with differential experience and knowledge must communicate with each other; they especially need to resolve the dilemma created by having distinctive goals in intervention. Interprofessional workshops and conferences would facilitate the exchange of information and cooperative efforts. Such educational programs additionally would provide opportunities for dispelling myths about elder abuse.

Research

Future research must survey large and representative samples of practitioners so as to more fully address the question of occupational perspective. Studies also are needed to examine how ageism and attitudes toward violence in American society affect the views of community professionals. Cultural bias has been an overlooked research area (Bookin & Dunkle, 1985).

Part III

POLICY

Chapter 11

FEDERAL INITIATIVES

Valerie Rinkle

Federal activity in the area of elder abuse has been marked by nearly a decade of legislative history. This history, however, has not produced special elder abuse social-service programs. This is primarily due to an ongoing debate among members of Congress and their staff as to the most appropriate means to prevent and treat this problem. Furthermore, Congressional attention has shifted away from elder abuse that occurs within families—as evidenced by recent activities that have focused instead upon institutional abuse and catastrophic health insurance as it relates to the relief of chronic illness and stress that are often associated with familial violence.

ELDER ABUSE LEGISLATION AND HISTORY

Federal interest in the area of elder abuse began in 1978 with the award of two research grants through the Department of Health and Human Services, and with the initiation of a special investigation conducted by the Select Committee on Aging of the U.S. House of Representatives. Two years later, the issue received more formal attention with a joint hearing of the Senate and House of Representatives special aging committees (U.S. House of Representatives, 1980). The hearing pursued early research findings and preliminary results from the Select Committee's special investigation that culminated in the report titled *Elder Abuse: An Examination of a Hidden Problem* (U.S. House of Representatives, 1981b).

This report represented the first attempt to define the problem of elder abuse as well as to identify the extent of the problem. However, as the Committee noted, its findings did not substitute for a statistically valid, national incidence study of elder abuse (U.S. House of Representatives, 1981a, p. 54). Several members of Congress and their staff believed that such a study, at a minimum, was necessary before a large-scale federal effort could be initiated to deal with the problem. Nevertheless, as a result of the Congressional interest spawned by the Committee's effort, several legislative proposals directed at the problem of elder abuse were developed.

In 1980, the House of Representatives (U.S. House of Representatives, 1981a) adopted legislation establishing a discretionary grant program that provided seed money to local community-based shelters to expand local domestic-violence prevention and treatment programs for victims of elder abuse. Although the provision failed in the Senate, the association of the problem of elder abuse with other types of domestic violence, and with their preferred intervention strategies, marked the beginning of a continuing Congressional debate over the most appropriate federal response to the problem of elder abuse.

Specifically, several members of Congress believed that strategies to prevent and treat elder abuse should be tailored after domestic-violence intervention methods, which recognize abused elderly as responsible adults with dysfunctional family systems. However, others believed that an approach modeled after child-abuse prevention and treatment strategies was more appropriate. This latter policy perspective, sometimes referred to as *mandatory reporting*, was supported by case studies available at the time that indicated abused elderly persons, like children, were typically dependent upon others for daily personal care and support. Advocates of mandatory reporting sponsored the

Prevention, Identification, and Treatment of Elder Abuse Act on January 6, 1981 (see H.R. 3833, 98th Congress, First Session, August 4, 1983 in the Legislative Information File, U.S. Library of Congress).

This bill proposed the creation of a National Center for Elder Abuse under the Department of Health and Human Services, providing monetary incentives for states to establish programs for mandatory reporting and investigation of elder abuse, and for the provision of protective services. In addition, the bill would have established immunity from prosecution for persons reporting incidences of elder abuse. The proposal was modeled after the Child Abuse Prevention, Identification and Treatment Act of 1974, including many of the same programmatic requirements and financial incentives to elicit state participation. The measure did not pass the 97th Congress, however, mainly because of the differing opinions regarding the most effective prevention and treatment strategy.

By 1983, research findings from studies of existing state elder abuse laws were published. The purpose of these laws was to enable the identification of abuse cases, and ultimately the correction of the situation. Most of these laws had been tailored after child abuse reporting laws. A study by the UCLA/ USC Long-Term Care Gerontology Center (Salend, Kane, Satz, & Pynoos, 1984) indicated that, with some exceptions, these laws did not fulfill their purposes because they failed to target specifically and/or to define elder abuse adequately. In addition, other critics of mandatory reporting laws (cf. Faulkner, 1982) noted that because most cases came to the attention of the "helping professions" outside of mandatory reporting, the laws authorized involuntary intervention without adequate cause. It was also noted that elder abuse statutes were based on age, and as such they acted to reinforce ageism. These findings supported the need for an alternative approach to the identification and treatment of elder abuse as advocated by those members of Congress who opposed mandatory reporting.

During the first session of the 98th Congress, the House of Representatives approved the Family Violence Prevention and Treatment Act as part of the 1984 reauthorization of the Child Abuse Prevention, Identification and Treatment Act. The act included several separate provisions designed to address elder abuse as a special component of the family-violence problem. One provision, aimed at recipients of funds under the act, prohibited discrimination against clients on the basis of age. The intent was to provide older persons access to the program established by the act. Another provision required the National Center on Family Violence, created by the act, to coordinate its activities with the Administration on Aging and the National Institute on Aging. Overall, the act provided for a domestic-violence or advocacy approach to the problem of elder abuse. This type of approach differed from the child-abuse/mandatory-reporting approach by supporting the independence of the victim through self-help groups and safe houses as well as use of the criminal courts, rather than family courts, to adjudicate abusers.

Specifically, the Family Violence Prevention and Treatment Act (October 9, 1984), which was enacted by both Houses of Congress and signed into law, authorizes the Department of Health and Human Services (HHS) to administer a state grant program for family-violence prevention and shelter programs; to operate a family-violence clearinghouse; and to coordinate family-violence activities within HHS and among other federal agencies. The act requires research and demonstration projects on family violence, including a study on the incidence of elder abuse. In addition, the act directs the Secretary of HHS to delegate to the U.S. Attorney General authority for providing grants to support training and technical assistance to local and state law enforcement personnel responsible for responding to incidences of family violence (H.R. 1904, 98th Congress, First Session, March 3, 1983). This act represented the first step Congress made to provide a direct federal role in combating elder abuse.

Another major step was the reauthorization of the Older Americans Act (October 9, 1984). Programs under this act still support the major social service activities that promote functional independence of the elderly within their own communities. Several members of Congress believed that these programs could supplement the provisions of the Family Violence Prevention and Treatment Act and provide another key vehicle for addressing the problems of abused elders and their families. The Older Americans Act Amendments of 1984 contained several new requirements related to elder abuse. The first required Area Agencies on Aging (AAAs) to identify local elder abuse programs and to assess the need for elder abuse prevention services; AAAs could provide services to victims where needed. A second provision required state agencies on aging to include elder abuse prevention and treatment programs in their Older Americans Act plans. These programs must conform to existing state laws and coordinate with existing adult protective-service activities. Further, a state could not permit involuntary or coerced participation in such programs. A third provision in the act required the Commissioner of the Administration on Aging to submit a report to Congress in 1986 on the need for elder abuse prevention services (S. 2603, 98th Congress, Second Session, October 9, 1984).

Early Congressional attention to the issue of familial elder abuse had been spearheaded by the House Select Committee on Aging, chaired by Representative Claude Pepper (later chairman of the Health and Long-Term Care Subcommittee of the Select Committee). The Committee's report provided the impetus for two major pieces of legislation concerning elder abuse—the Family Violence Prevention and Treatment Act and the Older Americans Act Amendments of 1984. Both pieces of legislation utilized the advocacy approach to elder abuse. One major reason for the success of these provisions was increased Congressional support for the advocacy approach generated by the Department of Health and Human Services' position in favor of local voluntary and community-based service programs to combat elder abuse (U.S. House of Representatives, 1985a, p. 61).

CURRENT ACTIVITIES

Late in 1984 and in early 1985, the Subcommittee on Health and Long-Term Care of the House Select Committee on Aging, chaired by Representative Pepper, conducted a follow-up study to its 1978 investigation on elder abuse. While preparing the report titled *Elder Abuse: A National·Disgrace* (U.S. House of Representatives, 1985a), the Subcommittee identified numerous cases of abuse occurring within long-term care institutions and began a separate investigation of this problem. The Subcommittee surveyed state nursing home commissions and long-term care ombudsman programs in addition to reviewing nursing home admission agreements and regulations affecting nursing homes and board-and-care facilities (U.S. House of Representatives, 1985b, pp. 1–3). The Subcommittee found that "about 1 out of every 7 institutionalized elderly persons may be the victim of physical or sexual abuse annually" (U.S. House of Representatives, 1985b, pp. 3). These findings were published in *Rights of the Institutionalized Elderly: Lost in Confinement*, a white paper presented at the Subcommittee's hearing in September 1985 (U.S. House of Representatives, 1985b).

As a result of these findings and the Subcommittee's follow-up investigation to the earlier work on elder abuse in the home, Representative Pepper endorsed a package of legislative proposals (June 20, 1985) aimed at both domestic and institutional abuse of the elderly: the Elder Abuse Prevention, Identification and Treatment Act (H.R. 1674); Bonding Required of Persons Handling Patient Funds (H.R. 2832), which required all nursing homes certified by Medicare and Medicaid to purchase security bonds to protect against mismanagement of patient funds that are handled by nursing home staff; and Medicaid Fraud and Abuse Units Against Abuse/Neglect (H.R. 2829), which authorized additional matching federal funds to state Medicaid Fraud and Abuse Control Units for the investigation and prosecution of all patient abuse and neglect complaints involving a violation of state criminal laws in Medicaid facilities (Congressional Record, 1985).

In addition to the Subcommittee's investigation of institutional abuse, another major study of nursing home care was released in February 1986 by the Institute of Medicine (IOM). The IOM study identified several problems among the nation's nursing homes that affect quality of patient care. This study confirmed the assumptions of many Congressional members concerning the need to reform nursing home regulation and financing. Several bills were introduced into both houses of Congress to provide for improved quality of care for nursing home residents (see, for example, the Nursing Home Resident Protection Act of 1985 [H.R. 4485] and the Long Term Care Patient Advocacy Act of 1986 [H.R. 5067]). Several of these bills proposed to strengthen the existing long-term care ombudsman program by providing staff with immunity from lawsuits pertaining to the performance of their duties, additional training, and improved access to facilities.

Although none of these legislative proposals passed the 99th Congress, they set the stage for continuing legislative activity in the 100th Congress. In addition, late in 1985 President Reagan charged the Secretary of the Department of Health and Human Services with the responsibility to study options for catastrophic health care. Several Congressional representatives were eager to pursue this type of health legislation as a means of protecting the elderly and their families from high medical costs and the stress of informal support. The increased attention to the issues of institutional abuse and catastrophic health care have changed the direction of federal initiatives regarding elder abuse.

FUTURE DIRECTIONS

Federal attention is now focused upon improved quality of care in nursing homes and on catastrophic health insurance. Interest in elder abuse has been partially subsumed in these larger issues. For example, several lawmakers assume that episodes of institutional abuse can be minimized with improved quality of care in nursing homes. The Department of Health and Human Services is adopting most of the Institute of Medicine's recommendations concerning nursing home regulation. In particular, emphasis on patient rights and a new Medicare requirement to investigate every patient complaint, in combination with state ombudsman programs, should protect against financial and other institutional types of abuses.

With regard to catastrophic care, many bills were introduced into the 100th Congress that would expand home health benefits under the Medicare program (see, for example, the Medicare Catastrophic Protection Act of 1987 [H.R. 2470], the Medicare Parts A and B Catastrophic Protection Acts of 1987 [H.R. 1280 and 1281], and the Medicare Catastrophic Loss Prevention Act of 1987 [S. 1127]). Instances of family abuse of the elderly are often associated with situations of heavy caregiver burden on the primary support person of the elderly person. An expanded home health benefit is viewed as a means to reduce the caregiver burden by providing insurance coverage for longer term home health care.

Currently, there are several social service programs in addition to the Older Americans Act and the Family Violence Prevention and Treatment Act that offer opportunities for elder abuse services. Programs aimed at elder abuse or at familial problems associated with domestic violence are also funded under the Social Services Block Grant (previously Title XX of the Social Security Act), the Alcohol, Drug Abuse and Mental Health Services Block Grant, and the Preventive Health and Health Services Block Grant, to name a few. However, activities directed at this problem are not as clearly focused as those for other types of family abuse, such as spouse and child abuse. One reason for this is the lack of national incidence data concerning the prevalence of elder abuse. Active interest in the issue cannot be generated without the perception that the problem is widespread. Another reason is the lack of a clear mandate from Congress to focus resources and attention on this issue. Even though the 1984 legislation allowed program resources to be used for elder abuse, it did not mandate specific activities to be funded with specified appropriations.

On November 29, 1987, the Older Americans Act Amendments of 1987 were signed into law (P.L. 100–175). The Amendments created a new Subpart G under Title III of the Act for elder abuse services. This subpart consolidates and reemphasizes the types of elder abuse prevention and treatment services appropriate for state agencies on aging to operate. The subpart did not expand the scope of those services; but it did authorize $5 million for the services. However, the authorization is subject to a special trigger protecting the base nutrition and supportive services of Title III. None of the $5 million can be appropriated unless the previous year's appropriation for Title III based services is increased by at least 5 percent. Since this did not happen for fiscal year 1987/88, no additional funds for elder abuse were appropriated. It is not likely that any funds will be appropriated in fiscal year 1988/89 for the same reason.

Given research findings that advocate use of intervention strategies that focus on the family and family systems, as opposed to policies that emphasize separate service programs unique to abused elders (Wolf, Godkin, & Pillemer, 1984, pp. 385–410), allowing states and local areas the discretion to use established aging programs to address elder abuse may be more effective than a special federal program. However, the lack of national incidence data is problematic for concerned individuals and social service organizations at the local level who are trying to garner the necessary support and resources to expand existing aging and family-violence programs. Current research supported by the Department of Health and Human Services should better define incidence, and this information will, more than any other, determine the direction of future federal initiatives in elder abuse.

ACKNOWLEDGMENTS

Background for this chapter was originally researched by the author during an assignment with the U.S. House of Representatives Select Committee on Aging's Subcommittee on Human Services. The author acknowledges the Subcommittee's Chairman and Staff Director, Representative Mario Biaggi and Mr. Robert Blancato, respectively, for permission to use this information.

Chapter 12

STATE ELDER/ADULT ABUSE AND PROTECTION LAWS

Marshelle Thobaben

This chapter presents a summary of recent elder/dependent abuse laws, and identifies their basic components. The data on the laws were collected by letter request and follow-up telephone calls to departments in the 50 states and the District of Columbia, as listed in the reference section at the end of this chapter. The laws were analyzed using the criteria that evolved from an earlier study by the author (Thobaben & Anderson, 1985).

Adult abuse and protection laws are premised on the legal precedent that society (in this case, represented by the state) has the authority to act in a parental capacity for persons who are unable to care for and protect themselves, and thus prevent them from suffering abuse, neglect, or exploitation by those responsible for their care or from self-abuse. The purposes of adult protection-service laws are to facilitate the identification of functionally impaired elders who are being abused, neglected, or exploited by others, to encourage expeditious reporting, and to extend protective services while protecting the rights of the abused.

There are two components of the following proposed

model statute that are widely contested: (1) victim rights and
(2) mandatory reporting. Civil libertarians believe that adult
protective services violate an adult's constitutional rights of
privacy and self-determination. Most state laws attempt to protect the constitutional rights of adults while upholding their
obligation to protect their abused dependent citizens. Generally, state adult protective services are voluntary, unless an
emergency situation exists or if the adult is declared incompetent. Even with those safeguards, achieving a balance between
protecting an abused dependent adult's rights and the state's
obligation to protect vulnerable adults is difficult.

There is also concern that mandatory-reporting laws may
violate the confidential relationship between a professional and
a client. Professionals are accustomed to adhering to strict legal
and ethical codes regarding confidentiality; thus reporting
possible abuse of a client without the client's permission is difficult. Professionals are concerned that such action will interfere with their client relationship. Unless the adult protective-
service system is perceived as adequate and beneficial in
meeting the needs of the abused elders sensitively, even with
penalties for not reporting, professionals are unlikely to report.

A model reporting statute should include the following
components:

1. Persons covered: Persons 18 and older who lack the
   functional ability to care for and protect themselves
   should be covered.
2. Reportable behavior: Clear definitions of abuse, neglect, and exploitation should be used.
3. Mandatory reporting: Reporting should be mandatory for all health and social services professionals
   who have reasonable cause to suspect or believe an
   incapacitated individual is a victim of abuse, neglect,
   or exploitation. Anyone else who has reasonable
   cause to believe or suspect abuse may report.
4. Failure to report: If a professional fails to report, he
   or she may be charged with a misdemeanor and
   reported to his or her professional licensing agency.
5. Immunity: All reporters should be immune from

civil and criminal liability if the report is made in good faith and without malice.

*6. Confidentiality: Reports should be confidential and disclosed only by the consent of the reporter involved, or by judicial process.

7. Time of report: The verbal report should be taken immediately and be accompanied by a standardized written report within a specified period.

8. Agency to receive report: A single state agency should be designated to receive and investigate reports, and to maintain a central registry. It should operate 24 hours a day and 7 days a week.

9. Initial investigation: The investigation for verification and assessment of abuse should be completed within a prescribed period of time.

*10. Service plan: Minimum content of a service plan should be stated.

*11. Services: Emergency response, placement services, guardianship procedures, and community-services inventory should be required.

*12. Funding: Funds for additional staff and services required to implement the law should be provided.

*13. Victim due-process protections: The law should state that a competent adult may refuse services and that incompetence must be proven through the state's appropriate judicial process.

*14. Caregiver penalty: Penalties for actions not covered by existent criminal laws should be stipulated.

*15. Education/training: Reporter/protective-service staff training should be required. Public-education programs that not only provide information on what abuse is, but that also educate caregivers about community resources that may alleviate the financial, emotional, and time demands, as well as other stressors that often contribute to abuse, should be required.

Table 12-1 summarizes the current status of elder/adult protective service laws with respect to the elements described

Table 12-1 Summary of State Adult Abuse and Protection Laws

State Year passed[a] amended[a]	Persons covered[b] (ages in numerals)	Reporters[c] (M = mandated; V = voluntary)	Penalty for failure to report	What to report — Abuse	Neglect	Exploitation	Other	When to report	To whom: Department responsible for investigation	Mandatory Time period to begin investigation	Central registry
AL 1976	Impaired 18+	M: Practitioners of healing arts	Misdemeanor, $550 or 6 mo in jail	X	X	X		Immediately verbal, then written	Pensions and security, law enforcement	3 days	No
AK 1983	65+	M: Wide variety of professionals V: Any person	Misdemeanor				Harm	24 hr	Health and social services, law enforcement	Promptly	No
AZ 1984/86	Incapacitated adults	M: Wide variety of professionals	Misdemeanor	X	X	X		Immediately verbal, written in 48 hr	Economic and security, law enforcement	As soon as possible	No
AR 1977/83	Incapacitated 18+	M: Wide variety of professionals V: Any person	Misdemeanor; civil liability for damages	X			Sexual	Immediately verbal, written in 48 hr	Central registry, human services	Promptly	Yes
CA 1983/86	Dependent 18–64; 65+	M: Wide variety of professionals V: Any person	Misdemeanor; $1,000 fine 6 mo/jail	X	may	Fiduciary (may)	Abandonment	Immediately verbal, written in 36 hr	County adult protective agency, law enforcement, nursing home ombudsman	Not specified	No
CO 1983	Incapacitated 65+	V: Wide variety of professionals	None	X (may)	X (may)	X (may)		Immediately	Social services	Immediately if adult consent in writing	No
CT 1977	60+	M: Wide variety of professionals V: Any person	Misdemeanor; $500 fine	X	X	X	Abandonment	Within 5 days	Human resources ombudsman	Promptly	Yes

(continued)

Table 12-1 (continued)

State Year passed amended[a]	Persons covered[b] (ages in numerals)	Reporters[c] (M = mandated V = voluntary)	Penalty for failure to report	Abuse	Neglect	Exploitation	Other	When to report	To whom: Department responsible for investigation	Mandatory Time period to begin investigation	Central registry
DE 1982/83	Infirmed 18+	M: Any person	None			X		Not specified	Health and social services	Promptly	No
FL 1978/86	Incapacitated 18+; 60+	M: Any person; wide variety of professionals	Misdemeanor	X	X	X		Immediately	Central registry, health and rehabilitation services	24 hours	Yes
GA 1981/84	Disabled 18+	M: Wide variety of professionals V: Any person	Misdemeanor	X	X	X		Not specified	Human resources, law enforcement	Promptly	No
HI 1981/82	65+	M: Wide variety of professionals V: Any person	None	X	X			Promptly verbal, written as soon as possible	Social services and housing	Not specified	Yes
ID 1982	60+	M: Any person	None	X	X	X	Abandonment	Within 24 hr	Health and welfare	Promptly	No
IL[d] 1984											
IN 1985	Endangered persons 18+	M: Any person	Misdemeanor		X	X	battery	Immediately	Aging and community services, law enforcement	Immediately if adult is in danger; 5 days otherwise	Yes
IA 1984	Dependent adult	V: Any person	None	Physical (may)		X (may)	sexual offense (may)	Not specified	Human services	Expeditiously	Yes

State/Year	Victim	Reporters	Penalty				Report timing	Agency	Investigation	Immunity
KS 1980/83	Adult resident of medical facility, care home, or family home	M: Licensed health and social professionals V: Any person	None	X	X		Immediately	Social and rehabilitation	48 hr	Yes
KY 1976/86	Dysfunctional 18+	M: Wide variety of professionals V: Any person	Misdemeanor	X	X	X	Immediately	Social services	As soon as practical	No
LA 1982/85	Impaired 18+	M: Any person	Misdemeanor; $500/6 mo jail	X	X		Immediately	Health and human services	Promptly	Yes
ME 1981/83	Incapacitated 18+	M: Wide variety of professionals V: Any person	Civil $500; Professional licensing board notified.	X	X	X	Immediately verbal, written 48 hr	Human services, mental health and corrections (Mentally Retarded Adults)	Promptly	No
MD 1984/85	Disabled adult	M: Wide variety of professionals V: Any person	None	X	X	X	As soon as possible	Human resources	24 hr in emergency, otherwise 5 days	No
MA 1982	60+	M: Wide variety of professionals V: Any person	Misdemeanor; $1,000 fine	X			Immediately verbal, written 48 hr	Elder affairs	24 hr in emergency, otherwise 7 days	Yes
MI 1982	Vulnerable 18+	M: Wide variety of professionals V: Any person	Civil; $500 fine, liable for damages from failure to report	X	X	X Endangerment	Immediately	Social services	24 hr	No
MN 1980/85	Vulnerable 18+	M: Wide variety of professionals V: Any person	Misdemeanor; liable for damages from failure to report	X	X		Immediately verbal, written as soon as possible	Welfare, law enforcement	Immediately	No

(continued)

Table 12-1 (*continued*)

State Year passed amended[a]	Persons covered[b] (ages in numerals)	Reporters[c] (M = mandated V = voluntary)	Penalty for failure to report	Abuse	Neglect	Exploitation	Other	When to report	To whom: Department responsible for investigation	Mandatory Time period to begin investigation	Central registry
MS 1986	Vulnerable 18+	M: Any person	None	X	X	X		Not specified	Welfare	48 hr	Yes; hotline
MO 1980	Unable to protect own interest 60+	M: Any person	None				Physical harm	Not specified	Social services	Promptly	Hotline
MT 1982	Impaired 60+	M: Wide variety of professionals V: Any person	Misdemeanor	X	X	X		Not specified, verbal or written	Social and rehabilitation services	Not specified	No
NE 1973	Incompetent or disabled adults	M: Wide variety of professionals V: Any person	Misdemeanor	X	X			Not specified, verbal then written	Public welfare, law enforcement	Immediately	Yes
NV 1981/85	60+	M: Wide variety of professionals V: Any person	Misdemeanor	X	X	X	Living in hazardous conditions	Immediately	Human resources, law enforcement	3 days	No
NH 1977/83	Incapacitated 18+	M: Wide variety of professionals	Misdemeanor	X	X	X		Immediately, verbal followed by written	Human services, law enforcement	3 days	Yes
NJ 1977/83	Resident of facility or institution 60+	M: Wide variety of professionals V: Any person	Misdemeanor; $500 fine	X		X		In a timely manner	State ombudsman	Promptly	Yes
NM 1978/82	Unable to protect self 55+	M: Wide variety of professionals, any person	Misdemeanor	X	X	X		Promptly	Human services	Immediately	No

State / Years	Persons protected	Who reports	Penalty			Protective service	Manner to report	Responsible agency	Response time	Registry
NY 1979/84	Endangered 18+	V: Any person	None	X			Not Specified	Social services, law enforcement	Not specified	No
NC 1973/85	Disabled 18+	M: Any person	None	X	X		Not specified, oral or written	Social services	Promptly	No
ND[c]										
OH 1981/85	Developmental disabled or mentally retarded 18+; Incapacitated 60+	M: Wide variety of health professionals; V: Any person	Misdemeanor; $500 fine	X	X	X	Immediately	Human services	Emergency 24 hr otherwise 3 days	No
OK 1980/85	Incapacitated 18+, 65+	M: Any person	Misdemeanor	X	X	Financial	Prompt	Human services	Promptly	Hotline
OR 1983/85	65+	M: Public or private officials	Misdemeanor; $500 fine	X			Immediately, oral	Human resources, law enforcement	Promptly	No
PA[c]										
RI 1981/82	60+	M: Any person	Misdemeanor; $500 fine	X	X	Abandonment	Immediately	Elderly affairs	Immediately	No
SC 1974/84	Developmental disabled, Mentally ill or senile 18+	M: Any person, wide variety of professionals	Misdemeanor; fine: $100–$1000/6 mos in jail	Physical	X	X	Immediately, verbal	Social services, law enforcement	3 days	No
SD 1986	Disabled adult 18+	Not specified	None	X	X	X	Not specified	Adult services and aging	Not specified	No
TN 1974/86	Dysfunctional 18+	M: Any person	Misdemeanor; $500/30-days in jail	X	X	X	Immediately	Human services	Emergency 24 hr, otherwise 5 days	No
TX 1981/83	Disabled 18+, 65+	M: Any person	None	X	X	X	Not specified	Human resources	24 hr	Hotline

(continued)

Table 12-1 (continued)

State Year passed amended[a]	Persons covered[b] (ages in numerals)	Reporters[c] (M = mandated V = voluntary)	Penalty for failure to report	What to report — Abuse	Neglect	Exploitation	Other	When to report	To whom: Department responsible for investigation	Mandatory Time period to begin investigation	Central registry
UT 1977/83	Disabled 18 +	M: Wide variety of professionals, any person	Misdemeanor	X	X	X		Immediately	Social services, law enforcement	Not specified	No
VT 1980/85	Disabled 18 +, 60 +	M: Wide variety of professionals V: Any person	Misdemeanor; $500 fine	X	X	X		As soon as practical, verbal; written, one week	Social and rehabilitation services	72 hr	Yes
VA 1974/86	Incapacitated 18 +, 60 +	M: Wide variety of professionals V: Any person	Misdemeanor; fine: $100–$500; subsequent failures fine: $1,000	X	X	X		Immediately verbal, written 72 hr	Social service	Promptly	No

WA 1984/86	Vulnerable 60+	M: Wide variety of professionals V: Any person	None	X	X	X	Abandonment	Immediately verbal, written 10 days	Social and health services	Not specified	Yes
WV 1981/84	Incapacitated 18+	M: Wide variety of professionals V: Any person	Misdemeanor; fine: $100/ 10 days in jail	X	X	X	Emergency situation	Immediately verbal, written 48 hr	Human services	Not specified	No
WI 1984	Infirmed 60+	V: Any person	None	X (may)	X (may)	material (may)		Not specified	Health and social services	24 hr	No
WY 1981/86	Disabled Adult 19+	M: Any person	None	X	X	X	Abandonment	Not specified	Health and social services, law enforcement	Not specified	No
DC 1984/85	Vulnerable 18+	M: Wide variety of professionals	Misdemeanor; $300 fine; Report to Professional Licensing Board	X	X			Immediately verbal	Human services, law enforcement	Promptly if life threatening, otherwise 10 days	Yes

[a] Amendment to State laws through July, 1986.

[b] Adult rights are protected in all states but AZ, HI, MN, MT, NE, OR, RI, SD, and WV.

[c] Reporters are immune from any criminal and civil liability on account or reporting adult abuse or giving testimony providing such action was in good faith and without malice. LA, ME, MD, MI, NY, OR, UT, and WY only offer protection from civil liability. DE, MO and SD do not offer such protection.

[d] Illinois has an Elder Abuse Demonstration Program Act 8-1-84 through 6-30-87.

[e] North Dakota and Pennsylvania do not have adult protection services or abuse-reporting laws.

above (those elements marked above with an asterisk have not been included). The tabular information is necessarily brief, but a copy of the reader's home state statute can be obtained from the state agency designated in the reference, from the local department of social services or aging, or from the local state legislator's office.

There is wide variability among the laws. In 14 states, reporting laws specifically cover abused elders; 34 states and the District of Columbia include the protection of the elderly within the protection of dependent adults, generally defined as 18 years of age or older. Illinois used an elder abuse demonstration program, designed to provide the knowledge necessary to write a law. North Dakota and Pennsylvania have neither an adult protective service nor an abuse-reporting law. Kansas and New Jersey's laws only cover residents of 24-hour residential facilities. Massachusett's law comes closest to the model law, except that it does not include exploitation in its definitions of abuse. Its law does provide a funding base for a comprehensive adult protection system, including educating the staff and developing community awareness of elder abuse.

The most effective statute provides the legal and funding bases to create a comprehensive adult protection system. One that defines, identifies, corrects, and prevents abusive situations while insuring the rights and expressed interests of the vulnerable victim has not been written.

SOURCES OF DATA

Data on state laws (listed according to their respective postal abbreviations) have been derived from the following sources:

AL Department of Pensions and Security. AL Code 38.9, Adult Protective Services Act of 1976 (Acts 1977, No. 780, §1.).

AK Department of Health and Social Services. Protection of the Elderly. AS 47.24, §1, ch. 36, SLA 1983.

AZ Department of Economic Security. 46 Ariz. Stat. Ann. ch. 4, art. 1. 1984, amended 1986.

AR Department of Human Services. AR Stat. Ann. 59-1310 et seq. 1983.

CA Department of Social Services. Division 9, Part 3 Welfare & Institutions Code, ch. 11. Abuse of the Elderly and Dependent Adults 1986.

CO Department of Social Services. 26 Co. Rev. Stat., art. 3.1. Disabled Adults in Need of Protective Services. 1983.

CT Department on Aging. 46a. CT Gen. Stat. ch. 814. Protection of the Elderly, 1977.

DE Department of Health and Social Services. DE Laws, ch. 39. Adult Protective Services, sec. 3901–3911. 1982, amended 1983.

FL Department of Health and Rehabilitative Services. FL Stat., ch. 415.101–113. Adult Protective Services Act. 1986.

GA Department of Human Resources. GA Code, ch. 5. Disabled Adults Protection Act, sec. 30.5.1–30.5.7. 1981, amended 1984.

HI Department of Social Services and Housing. HI Rev. Stat. ch. 349C, sec. 349C:1–349C:8. Elderly Abuse and Neglect. 1981, amended 1982.

ID Department of Health and Welfare. ID Code (39-5301) 39-5207. Elderly Abuse, Exploitation, Neglect and Abandonment Reporting. 1982.

IL Department of Aging. Public Acts 83-1259 and 83-1432. Elder Abuse Demonstration Program. 1984.

IN Department of Aging and Community Services. IN Code 4-27-7. Adult Protective Services. 1985.

IA Department of Human Services. 498 (Human Services) IA Code ch. 176. 1984.

KS Department of Social and Rehabilitation Services. KSA 39-1401 et seq. Reporting Abuse or Neglect of Certain Persons. 1984, amended 1985.

KY Department of Social Services. KY Rev. Stat. ch. 209. Protection of Adults, sec. 209.010–209.990. 1980, amended 1986.

LA Department of Health and Human Resources. Adult Protective Services Law. R.S. 14.403.2. 1982, amended 1985.

ME Department of Human Services. ME Rev. Stat. Ann. ch. 958-A. Adult Protective Services Act, sec. 3470–3492. 1981, amended 1983.

MD Social Services Administration. Title 14 of the Family Law Article. Adult Protective Services. 1984, amended 1986.

MA Executive Office of Elder Affairs. MA. Acts. ch. 604. Act Providing Further Protection of Elderly Persons. 1982.

MI Department of Social Services. Act 519. MI Pub. Acts. 1982.

MN Department of Human Services. MN stat. 626.557. 1980, amended 1985.

MS Department of Public Welfare. MS Vulnerable Adults Act of 1986.

MO Department of Social Services. Sen. Bill 576. 1980 MO Legis. Ser.

MT Department of Social and Rehabilitation Services. Title 53 MT Rev. Codes Ann. ch. 5, pt. 5. Elder Abuse Prevention Act. 1982.

NE Department of Social Services. NE Rev. Stat. 28-708. Offenses Involving the Family Relation. 1973.

NV Division for Aging Services. NV Rev. Stat. 200.509. Abuse, Neglect, and Exploitation of Older Persons. 1981, amended 1983.

NH Department of Health and Human Services. NH Rev. Stat. Ann. 161-D. Protective Services to Adults. 1977, amended 1983.

NJ Department of Human Services. Section 2 of P.L. 1977, c. 239 (c. 52: 27G-2). Mandatory Reporting of Adult Abuse to the State Ombudsman. 1977, amended 1983.

NM Department of Human Services. NM Stat. Ann. 27.7.1–27.7.13. Adult Protective Services. 1978, amended 1982.

NY Department of Social Services. Social Service Law, art. 9-B, sec. 473, 473-a, and 473-b, Adult Protective Services. 1979, amended 1984.

NC Department of Human Resources. Appendix III-A NC Adult Protective Services NC Gen. Stat. ch. 108A, art. 6. Protection of the Abused, Neglected or Exploited Disabled Adult Act. 1985.

ND Department of Human Services. Correspondence April 11, 1986.

OH Department of Human Services. OH Rev. Code Ann. 5101.61, 5123.61, and 5123.99. 1981, amended 1985.

OK Department of Human Services. OK Stat. Title 43A Mental Health, ch. 8. Protective Services For the Elderly Act of 1977, sec. 801–810. 1977, amended 1984.

OR Senior Services Division. OR Rev. Stat. 410.610 –410.700, 410.850, and 410.990. Reporting of Abuse of Elderly Persons. 1983, amended 1985.

PA Department of Aging. Correspondence May 6, 1986. Telephone interview June 30, 1987.

RI Department of Elderly Affairs. 42 RI Gen. Laws ch. 66. Department of Elder Affairs. 1981, amended 1982.

SC Department of Social Services. 43 SC Code ch. 29. Protective Services for Developmentally Disabled and Senile Persons. 1974, amended 1984.

SD Department of Social Services. S.D. C.L. ch, 22–46, Abuse or exploitation of disabled adults. 1986.

TN Department of Human Services. 14. Tenn. Code Ann., ch. 25. Adult Protection, §101–113. 1980, amended 1986.

TX Department of Human Resources. 48 TX Hum. Res., ch. 48. 1981, amended 1983.

UT. Division of Aging and Adult Services. Public Welfare ch. 19. Adult Protective Services 55-19-1–59-19-9. 1977, amended 1983.

VT Department of Social and Rehabilitation Services. 18 VT Stat. Ann. ch. 22. Reports of Abuse, Neglect, and

Exploitation of Elderly and Disabled Adults. 1980, amended 1985.

VA Department of Social Services. VA Code 63: 1-55.1–63.1-55.7, c. 604. 1974, amended 1986.

WA Department of Social and Health Services. Sec. 9, ch. 97, WA laws of 1984, and ch 74.34 RCW Abuse of Vulnerable Adults. 1984, amended 1986.

WV Department of Human Services. 9 WV Code art. 6. Social Services for Adults §1–15. 1981, amended 1984.

WI Department of Health and Social Services. 1983 WI Laws, Act 398. 1984.

WY Department of Health and Social Services. 1981 WY Sess. Laws. Adult Protective Services Act. 35-20-101–35-20-107. 1981, amended 1986.

DC Adult Protective Services Branch. DC Act 5-221. Adult Protective Services Act of 1984. 1984, amended 1985.

Chapter 13

TOWARD THE DEVELOPMENT OF ESTIMATES OF THE NATIONAL INCIDENCE OF REPORTS OF ELDER ABUSE BASED ON CURRENTLY AVAILABLE STATE DATA
An Exploratory Study

Toshio Tatara

Reliable national data on the nature and scope of elder abuse are critically needed to inform policymakers of public-policy options. It is believed that such data could be generated from several different sources through the application of sound research methodologies. Some of the possible data sources include: (1) a nationally representative sample of the elderly; (2) case records of various agencies dealing with elder abuse in a random sample of localities; and (3) statistics on reports of elder abuse collected from information systems of appropriate state agencies. In other human services fields, data generated from various sources have provided policymakers and program planners with useful national information. In the field of child abuse, for example, the National Center on Child Abuse and Neglect (NCCAN), the agency responsible for the administration of programs authorized by the Child Abuse Prevention and Treatment Act of 1974 (P.L. 93-247), has always relied on data on reports of child abuse and neglect

153

regularly provided by state child protective-service (CPS) agencies, as well as on information generated from national studies of the incidence and severity of child maltreatment, which have been conducted periodically. NCCAN's decision to support projects to produce both types of data makes good sense, because it is well recognized by CPS professionals that reports of alleged abuse or neglect received by CPS agencies represent only the "tip of the iceberg." Nonetheless, national data on child maltreatment—developed solely on the basis of reports of abuse and neglect—have played an important role in the national policymaking process in the past 10 years.

In elder abuse, since the 1970s, researchers have conducted many different types of studies, using a variety of data and different methodologies, to generate information about the nature and magnitude of the problem. Some of these studies surveyed a sample of the population (Block & Sinnott, 1979; Gioglio & Blakemore, 1983; Pillemer & Finkehor, 1988), whereas others reviewed agency case records (Lau & Kosberg, 1979) and surveyed or interviewed professionals working with elderly (Douglass, Hickey & Noel, 1980; O'Malley, Segars, Perez, Mitchell, & Knuepfel 1979; Senstock & Liang, 1982). Although some of these, as well as other studies, provided estimates for the national prevalence of elder abuse, most of them were exploratory studies based on a relatively small sample of people or records. The Pillemer and Finkelhor (1988) study involved over 2000 elderly persons and represented the "first large scale random sample survey of the problem," but its sample was chosen from the Boston, Massachusetts metropolitan area. Consequently, none of the previous efforts has used data on reports of elder abuse collected from public agencies to develop national information.

A recent study conducted jointly by the American Public Welfare Association (APWA) and the National Association of State Units on Aging (NASUA), with funding support from the U.S. Administration on Aging (AoA), was the first attempt to develop national elder abuse information on the basis of statistics on reports of elder maltreatment gathered from states (APWA/NASUA, 1986a). Building on the information collected by this study, the present chapter attempts to estimate the national incidence of reports of elder abuse on an exploratory basis.

STUDY METHODOLOGY AND DATA DEFINITIONS

In October 1985, APWA and NASUA jointly developed and distributed to the social service and aging agencies in 54 jurisdictions in the country the State Questionnaire on Elder Abuse in order to gather a wide range of information about policies and practices related to elder abuse. These two types of agencies in each state were asked to collaborate with one another to prepare a single response to the questionnaire. In the area of statistical data, states were asked to provide APWA/NASUA with four specific types of data—the number of substantiated reports; the total number of reports of institutional abuse and neglect; the total number of reports of self-abuse and neglect; and the number of reports of elder abuse and neglect by informal caregivers in domestic settings. Only the fourth type of data is pertinent to this paper, and figures were obtained for fiscal years (FY) 1983, 1984, and 1985.

Although it permitted states to combine "abuse" and "neglect," APWA/NASUA attempted to obtain a discrete count of reports of suspected abuse and neglect by informal caregivers in domestic settings from each state, separate from counts of institutional or self-abuse/neglect. It was the intention of APWA/NASUA to generate state-by-state incidence data on the basis of this "basic" definition of elder abuse/neglect, and states were therefore asked to use this definition in reporting their data.

ANALYSIS OF STATES' DATA

Not all of the 53 jurisdictions (including all 50 states, the District of Columbia, Guam, and Puerto Rico) that participated

in the APWA/NASUA study by returning the .survey ques-
tionnaires were able to provide statistical data. Further, it was
found, as was anticipated, that the definitions of elder abuse
specified in the statutes (on which reports of alleged elder
abuse or neglect are received and tabulated at the state level)
varied considerably among states (APWA/NASUA, 1986c). A
close examination of these definitions revealed that the definitions of some states are much broader than those of other
states, and it is therefore inappropriate to aggregate state-by-
state statistics to generate the national incidence on reports of
elder abuse/neglect. Also, it was found that a number of states
were not able to disaggregate their data to provide separate
figures for reports of suspected abuse/neglect by informal
caregivers in domestic settings.

In view of these circumstances, APWA/NASUA concluded
that the best way to understand the nature and the extent of
elder maltreatment based on these data would be to categorize
the participating states into four different groups according to
the following definitions:

> Group One: States that can provide the total number of
> reports of suspected elder abuse/neglect by informal
> caregivers in domestic settings.
>
> Group Two: States that include reports of self-abuse/ne-
> glect in the total number of reports of suspected elder
> abuse/neglect.
>
> Group Three: States that include reports of institutional
> abuse/neglect in the total number of reports of sus-
> pected elder abuse/neglect.
>
> Group Four: States that include reports of both self-
> abuse/neglect and institutional abuse/neglect in the total
> number of reports of suspected elder abuse/ neglect.

Presented below are the numbers of participating states in
each group which were able to provide their data for FY 1983,
1984, and 1985 to APWA/NASUA:

	FY 83	*FY 84*	*FY 85*
Group One	14 states	17 states	15 states
Group Two	11 states	13 states	14 states
Group Three	2 states	2 states	2 states
Group Four	6 states	7 states	9 states
Totals	33 states	39 states	40 states

Further, it is important to note that, although the majority of states were able to supply statistics for persons over 60 or 65 years of age, some states (which address elder abuse through their adult protective-service legislation and had difficulty in disaggregating data on the elderly) provided APWA/NASUA with an estimated percentage of elderly persons in their counts of reports of "adult abuse/neglect." APWA/NASUA calculated the numbers of reports of elder abuse/neglect based on these estimated percentages for several states.

INCIDENCE OF REPORTS OF ELDER ABUSE/NEGLECT AMONG STATES

Tables 13-1 through 13-4 present the incidence of reports of elder abuse/neglect for states for FY 83, FY 84, and FY 85 in four different groups based on the definitions described above. The incidence of reports is defined as the number of reports of suspected or alleged elder abuse/neglect received by state authorities for every 1,000 persons who are over 60 or 65 years of age.

The states shown in Table 13-1 are those able to provide the total number of reports of suspected elder abuse/neglect by informal caregivers in domestic settings. Only about 40% of the responding states (i.e., 42.4% for FY 83, 43.6% for FY 84, and 37.5% for FY 85) were able to follow this definition. It is interesting to note that the rates appear very similar among the states, showing a very small range from the lowest to highest. Further, only a small increase in the incidence of reports was

Table 13-1   Elder Abuse Incidence Rates for Group One States

State	FY83	FY84	FY85
California	——	1.9	——
District of Columbia	0.5	0.5	0.7
Hawaii	0.3	0.7	0.7
Iowa	0.7	0.9	——
Maine	0.7	1.0	1.1
Maryland	0.9	0.9	1.3
Massachusetts	——	1.4	1.7
Michigan	0.5	0.7	0.8
Minnesota	0.2	0.2	——
Montana	——	0.6	1.6
Nebraska	0.5	1.2	2.2
New Hampshire	0.7	1.0	1.4
Oregon	0.9	0.9	0.9
Rhode Island	0.9	1.1	1.3
Utah	2.4	1.5	2.0
Washington	1.4	1.4	2.1
Wisconsin	——	——	0.5
Wyoming	1.1	0.8	1.4
Number of states:	14	17	15
Mean average:	0.8	1.0	1.3

indicated from FY 83 to FY 85 in most of the states that were able to provide data for all three fiscal-year periods.

The states included in Table 13-2 are those which combined reports of self-abuse/neglect with reports of abuse/neglect by informal caregivers and which were unable to separate one type of report from another. Overall, approximately 30% of the responding states (33.3% for FY 83 and FY 84, and 35.0% for FY 85) used this method of reporting their data. On average, the rates in Table 13-2 are considerably higher than those presented in Table 13-1. However, this finding was expected because of the "lumping" of reports of self-abuse/neglect into those of abuse/neglect by informal caregivers.

Table 13-2   Elder Abuse Incidence Rates for Group Two States

State	FY83	FY84	FY85
Arizona	3.3	3.3	5.3
Connecticut	3.3	3.5	3.5
Delaware	3.2	3.5	——
Florida	1.2	1.2	1.9
Georgia	——	5.1	5.9
Louisiana	2.6	2.4	2.6
Mississippi	0.8	0.9	1.4
Missouri	7.2	8.0	7.3
New Jersey	——	——	0.9
Oklahoma	1.8	2.2	2.1
South Carolina	3.9	4.5	3.9
South Dakota	——	——	1.4
Texas	2.0	2.9	4.9
Vermont	1.2	1.3	1.5
Virginia	——	2.9	2.9
Number of states:	11	13	14
Mean average:	2.8	3.2	3.3

As shown in Table 13-2, the rates of Missouri (7.2 for FY 83, 8.0 for FY 84, and 7.3 for FY 85) stand out from others. However, these high rates are probably attributable largely to the fact that this state operates a statewide, 24-hour hotline for reporting suspected elder abuse, as well as strong public education/information programs. This raises the question regarding the impact of reporting systems and public education/information programs upon the actual reports of elder maltreatment received by authorities. Many states reported to APWA/NASUA that public education/information campaigns results in a substantial increase in the number of reports of elder abuse/neglect (APWA/NASUA, 1986b).

Only two states reported to APWA/NASUA that they combined reports of institutional abuse/neglect with those of abuse/neglect by informal caregivers (Table 13-3). It is notable that the rates of Nevada are substantially higher than those of

Table 13-3   Elder Abuse Incidence Rates for Group Three States

State	FY83	FY84	FY85
Nevada	2.4	2.1	2.0
North Carolina	0.4	0.5	0.7
Number of states:	2	2	2
Mean average:	1.4	1.3	1.4

North Carolina. However, available information is not sufficient to determine the nature of these differences.

The states shown in Table 13-4 included both reports of self-abuse/neglect and those of institutional abuse/neglect in the total number of reports transmitted to APWA/NASUA. As expected, the rates of these states are much higher than those of other types of states. As shown in the table, the rates of Alaska and Idaho are considerably higher than those of other states in this group. Both Alaska and Idaho operate a manda-

Table 13-4   Elder Abuse Incidence Rates for Group Four States

State	FY83	FY84	FY85
Alabama	——	5.6	3.3
Alaska	——	1.6	8.1
Arkansas	1.4	2.1	2.2
Colorado	3.6	3.3	3.3
Idaho	——	8.5	11.3
Kansas	2.3	2.8	3.2
Kentucky	2.9	3.4	3.0
Ohio	——	——	3.6
Tennessee	3.7	——	3.9
Virginia	2.7	——[a]	——[a]
Number of states:	6	7	9
Mean average:	2.8	3.9	4.7

[a]Virginia used the definition for Group Two for FY 84 and FY 85.

tory statewide reported system; however, whereas Alaska conducts ongoing public education/information activities on elder abuse, Idaho does not engage in such activities (APWA/ NASUA, 1986b).

ESTIMATES OF THE NATIONAL INCIDENCE OF REPORTS OF ELDER ABUSE/NEGLECT

The APWA/NASUA study calculated incidence rates only for states, and did not make any national estimates. For the purpose of this exploratory study, attempts were made to estimate four types of national incidence with the use of the average incidence rates for the four groups of states presented earlier. Although this type of method is often used in other human services fields, it has not been used in the elder abuse field to date because of the lack of appropriate data on elder abuse reports.

Further, for the sake of applying this particular method of estimation, two assumptions were made. The first assumption was that the number of "reports" of elder abuse/neglect can be interchangeably used with the number of "elderly persons." In other words, it was assumed that a report of elder abuse/neglect generally involves one elderly person. A brief review of some states' practices reveals that this assumption is valid in most states. The second assumption was that reports represent unduplicated counts within each fiscal year. Only one state indicated that an individual was counted twice (two reports) if a report of this individual was received from more than one source. Tables 13-5 through 13-8 present estimates for the national incidence of reports for FY 83, FY 84, and FY 85 for the previously mentioned four different definitions of elder maltreatment. Each table includes two sets of estimates; one for the U.S. population 60 years and older and another for the population 65 years and older. These two types of national estimates were made because both 60 and 65 years of age were used by states as the age cutoffs in their definitions of the elderly.

The national estimates in Table 13-5 are based on the

Table 13-5   Estimates of National Incidence of Reports of Elder Abuse/Neglect for Group One Definition

Age	FY83	FY84	FY85
60 years and up	31,000	39,000	51,000
65 years and up	22,000	28,000	37,000

most narrow definition of elder abuse/neglect among the four definitions discussed previously. These estimates show that there was a steady increase in the number of elderly persons reported as being victims of abuse/neglect from FY 83 to FY 85.

The estimates in Table 13-6 are based on the definition of elder abuse/neglect in which self-abuse/neglect is combined with abuse/neglect by informal caregivers. Again, a steady increase was indicated in the number of elderly persons involved from FY 83 to FY 85.

The definition of elder abuse/neglect that combines institutional abuse/neglect with abuse/neglect by informal caregivers was used to arrive as the national estimates in Table 13-7. It must be noted, however, that the average incidence

Table 13-6   Estimates of National Incidence of Reports of Elder Abuse/Neglect for Group Two Definition

Age	FY83	FY84	FY85
60 years and up	107,000	125,000	130,000
65 years and up	77,000	90,000	94,000

Table 13-7   Estimates of National Incidence of Reports of Elder Abuse/Neglect for Group Three Definition

Age	FY83	FY84	FY85
60 years and up	53,000	51,000	55,000
65 years and up	38,000	36,000	40,000

Table 13-8   Estimates of National Incidence of Reports of Elder Abuse/Neglect for Group Four Definition

Age	FY83	FY84	FY85
60 years and up	107,000	152,000	186,000
65 years and up	77,000	109,000	134,000

rate for this definition was calculated based on only the rates of two states. The estimates, therefore, should be treated as very tentative.

The national estimates in Table 13-8 were calculated on the basis of the definition that includes both self-abuse/neglect and institutional abuse/neglect in the reports of abuse/neglect by informal caregivers. As expected, the number of elderly persons covered by this definition is the largest among all four definitions. It is also significant that there was a steady increase in the number of elderly persons reported as being victims of abuse/neglect between FY 83 and FY 85.

QUALIFICATIONS

The various national estimates presented in this paper suggest that, nationwide, anywhere between 51,000 and 186,000 elderly persons were involved as victims in reports of abuse/neglect made to various public agencies during the FY 85 period, using 60 years and older as the age cutoff. If the age cutoff of 65 years or older is used, the national estimates would be between 37,000 and 123,000 for FY 85. The number would vary within these ranges, depending on which of the four definitions is used to make a national estimate.

In using these estimates (particularly if comparison with other national estimates is intended), several facts must be clearly understood. First, these estimates do not represent the national incidence of substantiated abuse/neglect per se. The number of confirmed reports (as well as the number of elderly persons determined as victims) would be much smaller than the numbers presented in this paper. It appears that the

APWA/NASUA study is the only source of information about substantiation rates of elder abuse/neglect available at the present time. The study calculated the substantiation rates based on data from a relatively small number of states, as follows: 79.2% (11 states) for FY 83, 74.5% (14 states) for FY 84, and 70,8% (13 states) for FY 85 (APWA/NASUA, 1986a, p. 41).

Second, there is an important distinction between incidence and prevalence, and one should not be confused with the other. "Incidence refers to the occurrence of a phenomenon during a specified period, to the onset of a situation, while prevalence refers to the number of cases of a particular phenomenon in a community or group at a given time" (Freeman & Sherwood, 1970, p. 43). Information presented in this paper is the national incidence of reports of elder abuse/neglect. On the other hand, most existing national estimates for elder maltreatment are based on prevalence studies of population samples. For example, based on a survey of over 2,000 elderly persons in the Boston metropolitan area, Pillemer and Finkelhor (1988) estimate that between 701,000 and 1,093,560 elderly persons in the United States had experienced some form of maltreatment (defined as physical abuse, neglect, or chronic verbal aggression).

Third, it is widely accepted that maltreatment of elderly is grossly underreported despite the existence of mandatory-reporting requirements in most states and, therefore, reported rates of elder abuse/neglect are substantially lower than rates estimated by population surveys. For example, Pillemer and Finkelhor (1988) suggest that about 1 out of 14 cases of elder maltreatment comes to the attention of appropriate authorities. Finally, the definitions of maltreatment vary widely from one study to another, and this makes it very difficult (sometimes impossible) to compare different studies. Also, it must be inappropriate to compare the results of an incidence study (such as one presented in this paper) with those of a prevalence study, because research methodology and sources of data are generally quite different between the two types of study.

Conclusions

Although there are many criticisms about the nature and effectiveness of mandatory reporting for elder abuse (Crystal, 1987; Faulkner, 1982; Salend, Kane, Satz, & Pynoos, 1984) mandatory-reporting requirements are now the law in over 40 states and in the District of Columbia (APWA/NASUA, 1986a). These, and several other states that operate some form of reporting program, have been collecting various data based on reports of elder maltreatment in the past several years. Although the technical capabilities of these states for providing reliable statistical data are still very limited, there is little doubt that the states are committed to improving their reporting programs and information systems in working with other states. Further, it is believed that statistics on elder abuse reports (which can be produced only by states) have potential for contributing to the development of national information that would be useful to policymakers and researchers.

This chapter presents estimates of the national incidence of reports of elder maltreatment calculated on the basis of rather incomplete state statistics. It can be assumed that, nationally, between 51,000 and 186,000 elderly persons were reported to authorities as being alleged victims of various types of maltreatment during FY 85. These figures represented an increase from previous years. Recognizing that elder maltreatment is considerably underreported, it is likely that there were actually many more cases of maltreatment that were not reported. These attempts to make national estimates are only explanatory, but it is anticipated that many more similar studies with better data and better methodologies will be conducted in the future.

Acknowledgments

The original APWA/NASUA study was supported, in part, as a subcontract of Grant No. 90-AM-0155 awarded to the University of Massachusetts Medical Center by the U.S. Administration on Aging in June 1985. Interpretations of the study results used in this paper are those of the author.

Chapter 14

THE ABUSED:ABUSER DYAD
Elder Abuse in the State of Florida

Richard B. Miller
and Richard A. Dodder

The concern within society for the safety of its members from violence at the hands of another has been illustrated in the past quarter of a century. Recognition of child abuse in the 1960s exposed a problem that at times has been considered one of epidemic proportions. The 1970s furthered this social awareness, with the recognition of wife abuse. This concern has spurred new laws and legal protection of a large segment of society that previously had little protection. What may be a logical progression in this escalating societal consciousness of domestic violence was addressed by Steinmetz (1978, p. 54) when she prophetically stated, "It may well be that the 1980s will herald the 'public' awareness of the battered aged-elderly parents who reside with, are dependent on, and battered by their adult, caretaking children."

The early gerontological research on elder abuse, although sparse, has played a significant role in public awareness of the phenomenon. Douglass (1979) suggested that the problem of elder abuse was real—but that little was known about it, and little was being done to combat it. Block and Sinnott (1979) attempted to connect the concern over child abuse with the need for concern over elder abuse when they suggested the concept of the *battered-elderly syndrome*. Rathbone-McCuan (1980) was one of the first to address how this new problem related to the whole issue of domestic violence and yet was a unique phenomenon to be examined separately.

However, as early as 1974, there were indications that the government was aware of the problem (U. S. Department Health, Education, and Welfare, 1974) and was attempting to do something about it. In 1978, the first Congressional hearings on elder abuse were convened. One of the earliest reports on elder abuse, which was produced jointly by the Special Committee on Aging and the Select Committee on Aging, was entitled *Elder Abuse* (U.S. House of Representatives, 1980). The report repeatedly cited existing research as an illustration of the growing new problem facing society in general and the elderly paticularly. However, it is a later report, *Elder Abuse: An Examination of a Hidden Problem* (U.S. House of Representatives, 1981), that has probably been the most widely read by the most researchers in elder abuse. Due to the exposure of this report and subsequent literature, there has been a growth in research and public concern about elder abuse.

In 1981, the Select Committee on Aging recommended that states create statutes that would address the issue of elder abuse. Prior to that point in time, Salend, Kane, Satz, and Pynoos (1984) stated that between 1973 and January 31, 1981, 16 states had passed statutes addressing adult abuse, including all adults aged 18 and older. They also indicate, however, that no laws were passed specifically to protect the elderly until 1977. Between 1977 and 1980, only 5 states had passed statutes aimed at the 60-and-older population.

Since the Select Committee on Aging's recommendation, Kerness (1984) and Traxler (1986) have both reported that as of 1985, there were 44 states (including the District of Columbia) that had passed adult-protective laws. Traxler (1986) mentions that since 1981, 19 states and the District of Columbia passed laws while an additional 11 states modified their statutes. Of these 44 states, only 22 specifically addressed protection of the 60-and-over population. Included in these statistics is New Mexico, whose statute is targeted at the 55-and-over population. This means that between the period of 1980 and 1985 there were 17 states that created a statute designed to protect the older adult.

Although the issue of elder abuse has only recently been called to the attention of gerontologists, legislators, and the public, there has been a rapid movement and growth in all aspects of our awareness of elder abuse. The literature that elaborates on the rapid growth and related problems of laws is plentiful (cf. Kerness, 1984; Salend, Kane, Satz, & Pynoos, 1984; Traxler, 1986), and studies that have critiqued the attempts to identify and categorize abuse are even more common (Douglass & Hickey, 1983; Pedrick-Cornell & Gelles, 1982; U. S. House of Representatives, 1981; Villmoare & Bergman, 1981). With this brief introduction to these issues, which are addressed in detail elsewhere in this book, this chapter analyzes a statewide-data set collected as a result of specific legal regulations, and compares the results of this analysis with past research and literature concerning the incidence and definitions of abusers and the abused.

THE FLORIDA STATUTE

With Florida's passing of an adult protection statute as early as 1973, it became one of the first states to address the concern for general adult welfare in society. The initial law was developed around the child protection laws and was designed to protect any adult of age 18 or older. However, various modifications to the statute took place in 1975, 1978, and 1983 in an effort to identify and meet the needs of the elderly population specifically. It was the creation of these laws that led to the establishment of the Adult Protective Service Program, which requires "that protective services be provided to those persons suffering from the infirmities of aging who have been abused, neglected, or exploited, and provides penalties for those violating this act " (Dept. of HRS, 1982, p. 3.3).

In an effort to coordinate the records and investigation of abuse reports, the state established the State Abuse Registry in Tallahassee, Florida. The registry maintains files on all reports of abuse and neglect in the state, regardless of the age of the victim. Any report of alleged abuse or neglect can be reported through a toll-free hotline number. Within 24 hours of the report, the allegation must be investigated by a trained protective-service worker from the district in which the referral was made. The worker then must file a written report citing what has been found and whether the allegation was substantiated, or was strongly suspected but unable to be substantiated, or was found not to involve abuse or neglect. A summary report must then be filed whith the registry, containing the evaluation and a list of any services or planned further action(s). The most frequently chosen forms of intervention are: referral for counseling with supervision or hospitalization (22.3%); counseling only (22%); hospitalization only (13.1%); referral to the prosecuting attorney (11.4%); placement of the victim out of the home (7.4%); and monitoring of the situation for further problems (2%).

RESEARCH DESIGN

For the purposes of this study, any case that involved an adult aged 60 or over who was reportedly abused or neglected in a 4.5-year period was examined. Only those cases were examined that the investigative protective service worker identified as "substantiated" or "strongly suspected but could not be completely substantiated." This produced a final sample size of 2,623 cases, of which only 7.5% were recidivist victims.

As alluded to previously, one of the more problematic concerns facing abuse research, and consequently legislation, is the definition and categorization of abuse and neglect in an acceptable, uniform, and applicable manner. This is illustrated by the disparity of projections of the prevalence of abuse in society, which have ranged from as low as 500,000 cases to a high of 2.5 million per year (Block & Sinnott, 1979; Lau & Kosberg, 1979; Pedrick-Cornell & Gelles, 1982; Wilcox, 1983). The overriding factor appears to be how narrowly or broadly abuse is defined. Consequently, a major flaw in the reporting and investigation of data is the subjective nature of the investigations. It may be impossible to cover objectively all possible situations; nevertheless, the human-discretion factor leads to a significant variation in substantiation by the investigators. For example, one case that was related to one of the authors involved a worker who was investigating a case where a family member had chained an 85-year-old parent to the bed. Family members admitted they did this, but reported that the parent was an alcoholic and that they did it to keep him from going down to a corner liquor store and getting drunk. The investigator decided this was an adequate reason for the behavior because it was done to protect the parent from himself, and reported the allegation of abuse to be unsubstantiated.

Using the data available, the researchers classified behavior in two general categories—abuse and neglect. In the case where a worker specified both abuse and neglect, the case was classified only as the form of behavior that was described as the primary concern of the investigator. This prevented the reporting of multiple codes for one victim. At no time was the worker's evaluation as to whether the victim was abused or neglected changed.

For research purposes, the authors have further delineated the types of abuse and neglect based upon the investigative worker's written summary of the incident. The five categories developed from the reports included three forms of abuse and two forms of neglect. The categories were:

> Physical abuse: Assaults on the individual's person, for example, slaps, beatings, bruises, broken bones, cuts, burns, or shootings.
>
> Psychological abuse: Verbal or emotional assaults, such as threats, insults, yelling, and intimidation.
>
> Financial abuse: Theft of money or of property, or fraud.
>
> Active neglect: Intentionally ignoring the victim's needs or withholding items necessary for the victim's well-being.
>
> Passive neglect: Neglect through ignorance or inability to care.

Florida does not specifically make a distinction between active and passive neglect but labels both under the generic term *neglect*. A distinction will be made here based on the difference in the behavior itself as well as the presumed intent that distinguishes the two, as outlined above.

RESULTS

The information gleaned from abuse and neglect research concerning the victim and the perpetrator has been surprisingly consistent over the past decade. Uniformly, the victim has been reported to be female, white, older than average (i.e., 75 years or older), has some form of physical or mental impairment, and is living with relatives. The perpetrator is likely to be female and a relative, usually the daughter (Block & Sinnott, 1979; Douglass, 1979; Lau & Kosberg, 1979; O'Malley, Segars, Perez, Mitchell & Knuepfel, 1979; Rathbone-McCuan, 1978, 1980; Steinmetz, 1978; Walker, 1983). The general findings of the literature are conflicting on the type of abuse and neglect that is most prevalent. Some studies have cited physical abuse as the most common (Kapp & Bigot, 1985; Lau & Kosberg, 1979; O'Malley, Bergman, Segars, Perez, Mitchell & Kneupfel, 1979;), whereas others have noted psychological abuse as the major form of abuse (Block & Sinnott, 1979). Still others report neglect as the major problem (Hickey and Douglass, 1981). Although these results are enlightening, one needs to be cautious in drawing conclusions from these studies. The primary criticism aimed at almost all of these studies is that they are generally conducted in very specific settings and have small sample sizes.

The preliminary results from the Florida data indicate that the earlier studies may have oversimplified the complexity of the relationship that exists between the victim and the perpetrator. Because past research has frequently lumped abuse and neglect together, as well as used different definitions of both abuse and neglect, the accuracy of the results must be questioned.

Table 14-1 illustrates that there are no significant differences between abuse and neglect in terms of the distribution of victim's age. As suggested by the earlier research, there is a trend for the elderly between the ages of 75 and 84 years to have the highest probability of being victimized, although the difference is not significant (chi square $[\chi^2] = 2.70$). Increasing abuse and neglect through the age of 84, followed by a rapid decline, may possibly be accounted for by an initially more rapid increase in dependency rate than mortality rate of the elderly with advancing age, followed by a mortality rate that outpaces the dependency rate beginning around 85 years of age.

As in the case of other research, the data show that when abuse and neglect are combined into one form of behavior, females are more likely to be victims, comprising approximately 67% of reports. This is much higher than the Florida elderly population, which contains 57% female (U. S. Bureau of the Census, 1980b). A plausible explanation for this tendency is that females are more likely to be living to more advanced years and therefore account for the majority of abuse and neglect cases. Still, when abuse and neglect are analyzed independently, a much better perspective of the complexity and prevalence of abuse and neglect against the elderly is gained. The data indicate that when abuse and neglect are analyzed separately, females are significantly more likely than men to be the victims of both abuse and neglect ($\chi^2 = 18.45$). In addition, the differences between men and women are greater in the abuse category (71.4% perpetrated against women) than in the neglect category (63.3% perpetrated against women).

Earlier research showed that the abuser was more often a female. These data do lend support to this contention, indicating approximately 47% of all abuse/neglect as being perpetrated by women, 43% by men with the remainder being perpetrated by both men and women together; however, the differences are not significant, When abuse and neglect are separated, moreover, a significant sex difference emerges ($\chi^2 = 39.82$), which is contrary to previous findings. Males are significantly more prone to be abusers than are females, with 50.1% of abuse being perpetrated by males compared with

Table 14-1   Chi Square (χ^2) Values for Abuse and Neglect on Selected Variables (in percentages)

Variables	Total $n = 2478$	Abuse total $n = 1174$	Neglect total $n = 1304$
Age of victim			
60–74	36.8	38.2	35.6
75–84	40.1	40.0	40.2
85 +	23.1	21.8	24.2
		$\chi^2 = 2.70$	
Sex of victim			
Male	32.9	28.6	36.7
Female	67.1	71.4	63.3
		$\chi^2 = 18.45*$	
Sex of abuser			
Male	43.5	50.1	37.5
Female	47.0	40.9	52.5
Both	9.5	9.0	10.0
		$\chi^2 = 39.82*$	
Relationship to abuser			
Spouse	9.3	13.3	5.7
Friend	5.7	9.1	2.7
Son	9.7	13.8	6.0
Daughter	6.9	10.1	4.0
Self	36.1	9.1	60.4
Staff	12.8	16.2	9.7
Caretaker	6.3	6.4	6.2
Relative	6.7	9.9	3.8
Other	6.5	12.1	1.5
		$\chi^2 = 711.22*$	
Type of injury			
Physical	31.5	58.9	6.8
Psychological	4.4	8.9	0.5
Financial	10.2	17.0	4.1
Active neglect	24.9	8.0	40.1
Passive neglect	30.0	7.3	48.5
		$\chi^2 = 1344.0*$	

$*p < .05.$

only 40.9% by females (the remaining are abused by both men and women together). With respect to neglect, females are more likely to be perpetrators (52.5%) than are men (37.5%). It is this drastic difference in neglect that makes females appear to be the probable abuser of the elderly victim. Because neglect is a more common problem than abuse, accounting for almost 53% of all reports, it appears that women are more likely to be the perpetrator when abuse and neglect are combined. Nevertheless, it should be remembered that this does not hold true in abusive situations. The explanation for the systematic differences between men and women in the type of abuse perpetrated may lie in that abuse requires, in most cases, a physical confrontation with the victim, whereas neglect requires overt or covert omission. Males, assuming that in general they are socialized to be more aggressive, might prove to be more prone to involvement in abuse.

Another area where these results contradict past results is the relationship of the abuser to the victim. Previous research concluded that a relative, usually a daughter, is the most likely perpetrator of abuse of an older parent. If abuse and neglect are distinguished in the analysis, we see that the relationship of victim and abuser is more complex. In abuse, a wide variety of relationships between abuser and victim may apply. Institutional staff account for the largest single group of abusers (16.2%), but the prevalence of sons (13.8%), spouses (13.3%), daughters (10.1%), and other relatives (9.9%) reinforces that, as a group, relatives of some sort are the most probable abusers. As can be seen, the contention that the daughter is the most common abuser is not substantiated here. In fact, she is the least likely among the nuclear family unit to perpetrate abuse.

On the other hand, when neglect is considered, there is a significantly different relationship of victim to abuser than was established in the abuse situations ($\chi^2 = 711.22$). Neglect by self is reported in over 60% of the cases, whereas neglect from family members accounts for only about 19% of the neglect cases. This conceivably explains why females are the likely perpetrators of neglect, as cited previously. With women generally outliving their male counterparts, the opportunity for self-neglect would be expected to be greater. Consequently, abuse appears to be more readily at the hands of another, ususally a family member or institutional staff, whereas neglect tends to be more of one's own doing.

Finally, if the breakdown of abuse and neglect show somewhat different abused:abuser relationships, it might be beneficial to examine the types of abuse and neglect taking place in an effort to gain a better understanding of the phenomenon. In support of the findings by Lau and Kosberg (1979); O'Malley, Segars, Perez, Mitchell, and Knuepfel (1979); and Kapp and Bigot (1985), physical abuse appears to be most commonly reported form of abuse, accounting for approximately 27.9% of the abusive behavior. This is followed closely by passive neglect (25.5%) and active neglect (21.2%). Because of the distinctly different nature of abuse and neglect, it is desirable to separate them and address which type of abuse and which type of neglect are most prevalent.

Table 14-1 shows that when abuse and neglect are separated, there is a significantly different type of injury resulting from abuse as opposed to neglect ($\chi^2 = 1334.0$). This in itself would be expected simply due to the definitions and the nature of each type of behavior. Although physical abuse accounts for approximately 28% of all abuse and neglect, it accounts for 58.9% of abuse alone. Financial abuse is prevalent in 17% of the abuse cases, with only 8.9% being attributed to psychological abuse. The difference in the magnitude of physical abuse compared with psychological abuse may be attributed to two factors. First, if most abuse is a spontaneous emotional reaction to stress, as is commonly believed, it would be expected that it would often involve a physical outburst. Psychological abuse, such as making threats or using intimidation, suggests persons more in control of thoughts and behavior. Second physical abuse is often used as a form of punishment or discipline. Consequently, it may be used with the justification that it is an appropriate response to a difficult or uncooperative elder.

Among the reports that were classified as neglect, passive neglect accounts for 48.5% of the behavior with active neglect explaining an additional 40.1%. This indicates that a majority of neglect is through unintentional behavior. It is likely that a large percentage of this is due to self-neglect. Nevertheless, a significant proportion of neglect is intentionally perpetrated. Again, this is probably influenced by the level of dependency of the elderly victims. Surprisingly, active neglect accounted for 8% of the abuse reports, and passive neglect for 7.3% which again illustrates the ambiguities surrounding the definitions used by investigators. If the definitions of abuse and neglect are mutually exclusive, which they should be for categorical and functional purposes, then we should not find any form of neglect reported under abusive behavior.

In summary then, the data reveal that the age of the victim, although showing a trend toward the 75-to-84-year-old group, is not significant. The findings substantiate that the most likely victims of abuse are females. Furthermore, if abuse is considered distinct from neglect, females are found to be proportionately more likely to be victimized by abuse than they are by neglect. The perpetrator, when abuse and neglect are combined, is likely to be female and a relative. However, the data show that males are more prone to be perpetrators of abuse, whereas females are the likely perpetrators of neglect, suggesting that the more common pattern for the abused:abuser dyad is a female victim, with a male perpetrator in abuse and a female perpetrator in neglect. This questions the strict female victim: female perpetrator relationship, which is so widely accepted in the literature. The relationship between the victim and the abuser show that relatives of some sort are most likely to be the abusers, followed closely by institutional staff. Among perpetrators of neglect, however, the victims themselves are the most common perpetrators. Consequently, it appears that in reality, elderly are more at risk from themselves than from any other single group of individuals.

The type of injury most prevalent from abuse and neglect suggests that physical injuries are the most prevalent, especially among abuse reports. Passive and active neglect are significantly less likely, but are respectively the first and second most common forms of neglect.

POLICY AND PLANNING IMPLICATIONS

The literature that cites the insufficient funding of adult protective-service programs is abundant. Since the creation of these programs, they have been underfunded, if funded at all. They are frequently the first programs to receive state and federal cuts in the budgets. The results are inadequate training, staffing, and community education. More adequate funding would go a long way to help ease the problems of elder abuse, and the reporting of it, but it would not eradicate the problems.

Because a majority of abuse and neglect occurs in the home environment, programs need to establish a better understanding of the intergenerational and familial relationships that might be addressed as a means of treatment and as a preventative tool, for control of elder abuse. This includes, but is not limited to, the victim's right to self-determination, understanding the stress factors involved in elder care rather than viewing it as strictly an abuser:abused dyad, as well as a more standardized and efficient networking of agency services.

In conjunction with this awareness, the standardization of the concepts of abuse and neglect needs to be reaffirmed. This is not only important for an understanding of the dynamics of the problem, but even more so in determining the investigator's response to the problem. Abuse appears to be similar to other societal forms of violence, such as domestic violence, whereas neglect appears to be largely self-inflicted. Not only is the origin of the problem different, but, theoretically, so should the response for intervention. Any vagueness or inconsistency in conceptualization could, and probably would, lead to inappropriate action.

Like most states, Florida spends little of the investigator-training sessions on the difficult but necessary component of making subjective evaluations and decisions. The point to be made here is not that all situations should be chronicled and spelled out to the letter, but that if there is going to be latitude for subjective evaluation in investigations, then there needs to be greater evaluation and training in the subjective situations in which the investigators are likely to find themselves. This may work toward alleviating the problem of inconsistency in the substantiation of reports.

Finally, it should be indicated that the development of Florida statutes, as with most state statutes, has been based on

the early findings of.a small collection of studies. If these studies, which dictated the direction of state investigations, are valid
in their estimates of abuse, then it would have to be assumed
that the states are overlooking a tremendous amount of abusive and even more neglectful behavior. This study illustrates
that the early studies oversimplified a very complex problem
through the failure to examine abuse and neglect separately in
determining the characteristics of both the abuser and the victim. Greater care needs to be taken to ensure that states are not
dictated in their investigations by the findings of unsubstantiated research, but that, rather the basic premises be used as a
guide for further learning.

Chapter 15

THE IMPACT OF PUBLIC POLICY DECISIONS ON ELDER ABUSE PROGRAMS
Missouri and Iowa

C. Edwin Vaughan

Service delivery and research interest in child abuse have led to a more general concern with family abuse. Out of this wider perspective emerged an awareness of and interest in the extent to which violence is perpetrated on older dependent adults. The increasing entry of women into the labor force, with second careers developing after childbearing, the increased cost of housing relative to family income, and the effect of decreased purchasing power on family budgets have all placed additional pressures on family members attempting to help care for relatives. More recently, the decline in medical and social services, both institutional and noninstitutional, may be contributing to economic and other strains on families caring for their elder members. Assuming that child and family violence should reasonably extend to include the elderly in its ambit, demographic changes alone would lead us to predict an increase in the incidence of elder abuse.

Whether or not this is the case, congressional committee testimony in both the House and Senate, called media attention to this phenomenon. Many sensationalistic articles have appeared describing incidents of extreme forms of elder abuse—

usually based on police or medical reports. The combinations of all these events—media attention, demographic and social change, and the interests of "moral entrepreneurs" (Becker, 1963) has, or so it would seem, been associated with the recognition of a new social problem. Laws have been passed to protect individuals in many states. Many public and privately funded programs have arisen to serve abused elders.

Pedrick-Cornell and Gelles (1982), among others, have criticized the scientific status of the purported data and research on elder abuse in terms of its definitional problems and flaws in research design. In particular, the definitional ambiguity and inconsistency surrounding the term *elder abuse* have produced two serious obstacles to our understanding of the phenomenon. First, the legislation and elder abuse programs sparked by the initial studies are only as valid as the methodologically weak and definitionally vague studies from which they were derived. Second, the problem of definition and the extent to which different definitions have been the basis of research data make comparisons of various state programs impossible (Douglass, Hickey, & Noel, 1980), and therefore make the search for the best practice model untenable.

Although these implications of definitional inconsistency have been repeated ad infinitum, it has often been overlooked that definitional consistency would do little in terms of allowing comparability of one state program with another, or of the incidence data collected by one state program with that collected by another. The process by which a case comes to be treated and counted as abuse in a protective-service program is influenced by many factors other than simply the definition proposed in the law. As Miller and Dodder point out, in Chapter 14 of this volume, the human-discretion factor of protective-service workers determines in part whether a case is substantiated or not. More importantly, besides being influenced by the individual caseworker, the data reported by varying state agencies are a function of the locally developed data-collection system, and the protective-service network in which it is embedded. These in turn are presumably the product of the moral entrepreneurs who legislate and institute the system. Because elder abuse legislation and programs have proliferated despite the lack of sound data, it is reasonable to ask, "Who is benefiting from the rapidly increasing interest in elder abuse?"

In this chapter, it is argued that differing definitions of abuse alone cannot account for differences in incidence reported between states. Pointing to definitional differences only begs the question as to why a state selected one defintion of abuse over another in shaping its elder abuse program. The impact of the structure of the elder abuse program, its niche within the service-delivery system, and the perceived role of its service providers have a bearing on both how elder abuse came to be defined and, consequently, on the magnitude of the elder abuse problem reported in the state. To illustrate the point, comparisons are made between the laws, investigative procedures, reporting systems, and resulting data of the elder abuse programs in Missouri and Iowa, the former state having 10 times the rate of elder abuse as the latter. The analysis demonstrates that state elder-abuse data sets, developed for internal organizational use, do not accurately reflect rates of incidence and prevalence of elder abuse within the states from which they are extracted, but that they do accurately reflect the public policy decisions and the interests of the political actors that primarily molded them.

THE MISSOURI STORY

In 1979, Missouri passed an elder abuse law, and beginning in 1980, the Missouri Division of Aging, under the Department of Social Services, began operating a toll-free elder abuse hotline. The hotline received reports of elder abuse concerning persons over the age of 60, either in the community or, in long-term care facilities. In recent years, this hotline has been receiving more than 10,000 reports annually.

Seventy-three percent of all reports of elder abuse in Missouri occurred for persons living in the community—the remainder were for persons receiving institutional care. Data are less readily available for elders in long-term care facilities. Cases of abuse in nursing homes have attracted considerable public attention in Missouri but tend to be politically and practically harder to resolve—with the only remedy being threats to close (or actual closing of) nursing homes.

Social workers assigned in each county make the judgment whether or not elder abuse has occurred. The investigating worker categorizes each reported case either as one there is "reason to believe," one that is "suspected," or "unsubstantiated." Among community-resident cases only, the proportion of cases judged to be abuse cases that is, those categorized under "reason to believe" (69%) or suspected (16%) cases, is higher than the overall percentage for community and institutional cases combined (Reiter,1987). Moreover, the proportion of all cases of abuse that are confirmed or suspected rather than unsubstantiated varies depending on the type of abuse. Table 15-1 presents the judgments made on six types of elder abuse generated by the Missouri reporting system, based on an accumulation of more than 40,000 cases.

The different rates of substantiation between community and institutional cases, and among different types of abuse, are noteworthy because services are provided for only two of the three categories—those that are confirmed (reason to believe) or suspected. The services that protective-service workers are able to directly deploy are least applicable to cases of institutional abuse and to cases of financial exploitation. As one would expect—though a causal link cannot be established—it is in these categories where the highest rates of unsubstantiated cases relieve the investigative worker of the responsibility of

Table 15-1   Judgments on Six Forms of Elder Abuse[a]

	Total %	Reason to believe	Suspected	Unsub- stantiated
Physical abuse	5.8	44.8	26.7	28.3
Physical neglect	61.2	57.8	19.9	22.1
Emotional abuse	7.9	49.7	29.0	21.3
Emotional neglect	11.5	55.0	27.0	18.0
Financial exploitation	5.2	20.9	34.7	44.4

[a]Data derived from "Missouri's Computerized Response to Elder Abuse," a paper presented by E. Reiter at the National Conference on Elder Abuse, Washington, DC, January 1987.

mobilizing services. The services at the disposal of the worker are most appropriate for the other abuse categories and include homemaker/chore services, home-delivered meals, respite, day care, personal care, and medical intervention.

The county elder abuse workers are staff members with direct administrative relationships to the Missouri Division of Aging; they are not administratively under Area Agencies on Aging. Furthermore, the program can boast an initial workforce of over 200 staff, many of whom were former Title XX purchase-of-service workers. This peculiar feature of the program is related to parallel transitions occurring at the federal level, as block grant allocation was implemented, and at the state level, where the Missouri Division of Aging was established as an autonomous division with its own reporting, accounting, and administrative focus.

The changes in Title XX of the Social Security Act to permit the Block Grant allocation of funds meant that instead of federal directives dictating the nature of and qualifications for service under Title XX, each state would be allowed to decide how it would use its resources. While the state was given greater latitude in the allocation of resources, the Missouri Division of Aging was simultaneously given greater latitude within the state by virtue of its being upgraded from a department under the Department of Social Services to a separate division. Many of the former purchase-of-service workers were assigned to the new Division of Aging. Workers now moved into a situation where the new law on elder abuse provided for direct intervention and project management. Rather than providing services under the general umbrella of service to families, as they had before the organizational change, they now had their own administrative apparatus and were free of the federal mandates for the allocation of their resources. As one administrator remarked, "We were in the right place at the right time." Missouri's protective-service law was passed with the attending public interest at a time when the Block Grant Assistance made possible the administrative decisions permitting reallocation of resources from general family-welfare programs to the newly developed program within the recently established Division of Aging. Missouri's Division of Aging, considering patterns of staffing and budgeting, became one of the largest in the nation.

THE IOWA STORY

In 1976, the legislature of the state of Iowa began to pursue legislation to protect adults from abuse. In 1977, the state of Iowa began a voluntary program for adult protection, using Title XX funds. The program, providing particular services to adults, continued using Block Grant discretionary funds until 1983. Parenthetically, these are the same Block Grant funds that in Missouri were used to provide staffing for the elder abuse program in the Missouri Division of Aging. The program that began to develop in Iowa was modeled after its child abuse laws and provided no protection for workers during the investigations, nor for the reporters of abuse. No additional legal sanctions for intervention were introduced. The only legal means for intervention were probate court or legal commitment procedures.

This temporarily authorized program served to build additional awareness of abuse and the need for legislation. It made use of data from the congressional hearings, the same hearings that have been the impetus for much of the national media attention on elder abuse and that have been used to support demand for legislation in a great many states. The Iowa legislature enacted Law 1250 (SF 2304) Section 117, 1982 Act, to become effective January 1, 1983. During a 6-month trial period, staff provided weekly statistics of reports of abuse that were made possible under the temporary legislation; this additional recording of statistical information led to permanent legislative enactment, the passage of Chapter 153 (SF 541, 1983 Session Act). The Department Abuse Program became an ongoing program of the Department of Human Services. The new law provided protection for reporters and investigators, time-limit requirements for investigation, and a system for tracking reports. (The history of Iowa legislation is based on a report prepared by the Iowa Commission on Aging for Governor Branstad in January 1984, as related through personal communication with Iowa staff member Vince Weber, August 27, 1987.)

There are a number of differences between the law in Iowa and in Missouri, including the definition of abuse (see Chart 1). The Iowa statute does not include neglect in its definition. In addition, Iowa's laws provide protection throughout the life cycle, whereas Missouri does not provide protective services for the nonhandicapped who are aged 18 to 60. Recent changes in the laws in Iowa will require reports of abuse by police, physicians, and other professionals, but unlike Missouri, Iowa has had a voluntary rather than mandatory system of reporting and does not operate a hotline.

In fiscal year 1986, Missouri's elder abuse reporting system recorded 7,257 reports of elder abuse, with physical abuse accounting for one of the smallest categories of abuse. This is nearly 10 times the number of reported abuse cases as in Iowa. It is not surprising that Iowa has a fraction of elder abuse cases that Missouri has, in light of its voluntary reporting system and its more restricted definition of abuse. Why would Iowa choose a more circumscribed approach to dealing with its elder abuse problem? It is unlikely that the Missouri citizenry is so much more abusive that an expanded response system is required. The answer would seem to lie in the lack of moral entrepreneurs in whose interest a large-scale response to elder abuse would lie.

Although Iowa upgraded its former Commission on Aging to a Department of Elder Services, it is comprised of only about 30 persons, and does not handle the investigation and intervention in elder abuse cases. The Department of Human Services, which must respond to a wide variety of human service needs, has been delegated the responsibility (personal conversation with Vince Weber, staffperson of the Iowa Department of Elder Abuse, August 27,1987). Therefore, while the Missouri Division of Aging provides its own protective-service and reporting system, the Iowa Department of Aging, a much smaller entity, educates and advocates but does not provide protective services. These are provided by another department of equal standing in state government. In addition, the Iowa state program must respond to service needs arising from any

Table 15-2 **ELDER ABUSE IN MISSOURI**

M I S S O U R I

LEGISLATION

GROUPS COVERED

The State of Missouri has two laws which relate to elder abuse: the Protective Services for Adults Act (EPSL) and the Omnibus Nursing Home Act (ONHA). The Protective Services for Adults Act provides protection for persons age 60 and older who are unable to protect their own interests or adequately perform or obtain services which are necessary to meet essential human needs. The omnibus Nursing Home Act provides protection for residents of any residential care facility I, residential for residents of any residential care facility I, residential care facility II, care facility, or skilled nursing facility.

DEFINITIONS

Serious Physical Harm

(EPSL) "Likelihood of serious physical harm: means one or more of the following:

(a) A substantial risk that physical harm to an eligible adult will occur because of his failure or inability to provide for his essential human needs as evidenced by acts or behavior which have caused such harm or which give another person probable cause to believe that the eligible adult will sustain such harm;

(b) A substantial risk that physical harm will be inflicted by an eligible adult upon himself, as evidenced by recent credible threats, acts, or behavior which have caused such harm or which place another person in reasonable fear that the eligible adult will sustain such harm;

(c) A substantial risk that physical harm will be inflicted by an eligible adult upon another as evidenced by recent acts or behavior which have caused such harm or which give another person probable cause to believe the eligible adult will sustain such harm;

(d) A substantial risk that further physical harm will occur to an eligible adult who has suffered physical injury, neglect, sexual or emotional abuse, or other maltreatment or wasting of his financial resources by another person."

(ONHA) Not addressed in the law.

Abuse

(EPSL) Not addressed in the law.

(ONHA) "Abuse" means the infliction of physical, sexual or emotional injury or harm.

AND IOWA: A LEGISLATIVE COMPARISON

I O W A

LEGISLATION

GROUPS COVERED

Elder abuse is covered by Iowa Code Chapter 235B, Adult Abuse Services. The law provides protection to dependent adults. Dependent adults are those persons unable to protect their own interests or unable to perform or obtain essential services.

DEFINITIONS

Dependent Adult Abuse

"Dependent adult abuse" means:

(a) any of the following as a result of the willful or negligent acts or omissions of a caretaker: (1) physical injury to or unreasonable confinement or cruel punishment of a dependent adult; (2) the commission of a sexual offense with or against a dependent adult; (3) exploitation of a dependent adult which means the act or process of taking unfair advantage of a dependent adult or the adult's physical or financial resources for one's own personal or pecuniary profit by the use of undue influence, harassment, duress, deception, false representation, or false pretenses; (4) the deprivation of the minimum food, shelter, clothing, supervision, physical and mental health care, and other care necessary to maintain a dependent adult's life or health.

(b) the deprivation of the minimum food, shelter, clothing, supervision, physical and mental health care, and other care necessary to maintain a dependent adult's life or health as a result of the acts or omissions of the dependent adult.

(continued)

Table 15-2

Neglect

(EPSL) Not addressed in the law.

(ONHA) "Neglect" means the failure to provide, by those responsible for the care, custody, and control of a resident in a facility, the services which are reasonable and necessary to maintain the physical and mental health of the resident, when such failure presents either an imminent danger to the health, safety or welfare of the resident or a substantial probability that death or serious physical harm would result.

Exploitation

(EPSL) Not addressed.
(ONHA) Not addressed.

REPORTING

Who Must Report

(EPSL) Any person having reasonable cause to suspect that an eligible adult presents a likelihood of suffering serious physical harm and is in need of protective services shall report.

(ONHA) Any physician, dentist, chiropractor, optometrist, pediatrist, intern, nurse, medical examiner, social worker, psychologist, minister, Christian Science practitioner, peace officer, pharmacist, physical therapist, facility administrator, nurse's aide or orderly in a facility, or employee of the Department of Social Services or of the Department of Mental Health with reasonable cause to believe that a resident of a facility has been abused or neglected shall report.

Who May Report

(EPSL) Not addressed in the law.

(ONHA) Any person having reasonable cause to believe that a resident has been abused or neglected may report.

Procedures

(EPSL) Reports are made orally or in writing to the Department of Social Services. The time frame for making reports is not specified.

(ONHA) Reports are to be immediately made to the Department of Social Services. The method of making the report is not specified.

(Continued)

REPORTING

Who Must Report

Not addressed in the law.

Who May Report

Any person who believes that a dependent adult has suffered abuse may report the suspected abuse.

Procedures

Reports of suspected abuse are made to the Department of Human Services. The timing and manner of making reports is not addressed by the law.

Table 15-2

Central Registry

(EPSL) not addressed in the law.

(ONHA) The law requires the Department of Social Services to keep a record of names of persons determined by the department to have knowingly abused or neglected a resident while employed in any facility. The names listed are provided to licensed operators who are prohibited from knowingly employing, in direct resident care, any person who have been determined to have abused or neglected a resident and whose name is listed in this record.

INVESTIGATION

(EPSL) The Department of Social Services is required to make a prompt and thorough investigation of a report upon receipt. If there is a likelihood that an eligible adult has or will suffer serious harm and the department is unable to conduct an investigation because access to the eligible adult is barred by any person, the director of the Department of Social Services may petition the court for a warrant to enter the premises and investigate the report.

(ONHA) The Department of Social Services is required to initiate an investigation within 24 hours of the receipt of the report. Access to the facility to investigate a report is not addressed by the law.

SERVICES

(EPSL) Protective services are defined as those services necessary for the eligible adult to meet his essential human needs. The Department of Social Services is responsible for providing:
identification of the eligible elder adult and determination that the eligible adult is eligible for services; evaluation and diagnosis of the needs of eligible adults; provision of social casework and counseling; assistance in locating and receiving necessary protective services; assistance in locating and receiving alternative living arrangements as necessary; coordination and cooperation with other agencies (state, public and private) in exchange of information and the avoidance of deprivation of services.

(Continued)

Central Registry

The department shall receive dependent adult abuse reports and shall collect, maintain and disseminate the reports by expanding the central registry for child abuse to include reports of dependent adult abuse.

INVESTIGATION

Evaluations of reports are required to be made expeditiously by the Department of Human Services unless the alleged abused is a resident of a health facility in which case the state Health Department has the responsibility for evaluation and investigation. Upon a showing of probable cause, a district court may authorize the designee of the department to make an evaluation, to enter the residence of, and to examine the dependent adult.

SERVICES

The law authorizes the department to provide necessary protective services, make appropriate referrals to services and, if determined to be in the best interest of the dependent adult, initiate action for the appointment of a guardian or conservator or for admission/commitment to an appropriate institution or facility.

(continued)

Table 15-2

EMERGENCY/INVOLUNTARY
INTERVENTION

(EPSL) If the eligible person is unable to give consent and the guardian refuses to provide or permit essential services to be provided, the Department of Social Services must inform the court having jurisdiction over the guardian. The court may take such action as it deems necessary.

When a peace officer has reasonable cause to believe that an eligible adult will suffer an immediate likelihood of serious physical harm if not immediately placed in a medical facility and the adult is incapable of giving consent, the officer may transport or arrange to transport to an appropriate medical facility. The peace officer must notify the next of kin and the Department of Social Services.

If immediately upon admission to a medical facility a person legally authorized to give consent for the eligible adult has not given or refuses to give consent for medical treatment and it is the opinion of the medical staff of the facility that treatment is needed to prevent serious harm, the head of the medical facility shall file a petition with the court. If the designated licensed physician at the facility determines that the life of the eligible adult would be jeopardized by the delay caused by the hearing, the medical facility may provide treatment before the hearing.

(ONHA) The Department of Social Services, the local prosecuting attorney, or the attorney general may petition the circuit court for an order giving the Department of Social Services authority for the temporary care and protection of the resident for a period not to exceed 30 days.

(Continued)

EMERGENCY/INVOLUNTARY
INTERVENTION

In the event of an emergency situation, a law enforcement agency may be called. Law enforcement agencies are authorized to take any lawful action necessary or advisable for the protection of the dependent adult. Involuntary intervention may also be ordered by the district court.

(continued)

abused adult, aged 18 to 60. Missouri, in contrast, has been able to concentrate on services to only those aged 60 +. If it had to staff a comprehensive adult protective-service program, it might have had fewer resources with which to develop its elder abuse program. As in those categories of abuse where Missouri workers have the fewest services available, the proportion of substantiated cases might be expected to decline under circumstances of more thinly spread service alternatives.

It should be noted that because Missouri subsumes its elder abuse program under its Division of Aging, budget information concerning staffing may be misleading. For example, it was reported in the Elder Abuse Project (American Public Welfare Association/National Association of State Units on Aging, 1986b, p. 14) that only 11 states have discrete funding categories to provide protective services. Missouri is not listed in this report as one of those 11 states; yet, Missouri has approximately 200 social workers and 10 people staffing the hotline, whose primary work is to provide protective services for abused elders living in community settings. Additionally, workers are responsible for institutionally based cases. This large force involves a budget of approximately $2,700,000 which is part of the operating budget of the Missouri Division of Aging.

CONCLUSION

A comparison of elder abuse in Iowa and Missouri reveals that the elder abuse system and its data-collection procedures can create the very phenomenon they are meant to identify and enumerate. Iowa's system has produced a much lower profile elder abuse problem, it is argued, because of certain dimensions of its program—the omission of neglect from its definition, the voluntary reporting aspect, the lack of a hotline, and the dilution of the elder abuse problem within an adult protective-service system. These dimensions in turn reflect that elder abuse is not the raison d'être of a single administrative agency.

What is striking about the differences is that commonly, when one state has been in the process of passing an elder abuse law, it has typically made reference to the laws and experience of other states. In generating background information for the law passed in Iowa, as a case in point, staff sought information on the experience of programs developed from recently enacted laws in Nebraska, Missouri, and Kentucky (personal communication with staff of the Iowa Commission on Aging, April, 1984). The divergence that ensued indicates that although the content of an elder abuse law or program may be borrowed, its ultimate form will depend on how it is grafted onto the existing aging network and human-service-delivery system. In Iowa, the elder abuse program was incorporated into a department in which it had to compete (with other aging and nonaging issues) for allocation of resources. Through a series of public-policy decisions, Missouri focused a relatively large portion of its Title XX Block Grant discretionary resources to support its elder abuse protective-service program. These decisions, and others, gave Missouri, particularly when statistics are controlled for population, one of the largest divisions of aging, elder abuse programs, and incidence of elder abuse in the United States.

Chapter 16

THE ILLINOIS PLAN FOR A STATEWIDE ELDER ABUSE PROGRAM

Melanie Hwalek, Bette Hill, and Caroline Stahl

Over the past 10 years, state and national attention has focused on the issue of abuse and neglect of the elderly, resulting in many states having passed elder-abuse-reporting legislation. According to Traxler (1986), in 1986 over 40 states had reporting laws, by far the majority of which mandated the reporting of elder abuse by professionals. Common among these laws has been the failure to establish a comprehensive system for managing cases of elder abuse and providing resources for assisting victims and their families once abuse is found.

The state of Illinois has been unique in its approach to statewide elder abuse programming. Instead of adopting legislation patterned after other states, Illinois decided to first gather critical information about the extent, cost, and effectiveness of providing for community elderly who are victims of abuse, neglect and/or financial exploitation (State of Illinois, PA 83-1259 and PA 83-1432). Over the past 3 years, an evaluation of four state-funded elder-abuse demonstration projects provided information to the legislature and the Illinois Department on Aging regarding the characteristics of elder abuse victims, issues addressed by program staff, and the cost implications of three different models of elder abuse intervention. Using data from the evaluation as a base, in 1987 the Illinois Department on Aging proposed to the legislature a plan for a statewide elder abuse program. This chapter describes the plan recently passed by the Illinois legislature for managing elder abuse cases in the state.

BACKGROUND OF ILLINOIS' COMMUNITY SERVICES AND DEMONSTRATION PROJECTS

The information obtained from the evaluation of the demonstration projects regarding the types of abuse, the victims, and the relationship of victim to abuser was used in the development of the statewide program. Between May 1984, and March 1987, over 500 reports of abuse and neglect were received from the four demonstration projects. Professionals were the major sources of referrals for reports with social workers, nurses, and paraprofessionals accounting for over 50% of reports. In the one site with mandatory reporting, paraprofessionals accounted for a larger proportion of referrals than in the other sites, but this need not indicate the impact of mandatory reporting because there was in addition, considerable emphasis on coordination efforts at this site.

The data collected provide the following information about victims and abusers. The average victim is 77 years old, female, and widowed. About two-thirds of victims had a chronic health condition and one-third were reported to be disoriented. The majority of victims lived in their own homes with others, or in the home of a relative; only 10% lived at home alone. Psychosocial data on substantiated versus nonsubstantiated cases of abuse indicate family discord is more likely among those who are abused. In addition, confirmed victims are more likely to report someone who is trying to force actions against their will, take property from them, or threaten them. The average abuser was a relative of the victim, and about 48 years old. Where the abuser was the spouse, physical abuse was more likely. Where the abuser was a child or other relative, financial abuse was more likely.

Definitions of Elder Abuse in the Demonstration Projects

The demonstration projects used the following definitions of elder abuse:

Physical abuse: The infliction of physical pain or injury.

Confinement: Confinement for other than medical reasons.

Sexual abuse: Touching, fondling, or penetration of the elderly person for the purpose of sexual gratification without consent of the elderly or with use of physical force.

Deprivation: Withholding service or medical treatment necessary to maintain physical health.

Financial exploitation: The use of an elderly person's resources to the disadvantage of the elder or for the profit/advantage of a person other than the elder.

Neglect: Failure to provide for the physical or psychological needs of the elderly either through commission (*active neglect*) or omission (*passive neglect*).

The evaluation data on substantiated cases revealed that financial exploitation was the most common type of abuse reported (53%). Physical abuse (29%), deprivation of services (21%), and passive neglect (19%) were also commonly reported. Confinement (12%), sexual abuse (less that 2%) and self-neglect (11%) were least likely to be reported. Another important finding was that victims often experienced more than one type of abuse. This empirical analysis of the demonstration-project data helped set the stage for examining critical questions addressed below.

Considerations for Statewide Programming

The evaluation data revealed several issues that should be considered in designing a statewide program. The most critical issues were:

1. Does the state's current service system address the needs of abused elderly? One primary aspect of the research has been to examine the service needs of abused elderly in comparison with services already available from the aging network and administered through the Department on Aging. In fiscal year (FY) 1984 Illinois implemented a statewide case-management system whereby the responsibility for client intake, assessment of needs, and ongoing case monitoring for frail, vulnerable elderly was given to local agencies called Case Coordination Units (CCUs). The CCUs provide case-management services to over 40,000 elderly per year. The Community Care Program, funded with state general revenue funds and a Medicaid 2176 waiver, is one of the largest in-home care programs in the nation, providing services to 22,000 older persons each month, with a budget of over $90 million per year. Community Care Program services include chore, homemaker and adult day care. Services such as home-delivered meals and transportation are also funded extensively by the Area Agencies on Aging under Title III of the Older Americans Act at a level of $30 million annually. In short, Illinois has a rather extensive community-based services and case-management system in place, which required the state to ask whether this system was already adequately serving elderly victims of abuse and neglect.

2. Should the state have mandatory or voluntary reporting of elder abuse? Mandatory reporting acknowledges the need for involuntary intervention by the state in cases of suspected abuse. It can be useful when the victim is reluctant or unable to reveal abuse. It can also be useful when professionals are reluctant to report abuse among their clients. Mandatory reporting emphasizes case-finding activities and usually requires the development of a central registry for tracking reports.

Some legal experts have not recommended mandatory reporting (Faulkner, 1982; Regan, 1985). Mandatory reporting can invade the privacy of individuals and families. The reporting process can interfere with professional-client rapport and confidentiality, because the professional must inform the client that a report to authorities is required. Further, mandatory reporting can create needless investigation and expenditures on resources when the caseworkers are not suitably trained to identify abuse. And the psychological stress of the investigation process on the elderly and their families can be devastating when alleged abuse is unfounded.

On a more practical level, even when mandatory reporting exists in a state, many professionals are not aware of the legislation, and lack the awareness of symptoms to clearly identify victims (O'Brien & Greenblatt, 1985). Further, the cost of administering a central registry can severely limit the development of needed services.

3. Should the client in a statewide program be the victim, both victim and abuser, or the entire family/abuse unit? Evidence from the evaluation of Illinois' demonstration projects indicates that the abuser is most often a family member or relative of the victim. Elder abuse was most likely to occur in the victim's home. And a large percent of the victims were physically frail and in need of assistance.

Considering the victim as the client may, in the short run, be less costly than providing services to the entire family. However, in the long run, without family support the victim could be eventually placed in a long-term care facility at considerable expenditure to the families and, eventually, to the state. Considering the abuser as part of the client system can place great strain on the caseworker, who must provide assistance to both the victim and abuser. Including the abuser in the client-system could also result in resistance from the legislature in funding necessary services, because the public is likely to view abusers as criminals who need punishment more than therapeutic intervention.

4. Should self-neglect be included in a statewide program? Although self-neglect is a serious and frequent type of elder abuse that was reported to the four demonstration sites in Illinois, cases of self-neglect are already handled by the existing statewide case-management system. However, even though self-neglect need not be included in a statewide elder abuse program, victims of self-neglect uncovered through the program must be referred for other statewide resources. Therefore, a statewide elder abuse program must make provisions for interfacing with the case-management system.

5. Should there be age and/or financial eligibility requirements for inclusion in a statewide elder abuse program? If an elder abuse program is to be administered by a department on aging, age restrictions should be considered because age is a requirement for eligibility into other programs of the department. On the other hand, domestic violence is not limited to those over age 60. Therefore, any adequate statewide program should have provisions for making referrals for assistance to victims of any age.

Similarly, elder abuse is not limited to low-income individuals. Many studies have indicated that elder abuse is prevalent in other socioeconomic classes (cf., Hwalek, 1986; Pillemer & Finkelhor, 1986). Assistance to victims is a major focus of elder abuse programming, but pragmatic and economic constraints limit the extent to which all needed services can be supported by the state. If victims and their families can afford to pay for services, the public should not be required to provide state-supported services. On the other hand, if the abuser is controlling the victim's resources, having assets does not mean that the victim is in a position to be able to pay for needed assistance.

Components of the Proposed Statewide Elder Abuse Program

In developing the statewide program, the Department on Aging examined the aforementioned issues. The department decided to recommend legislation that would create an elder abuse intervention program based on the *advocacy/voluntary-reporting model*. This intervention model recognizes that the victim of elder abuse and neglect is an adult in a vulnerable position and assists elderly persons by intervening on their behalf for the purpose of serving as an advocate in guaranteeing protection of elders' rights and obtaining needed services. This model was one of the models of elder abuse analyzed and originally promoted in an early study of elder abuse in Illinois (Crouse, Cobbs, Harris, Kopecky, & Poertner, 1981). The program assumes that existing family supports, legal mechanisms and community service can be used to assist abused older persons and their families. Illinois' current service system for the elderly became a critical asset to the development and implementation of plans based on this advocacy-voluntary model.

The decision to propose a voluntary-reporting model was also based on the experience of testing both mandatory reporting and voluntary reporting at the demonstration program sites. Because there were a number of factors unique to each site, the difference in reporting statistics between the voluntary-reporting and mandatory-reporting sites could not be causally linked to either mechanism. Therefore, the Department on Aging believes that a voluntary-reporting system, supplemented with public-education materials developed for those professional groups most likely to encounter abuse situations, is the least restrictive approach to assisting abused older persons in Illinois and can be more effective than mandatory reporting.

The decision was also made that the elder abuse intervention would be approached in terms of a family situation or problem. However, the alleged victim must be 60 years of age or older to receive intervention; younger victims of spouse abuse are assisted under the Illinois Domestic Violence Act. In addition, no income requirements for admisssion in the program were set, recognizing the need that older persons who are abused or neglected, regardless of income, should have access to an advocate to assist them in obtaining needed services. However, certain supplemental services would be available to victims but only if their resources are insufficient or unavailable to purchase them.

Assessment of cases will be paid through state general-revenue funds. The statewide program will provide a systematic, standardized format to receive and respond to reports of abuse and neglect, to determine whether abuse has occurred, and if so, to determine the competency of the alleged victim and the services needed. All reports of abuse and neglect would receive this standardized assessment, which is now being developed and field-tested by the Department on Aging.

The proposed program would involve victims of the following types of abuse: physical abuse, neglect, sexual abuse, confinement, psychological abuse, and financial exploitation. This comprehensive definition includes all possible types of elder abuse. Self-neglect would be referred to the CCU. Unsubstantiated cases who are in need of community care service would also be referred to the CCU.

Intensive casework activities would be provided for substantiated cases. Casework would include the development and implementation of a care plan, and stabilization of the abuse situation following the assessment. Casework would continue for an average of 3 months following the assessment. After stabilization, a face-to-face follow-up would continue on at least a 3-month basis for a 1-year period. If abuse or neglect has not occurred at the end of the 1-year period, the case would be closed. If continued monitoring of in-home services is necessary, the monitoring would be continued through the CCU. Figure 16-1 illustrates the flow of cases through the proposed program.

Although existing community services in Illinois met the needs of the majority of abused elderly and their families in the demonstration program sites, there were cases where the victim lacked access to available resources, where processing delays threatened the health and safety of the victim, or where gaps existed in publicly supported services. Therefore, the Department of Aging determined that the service system de-

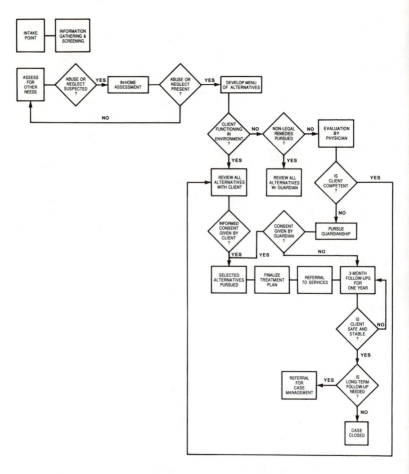

Figure 16-1. Proposed flow of clients in statewide elder abuse program.

signed to assist elder abuse and neglect victims must have available at the local level the flexibility to purchase specific services on a short-term and emergency basis to meet victims' needs. A key component of the Illinois program is the availability of supplemental services, which will include emergency aid, respite care, legal assistance, and housing. It is the intent that these services be available to suspected and substantiated victims who are in immediate, life-threatening situations and are in situations where community resources are insufficient or unavailable to purchase needed services. Five hundred dollars will be made available to the designated provider agencies per case for supplemental services. For those cases in which more than $500 is needed, a waiver could be granted with prior approval of the regional administrative agency.

Although not directly provided to the older person, public education would also be developed under the statewide program. Public education would increase knowledge and understanding by professional groups and the general public of the risk symptoms of abuse and methods of accessing assistance. Public education was seen as particularly important to a voluntary-reporting system in order to elicit moral obligations of professionals to report, because legal obligations do not exist. Because of the relationship between public education and volume of reports seen at one model site, the state would proceed cautiously and prudently in pursuing public education efforts to ensure that the newly created elder abuse program is not overwhelmed with reports of abuse and is therefore not able to adequately deal with them

ADMINISTRATIVE STRUCTURE OF THE STATEWIDE PROGRAM

The Department on Aging would assume overall responsibility for designing, implementing, and administering the statewide elder abuse program. Regional Administrative Agencies (generally Area Agencies on Aging) would be responsible for specific administrative and systems-development activities within their planning and service areas. They would work with the state department in coordinating elder abuse activities at the regional level and assist in developing and administering services under the Elder Abuse and Neglect Act. Provider agencies would be selected by the regional administrative agencies to provide direct services to alleged and substantiated cases of elder abuse and neglect. Provider agencies woud include CCUs, domestic-violence agencies, outreach agencies, legal agencies, counseling sevices, and the like.

Conclusions

On June 30, 1987, the Illinois legislature passed the Elder Abuse and Neglect Act directing the Illinois Department on Aging to implement a statewide abuse and neglect program by September 30, 1987. The Department on Aging will seek funds from the legislature in the spring of 1988. The passage of this legislation illustrates the impact a well-developed, adequately evaluated demonstration program can have on convincing legislators of the need for a statewide elder abuse program.

The Illinois program appears to be unique in many ways. It is based on evaluation data that allow for a projection of the number of cases likely to be reported in a statewide program. The Department on Aging projects that when the statewide program is fully operational, elder abuse would be reported at a rate of 2.31 per 1,000 elderly. Evaluation data also allow the state to estimate the cost of operating a statewide program based on voluntary reporting.

Another unique component of this program is the development of a system for funding supplemental services. The use of supplemental services guarantees the emergency needs of elder abuse victims will be adequately addressed.

Finally, the Illinois program has a strong focus on intervention. Unlike many mandatory-reporting laws that focus on reporting and investigating cases, the Illinois plan recognizes the importance of sufficient and appropriate intervention strategies in addressing the problem of elder abuse.

Acknowledgments

The authors would like to acknowledge the Illinois Department on Aging and the Illinois legislature for their support of the research related to this paper. The authors would also like to acknowledge Sally Petrone, Elder Abuse Specialist at the Illinois Department on Aging, and Dr. Mary C. Sengstock, Professor of Sociology at Wayne State University for many of the ideas contained within this paper.

The opinions expressed in this paper are those of the authors and may not represent the opinions of the Illinois Department on Aging. Further information about the Illinois Elder Abuse Program can be obtained from Carolyn Stahl, Illinois Department on Aging, 421 East Capitol, Springfield, IL 62701.

Chapter 17

THE POLITICS OF MICHIGAN'S RESPONSE TO ELDER ABUSE

Sharon R. Medved

It is an undeniable fact that abuse of the elderly exists. Although research on this issue is minimal, estimates of the magnitude suggest that 4% of the elderly among the United States population may be victims of abuse that ranges in type from passive neglect to the violation of rights, to verbal, financial, sexual, and physical abuse (Phillips, 1983b; U. S. House of Representatives, 1985a). Given the interest displayed from pressure groups, academics, researchers and politicians for the multiple special issues surrounding the elderly and the severe examples of abuse presented in past congressional hearings, it would seem logical to assume that concern about abuse would evoke the strong reactions necessary to lead toward the development and implementation of a policy solution. To be sure, research has occurred, some legislation has been passed, and proposals for solutions have been made, but key elements that would push forth a comprehensive program are missing. Before addressing this directly, it is important to review the background of the attempt to develop a policy solution in Michigan.

HISTORY

Between 1978 and 1980, two Michigan researchers, Richard Douglass and Thomas Hickey, undertook an extensive study on elder abuse within the state of Michigan (Hickey & Douglass, 1981a). Hypotheses for the causes of abuse, uncovered in the earliest studies centered around intergenerational relationships that were greatly stressed due mainly to the difficulties of providing care for a physically impaired elderly relative who is dependent upon a family that lacked either the skills or resources to provide the needed care. The ensuing conflicting emotions that resulted were prime contributors to any abuse. It was also suggested that substance abuse and/or the presence of learned abusive behavior within the family contribute to the conflicts that result in abuse of the elderly (O'Malley, Everitt, O'Malley, & Campion, 1983). Given the relative newness of the subject and the preliminary nature of the research, most recommendations included suggestions for further study while attempting to suggest several means to alleviate the intergenerational stresses.

At about the same time, concern with somewhat related issues was growing. Michigan, facing severe economic problems, was cutting back on funding for care of the developmentally disabled and mentally ill while attempting to continue with the deinstitutionalization of care for this segment of the population. This caused many difficulties in providing adequate community support programs as well as institutional care for those who could not be discharged. Strongly organized groups involved with lobbying for this population (particularly for the developmentally disabled) became more concerned about the potential for abuse with the advent of dwindling resources. These groups, although not involved with seniors' issues directly, were strongly supportive of a mandatory reporting law. Other individuals, such as physicians, nurses, and social workers, with an interest in gerontology, plus groups such as Citizens for Better Care (who were overseeing institutions and nursing homes) and the Gray Panthers, lent their support through lobbying efforts (J. Lindsay, personal communication, March 24, 1986). It must be noted here that even though there were several groups, pushing for the passage of the mandatory-reporting law, their main objectives were unrelated and so a cohesive network was not formed, which was significant for future events.

In 1982, Michigan legislators, seeing the type of constituency support generated by various groups, along with the legitimization of the issue through congressional hearings and research evidence of the problem, passed a mandatory-reporting act into law (Michigan Senate Bill No. 223). The act, which requires both those who are employed by agencies providing as well as those licensed to provide health care, social welfare, mental health, or other human services, to report suspected adult abuse to the county Department of Social Services, was a relatively simple measure to deal with elder abuse. Further, by including law-enforcement officers and employees of the medical examiners' offices as professionals required to report, links for gathering evidence were established for possible follow-up prosecution. Interestingly, due to a strong lobbying effort, physicians were exempted from reporting unless they believed it to be in their patient's best interests. The flaw, however, in expecting the mandatory-reporting law to deal with the problem and do what it was intended to do was that appropriations for the Department of Social Services Adult Protective Services were minimal, thereby hampering implementation (L. Kole, personal communication, March 26, 1986).

THE LACK OF POLICY-SOLUTION FORMATION

The relative speed with which the mandatory-reporting act was passed was deceiving. Surface appearances seemed to indicate that momentum was being gained and that further steps would be taken to deal with the problem. Occasional media attention was given to stories that suggested reporting procedures were helpful in uncovering cases that should be prosecuted. Several legislators began describing proposals for tax credits and other programs to help relieve the stress on caregivers of elderly relatives (May, 1982). However, community groups that supported the reporting act, as previously stated, were neither a cohesive unit nor an organized movement. They had been a collection of interest groups supportive of a measure that would benefit each of them in some way. Each group had its own major issue and there no longer appeared to be a common ground between groups. In a climate of economic recession and budget cuts, the differences in focus for the various groups put them into competition with each other for limited resources.

A further sign that continued response to the problem would be slow is that little of the social-services budget was ever actually allotted to Adult Protective Services. The result was obvious—an understaffed organization was charged with investigating reports of suspected abuse and neglect, but had minimal resources available for investigation and education of the public, and even fewer resources available to provide for intervention. Additionally, Department of Social Service workers were finding that much of their ability to intervene was based upon, not only the availability of in-county service, but more importantly, the elder's willingness to accept intervention. Department of Social Services workers began to feel much frustration with the conflict over protecting an adult's rights while wanting to protect them from harm. They were also finding that the public's awareness of the problem and the law was minimal—but they had few ways to educate them. Lastly, interdepartmental issues arose around services for those who exhibited self-neglect and were in need of mental health services (L. Kole, personal communication, March 26, 1986). In essence, many more problems were becoming evident.

By 1986, Michigan's political agenda was still strongly focused on economic recovery, tax and budget cuts, and issues related to mental health, education, and children. Further, various community agencies and senior-citizen organizations were attempting to hold their own in the face of federal budget cuts due to Gramm-Rudman and concern about spiraling costs. Gramm-Rudman legislation is properly identified as Public Law 99-177. This law was intended to provide for a balanced federal budget by 1991 through set budget reductions each fiscal year. Medicare was exempted from any cuts; however, other programs that would benefit seniors were not directly protected. The Michigan Gray Panthers were looking for support for programs aimed at improving and maintaining the health and independence of seniors within the state (J. Lindsay, personal communication, March 24, 1986). At the same time, individual legislators, having their own agenda on seniors-related issues, introduced several bills that ranged from granting department status to the Office of Service to the Aging, to requiring insurers to offer coverage for home health care, to tax credits and subsidies for families caring for the elderly (Ablan, 1986). In this climate, elder abuse, although still acknowledged as a problem by most professionals and seniors' organizations, was not a priority issue.

Even though little significant legislation has been enacted since the passage of the reporting act, it would be both unfair and an oversimplification to state that this has occurred due to loss of interest in the subject, or to the state's economic condition, or even to interest-group competition for limited resources. The lack of major agenda status for the issue of elder abuse is really much more complex, involving all of the participants who played a part in the mandatory-reporting law, and also encompassing a lack of convergence of what political scientist John W. Kingdon (1984) calls the problem, policy, and political streams.

THE PROBLEM STREAM

To understand why there has been no convergence, it is crucial to first look at the components of each stream separately. Kingdon describes the *problem stream* as indicators of the magnitude of the problem as well as the focusing events that push attention toward a specific problem. Personal experiences as well as crises can act as focal events. Early on, in the case of elder abuse, one can clearly point to the testimony before the United States House of Representatives' Subcommittee on Aging to find a shocking crisis. Michigan, with its own examples of abuse toward institutionalized adults as well as those living in the community, had sufficient experiences available to be moved toward action. Given the lack of definitive numbers describing the magnitude of the various types of abuse, what resulted was an identification of a problem, shocking in nature, that required action, but was lacking in concrete information about its causes, magnitude, and solutions.

The Policy Stream

The *policy stream*, in Kingdon's view, is of prime importance in developing ideas and establishing the range of solutions. For researchers, elder abuse was both a new area for investigation and one that dovetailed nicely with past work on child and spouse abuse. Michigan, with its universities and specialists in gerontology, should have been a prime site for the policy stream to develop its idea networks, conduct research and generate potential solutions.

The Political Stream

Kingdon's *political stream* is a complex combination of actors involving those in government, the bureaucracy, and those groups that make up a constituency. Through feedback mechanisms (polls, letters, etc.), legislators are able to gauge the public mood on an issue. The political stream in Michigan contained several legislators who were receptive to seniors' issues as well as a bureaucracy that administered multiple state and federal programs aimed at seniors such as Meals-on-Wheels, the Foster Grandparent Program, and the like. The Office of Services to the Aging, set up as a part of the Department of Management and Budget, oversaw these state and federal programs through five Area Agencies on Aging, provided referral information, and published newsletters to educate the public on pending legislation of interest to seniors (C. Mollison, personal communication, April 14, 1986). The shock of severe abuse could have been used as a triggering event to focus attention on the needs of the elderly. Instead, it became identified as the main problem. The simple response of enacting a reporting law diverted attention away from the larger picture in a state that was experiencing severe economic difficulties.

In essence, there was an error in that the "wrong" problem was identified. Elder abuse should have been seen as a condition, severe and worthy of correction, but not the main problem. Properly identified, the problem should be seen as the complex set of factors (i.e., the lack of resources and services) that creates the stresses in households that result in acts of neglect or violence. Seen in this light, the passage of the mandatory-reporting act should have been viewed as a preparatory, facilitating process while providing the policy stream with details as to magnitude and causative components. With the wrong problem identification occurring in Michigan, the act's passage was an end in and of itself, seen by many as the mechanism for taking care of the problem.

MOVEMENT TOWARD A POLICY

Several things are currently happening to suggest that a policy can be developed. Since reporting began, statistics are indicating that neglect and self-neglect are of a much greater magnitude than is physical abuse (and much of this results from a lack of services). It may be assumed, as a result, that the groundwork for correcting the erroneous problem identification has been set. Further, the policy stream now appears to have a consensus on the types of abuse and neglect and the basic causes. However, an idea network within Michigan must still be developed where research findings from various fields— encompassing social and health services, plus delivery model— are discussed. The focus of elder abuse research should be geared toward identifying preventive sevices that would assist the entire family of those caring for the elderly. Also, the emergence of several policy entrepreneurs is needed to continue and expand the interest in seniors-related issues. This will be extremely important for future action if the current concern over the costliness of service is to be balanced and the isssue kept alive.

Another serious issue to be addressed is the need to build

broadly based public support. Further, by having focused on abuse of the vulnerable, frail, dependent adult, and then modeling a corrective action after the type used in child abuse cases, the stage was set to possibly alienate potential advocates who would have fears that this negative characterization of seniors could become generalized to all seniors. The trick is to find a balance between presenting some of the potential consequences of a lack of services for the elderly in need while promoting the fact that the majority of elderly adults are competent individuals. Focus must also be placed on assessing the seniors' health and service needs in each community, and then educating the public as well as the professionals who work with seniors.

Currently, a recently completed report by a Michigan task force may be an impetus for beginning this type of action. The task force was a joint effort between the Michigan Office of Services to the Aging and the University of Michigan Department of Social Work. The survey found that the elderly live in a wide variety of geographic settings, requiring flexibility in service delivery systems to meet their different needs (Dluhy, 1987). The services identified as most needed by the elderly were transportation services, home delivered meals, home health aides, chore services, and health screening. In addition to these services, the researchers suggest there is need for more education about caregiving and more respite care services, given the extensive provision of caregiving by relatives uncovered in their survey.

Coalition building is another important step in gaining momentum around a policy idea. The links between individuals, groups, and legislators, plus those within areas of the bureaucracy need to be strengthened. Discussions that illustrate the need for action, the availability of solutions, and the potential for wide support are essential. Currently, attempts in this area are being made by the Michigan Gray Panthers to include state representatives and gerontology specialists from the University of Michigan in a coalition to promote further development of seniors' health services (J. Lindsay, personal communication, March 24, 1986). Once firmly established, other groups should be included to maintain continued expansion of support for action.

RECOMMENDATIONS FOR FUTURE ACTION

Given that the stage is being set in regard to senior-related issues, questions arise concerning what to do with existing programs and how to avoid wasteful duplication. One of the first moves that could help to provide a coordinating role would be to enact the bills aimed at raising the Office of Services to the Aging to department status. This would provide the prestige necessary for further attracting competent personnel and, it is hoped, a sufficient budget.

Within the hierarchy, the Area Agencies on Aging would continue to administer the programs they now provide. However, grants should be sought to pilot demonstration projects dealing with the provision of services under alternative payment methods. Because 97% of Michigan's elderly are enrolled in Medicare, and Medicare social-health-maintenance organizations have been suggested and successfully piloted elsewhere in the country (Diamond & Berman, 1981; Zawadski & Ansak, 1983,), this form of prepaid comprehensive service delivery should be investigated. (If viable, the SHMO could, through a case management gatekeeper, set up needed service packages for individual enrollees, maintaining independence and thereby minimizing the vulnerability to abuse for at-risk seniors.)

With regard to the type of services that are actually needed, it appears that respite care, home care, home-delivered meals, and transportation are all necessary. Mental health services are also needed for both seniors who are at risk and their caregivers. In many of these services, senior volunteers or postretirement employees would add a special benefit in that they would help to encourage acceptance and use of these services. It has been shown in several studies (Pynoos, Hade-Kaplan, & Fleisher, 1984; Silverstein, 1984) that service utilization is increased through the use of the informal word-of-mouth network, with those making up the network being family, friends, and/or peers. In order to assist with service delivery of programs that fall under the jurisdiction of other departments, agreements between what would be the department of services to the aging, the department of social services, and the department of mental health should be drafted so as to help refer identified seniors in need to appropriate services.

One comment must be made about the current bills aimed at granting tax credits to caregivers of seniors. Although they could be considered as a form of cash aid, allowing the family to purchase services in a competitive market (and thus appealing to those who believe that this is a more equitable and dignified method of redistribution), these bills avoid dealing with the basic issue—the lack of services and the maldistribution of some needed services. It would not help to be able to afford a service if that service were too far away to be practical, or if it did not exist at all. Tax credit should really only be viewed as a supplement to the family income and, dependent upon the values and problems within the family itself, this tax relief may not relieve the emotional stresses that could contribute to abuse. Therefore, credits and subsidies are only adjuncts to the main solution of developing comprehensive services for the elderly.

Clearly, what is being recommended to deal with the problem of elder abuse is an addition of services and a change in the delivery system. Given the current existence of various types of programs and the uncertainties of financing, change will more than likely occur slowly and incrementally. The key will be to have the end result (an organized comprehensive set of programs) clearly in mind while changes are being implemented. Imperative with this type of change will be the demonstration of a financing mechanism that will help to contain costs as well as the emergence of policy entrepreneurs to maintain a course of change so that the end goal will ultimately be reached.

ACKNOWLEDGMENT

The author wishes to acknowledge the help and encouragement given by Professor Barry Rabe in the preparation of this chapter.

Chapter 18

ELDER ABUSE AND PREVENTION
A Holistic Approach

L. Rene Bergeron

This chapter suggests a holistic approach for the intervention of elder abuse and prevention. It outlines the mandatory-
reporting law of New Hampshire; the response of the Division
of Elderly and Adult Services to reports of abuse, neglect, and
exploitation; the misconceptions concerning the law and response system; the role of community service providers; and
the development of a community-based task force.

THE NEW HAMPSHIRE REPORTING LAW

New Hampshire has had a reporting system for abuse
and neglect of the adult with incapacities since the middle
1970s, currently called RSA 161-D (Department of Health and
Human Services, 1986). Informally, those of us providing services to the elderly have come to refer to it as our "elderly protection law" when in fact the term *elderly* is not used. This is
symbolic of how human services workers in New Hampshire
have come to view the intent and purpose of the law; that is, we

associate the law with those adults over the age of 65 and use it accordingly.

New Hampshire charges the department of health and human services, formally called the Division of Health and Welfare, with administering the Protective Services to Adults law. Within that department, the Division of Elderly and Adult Services has the responsibility of investigation of filed reports and of follow-up. Although the law allows the department flexibility in whom it assigns as an authorized representative in investigations, it is the policy of the department to have one of its own social workers (from the Division of Elderly and Adult Services) carry out all investigations and oversee the subsequent actions taken.

The law defines *adults* as persons 18 years of age and older. It is targeted for *incapacitated* adults, defining incapacity as "limited mental or physical function" (Department of Health and Human Services, 1986, p. 32.19). It is within this definition of incapacity that we incorporate our vulnerable elderly population.

The law concerns itself with abuse, neglect, and exploitation, defining *abuse* as "intentional use of physical force, non-accidental injury as the result of acts or omissions, mental anguish or unreasonable confinement"; *neglect* as "a pattern of conduct rather than action or omission which results in deprivation of services that are necessary to maintain minimum mental and physical health"; and *exploitation* as "the illegal or improper use of an incapacitated adult or his resources for another's profit or advantage" (Department of Health and Human Services, 1986, p. 32.19).

The New Hampshire law is a mandatory-reporting one, requiring anyone who suspects abuse, neglect, or exploitation to report it to the division immediately. The law specifically identifies health care professionals, hospital personnel, social workers, clergy, law enforcement officials, protection officers, volunteers, or persons residing in the home of the suspected abused adult as sources obliged to report. It recognizes the privileged communication between attorney and client only. The law clearly states that any suspected abuse, neglect, or exploitation must be reported, and it carries a misdemeanor if anyone is found guilty of knowingly not reporting abuse. Therefore, it does provide immunity with respect to participation in judicial proceedings, as well as protection from civil or criminal liability for those who in "good faith" file a report (Department of Health and Human Services, 1986, p. 32.20).

The law requires a state registry, containing case material adhering to the division's rules of confidentiality for verified reports. The division's central registry now publishes statistical data on filed reports giving access to such data as the number of cases involving clients over age 65, number of cases involving institutional abuses, and number of unsubstantiated cases.

All reports must be investigated, and if a reported adult does not allow the worker on his premises when there is probable cause, the worker may order a police officer or probate-court official to conduct the evalution. The law also allows for guardianship procedures, conducted pursuant to RSA 464 ("Mentally Incompetent Persons, Spendthrifts, Etc., Conservators," revised 1984), if the client is found to be mentally incompetent (Department of Health and Human Services, 1986, pps. 174.1–174.28). Psychiatric/mental health and physical examinations may be ordered through probate court if the client refuses to submit to needed evaluations.

THE DIVISION OF ELDERLY AND ADULT SERVICES: RESPONSE TO REPORTS

Although the law addresses incapacitated adults, those adults who are in need of supportive services because they are mentally ill or developmentally disabled are generally referred to mental health agencies within the Division of Mental Health and Developmental Services. For the remaining cases, coming under the aegis of the adult protective-service authorities, reports of abuse are typically given over the telephone. If the report is filed by a professional person or by an institution, a written report is requested to follow the oral report. Once the division receives the report, oral or written, it must respond with an investigation within 3 days (Department of Health and Human Services, 1986, p. 32.19). If the situation is suspected to involve serious, life-threatening abuse or if a perpetrator is implicated, the investigation tends to occur sooner.

According to the Division of Elderly and Adult Services, the purpose of the investigation is to assess the client, the situation, and the persons involved with the client, and to verify the report. The worker must gain access to the client in order to do this. In the event that the client is living with someone, especially if that person is the perpetrator, this may not be an easy task. Because the law (RSA 161-D: 1) clearly states that the intent of the law is to protect the adult and that the philosophy of the law is to strengthen the family unit whenever possible, the worker must try to conduct an investigation in a non-threatening manner. To attain these ends, the worker has no obligation to file criminal charges on behalf of the client with the local police, though the police must file a report with the division if they receive a complaint from an adult (Department of Health and Human Services, 1986, p. 32.20). The social worker may advise the client of his or her right to press criminal charges, but that decision and responsibility rests with the client. It is also expected that the social worker will attempt to work with the perpetrator, or with any persons living with the client. Therefore, when a worker conducts an investigation, the client population may well include the abused, the perpetrator, and/or other family members.

The social worker investigates several factors of the abusive situation. The worker observes clients' general health, physical appearance, and mental competency. The living situation is observed, as well as the appearance of other members within the clients' households. During the interview process, the worker assesses communication skills, affect, and whether clients are realistic about their current and future situation. The worker considers the isolation of the client, noting involvement with others outside the home. A financial assessment is obtained to see what the client can afford and what the client may be eligible to receive in terms of benefits or services. The worker may seek information of the client's situation from involved professionals, family, or neighbors. The worker then compiles this information into a written report and recommends a course of action to the client.

Upon noting abuse, neglect, or exploitation, the worker's goal is to bring needed services to the targeted client(s). However, unless the clients are found to be mentally incompetent, they remain in control of the situation. Abused persons may decide to continue in their current situation without intervention, or with minimal services, and the social worker must respect the clients' rights to self-determination.

The social worker is obligated to bring cases of gross abuse, neglect, or exploitation to the attention of the attorney general's office. The attorney general will decide whether or not to prosecute based on the worker's report (Department of Health and Human Services, 1986, p. 32.22).

Obviously, the individual worker's approach, experience, knowledge, energy level and caseload, the availability of community resources, and the commitment to the elderly by the local division will determine how successful the investigation and intervention will be in alleviating the oppressive situation.

Misconceptions of the Law and Intervention Process

There are several misconceptions about the law and the intervention process that exist. The first misconception is that a filed report ensures that the client's situation will be alleviated and that services will be initiated. It does not. Unless the client is found to be mentally incompetent, the client remains in control of the situation and may refuse intervention and services.

The second misconception is that if a client is found to be mentally incompetent, a guardian will be provided in a timely manner. That may not occur. The guardianship procedure, particularly if initiated by the worker, is painfully slow. Furthermore, even if the court decides guardianship is in the best interest of the client, there may not be a guardian to assign unless a willing family member or friend is found. New Hampshire's Public Guardianship Program has a waiting list, and volunteer guardians are precious and few.

The third misconception is that because we have a law and

an investigation procedure, we have adequate services to offer clients. We do not. New Hampshire funds little in the line of human services. Services that are funded may not be available because service providers do not come forward to enter into contracts with the state. For example, an elderly client may qualify for in-home care, but because of a lack of service contracts for in-home care, the client will not receive it. There is also an unequal distribution of resources, with rural areas disadvantaged compared with urban areas.

The fourth misconception is that a report ensures continued social work intervention and monitoring of the abused, neglected, or exploited elderly client. It does not. Depending on the worker's approach and frequency of contact, the elderly client may not accept needed services. Even if the elder agrees to services, and services are provided, contact by the worker to monitor the continued well-being of the client may not be adequate to prevent future abuse, neglect, or exploitation. The resistant elder who refuses "reasonable" suggestions for services may be terminated for service, because the division tends to promote the delivery of concrete services, and does not tend to promote long-term counseling for acceptance of services.

There are clearly unrealistic expectations of division workers. Ideally we expect the adult service worker to work simultaneously with the abused, abuser, and family unit; we expect the worker to promote services and to develop those services that do not exist; we expect long-term counseling and monitoring to assist the client and family in changing maladaptive life patterns. We expect case-management services. We assume many times that our responsibility in the elderly abuse intervention process ends once we file a report. This is the final misconception, for it does not.

THE ROLE OF HUMAN SERVICE PROVIDERS

The law is the law. It states we must report known and suspected abuse, neglect, and exploitation to the department of health and human services. As we become better acquainted and more comfortable with the law, we are reporting with greater consistency (excluding physicians, who remain consistently resistant to filing reports). Statistical data from the department's central registry (Table 18-1) show a 20% increase of reports from 1983 to 1984, and an amazing 85% increase from 1984 to 1985. According to statistics taken from the 1986 Adult Protection Report (Form 620 Activity), in 1986 reporting continued to increase and was approximately 47% over the 1985 figures.

Many of the reports come from human service providers such as visiting nurses, homemaker/home health workers, community action workers, drug and alcohol counselors, and mental health clinicians. Yet there is a lack of integration of the adult protective-service system with the human service providers who are so critical in both the reporting and responding stages of the process. Without a protocol stipulated by law for effective reporting, many agency personnel, including those trained in the field of social work, wish to remain anonymous and never prepare the client for the division worker, the investigation, or follow-up. We leave the uncomfortable task of confronting the client to the division worker. The end result is that the client is suspicious, resistant, and often terminates association with all human service providers. Moreover, once the protective-service worker identifies necessary services, she or he is not in the position of directly deploying them, but must seek the cooperation of service providers in the community.

A holistic approach is necessary if one is truly going to serve the elderly. It is essential that we educate ourselves regarding effective intervention, and that we develop consistent approaches with the elderly clientele. We cannot work in isolation from each other, but we should rather jointly devise good reporting and intervention systems that allow for immediate reporting but give consideration to the elderly client's rights, facilitate the initial contact of the adult service worker, and guarantee an optimal package of services that are necessary to assist the older adult. A community-based program that strengthens services, promotes good casework, and forges linkages among providers not only can assist in

Table 18-1   1986 Statistical Data on New Hampshire Elderly and Adult Abuse and Neglect[a]

Number of cases reported	
Total number of reported adult abuse and neglect	1,000
Number of substantiated cases	597
Number of unfounded cases	403

33% of reported cases—Male 67% of reported cases—Female

72% of reports involved elders

Number of cases reported by age	
18–59 years	276
60–69 "	151
70–79 "	241
80–89 "	267
90 and over	65
Total number over 60	724

Cases involving 18- to 59-year-olds primarily involved adults with mental retardation/emotional disturbances

Number of reports by types/categories:		
	18–59 years	60 years and over
Exploitation (financial/property)	14	39
Neglect (inflicted by caregiver/significant other)	48	136
Self-neglect	132	371
Physical abuse	36	91
Emotional abuse	29	78
Sexual abuse	17	9

[a]Figures approximated, based on percentages. The information in this table is derived from cases reported to the Division of Elderly and Adult Services, New Hampshire Central Registry, Concord, NH 03301; January 1986 to December 1986.

reporting valid cases, but may also prevent cases of abuse and neglect.

DEVELOPMENT OF AN ELDER ABUSE AND PREVENTION TASK FORCE

My own involvement in developing a task force in the seacoast area of New Hampshire suggests that it is a viable means of accomplishing a holistic approach. The task force began in 1982, was formalized in 1985, and is functioning well with a membership of 13 human service agencies, covering fifteen municipalities. The following guidelines are based on the New Hampshire experience.

The primary purpose of a task force on elder abuse and prevention must be to network with service organizations, and to create a common language and approach to elder abuse, neglect, and prevention. It should not be statewide, but rather regional, so as to meet the needs that may be unique to the area.

There should be a sponsoring organization willing to assume the cost, or to apply for funding that will cover the cost, of the task force. Preferably, the sponsoring organization should not be a department of health and human services, but rather an independent service provider. The rationale for this is to take the focus off the department as the sole responsible agency. In our case, the sponsoring agency was the Portsmouth Community Council of Senior Citizens, which assumed and still maintains sponsorship.

A core group of service providers needs to be identified. A suggested listing is:

> Legal Aid Services/Senior Citizen Law Project
>
> Visiting nurse agencies
>
> Homemaker/home health
>
> Division of Elderly & Adult Services (or the agency designated by law to carry out investigations)
>
> Long-term care ombudsman programs
>
> Seniors centers agencies

Housing authorities
Drug- and alcohol-counseling centers
Mental health centers
Legislators
Hospital social workers and emergency-room personnel

The task force must address issues of elder abuse that the law, if there is a law, does not. Issues such as agency and client responsibility, approaches to the resistant client, creative intervention, new programs to meet client needs, among others, must be on the agenda.

To be effective, the members must decide upon their primary purpose. In our case, the stated purposes were education of area service providers, identification of hard-to-reach elders, promotion and development of needed services, and dissemination of free educational services to the general public by means of open public forums.

Specified meeting dates must be agreed upon and be consistent (e.g., the third Wednesday of every second month at 8:00 A.M.). A designated meeting place, central to all, is helpful, although rotating meetings among service providers may stimulate interest in and serve to educate the task force on the roles of different service providers.

The sponsoring organization must keep records of the meetings, send meeting notices, set the agenda, and keep the members of the task force up to date on its own activities.

The merit of the task force is that it allows for providers to share openly their frustration with the system and to devise a set of intervention processes that can meet the unique needs of its region while still adhering to the guidelines of the law. Service providers need to realize that there are methods of intervention to help prepare a client for an impending report. In cases where this might endanger the client, the service provider needs to claim responsibility for filing a report, give a clear explanation for the report, and be encouraged to work with the adult-service workers. Sometimes even being present during the investigation can make the process less threatening to the client. The view that many service providers hold, namely that filing reports of abuse and neglect will hurt their rapport with the client, is invalid if good casework skills are employed. It may even help in keeping human service providers more "honest," because with the focus on promoting collective services to the elder client, service agencies are less apt to discontinue services to the difficult client and will instead try new approaches.

The task force can also serve in providing supportive services to the providers, giving encouragement to novel ideas (e.g., respite day care for Alzheimer patients), writing letters of support for funding, and sharing information on funding sources. Probably the single most important achievement of a task force would be its initiation of a process of sharing responsibility in order to provide a unified approach to elder abuse and prevention, as well as a common working language of abuse and neglect. By virtue of human service providers' becoming members of a task force, they recognize that they are a part of a broad solution and begin the commitment of defining and developing that solution beyond what the law mandates. They can no longer simply file a report and then attempt to avoid the responsibility of the outcome, because they are part of that outcome.

ACKNOWLEDGMENTS

I am grateful for the assistance of the Elder Concern and Abuse Prevention Task Force, Community Council of Senior Citizens, Portsmouth, NH 03801, and Portsmouth Division of Elderly and Adult Services, Department of Health and Human Services, 30 Maplewood Avenue, PO Box 550, Portsmouth, NH 03801.

Chapter 19

MAKING POLICY RESEARCH COUNT
Elder Abuse as a Legislative Issue

*Jeffrey M. Anderson
and John T. Theiss*

The tragedies of elder abuse are not new, but public concern about the problem and state legislation in the area are recent phenomena. The most serious cases—incidents of physical abuse and caregiver neglect that result in death— capture the newspaper headlines and inspire editorials that urge more vigorous prosecution and new laws. These atypical accounts influence public perceptions. They are often a major focus in the policy process, and lead to adoption of solutions with limited utility.

Research can help provide more balanced input into the policy-development process. This chapter describes the Texas legislature's decision to deal with elder abuse, and the role of a research project in the Texas legislative process. A sensationalized story on elder abuse sparked the Texas legislators' interest and suggested a criminal-justice approach to the problem. The research helped redefine the problem and secure consideration of solutions other than punishment.

The research questions asked, the methodology used, and the data sources tapped were important determinants of the study's useability, credibility, and feasibility. The study findings made a case for community services that became part of the Texas Senate Select Subcommittee on Elder Abuse recommendations to the full senate. The research broadened legislators' understanding of elder abuse and helped expand the range of potential solutions to which they gave serious consideration.

The survey did not have immediate and dramatic effects on service structure or delivery. Many other forces, in particular a severely restricted state budget, shaped policy decisions of Texas' 70th legislature. The senate put aside many of the subcommittee's recommendations for future consideration. But the legislature increased appropriations for adult protective services and other services crucial to elderly Texans.

LINKING POLICY RESEARCH TO POLICY CONTEXT

Researchers and politicians proclaim the importance of linking social-science research and public policy, but few researchers have explored the nature of those linkages. John Kingdon's (1984) research on policy development is a notable exception. He identified many forces that help determine which issues become part of the federal policy agenda; what solutions legislators consider; and what decisions they make. The model developed from his research provides a context for development of policy-focused research and a framework for examining the Texas situation.

Problems, Policies, and Politics

The Kingdon model identifies three processes: problems, policies, and politics.

Problems: The model examines how a given condition becomes defined as a problem for which government action is an appropriate remedy. Empirical indicators of a problem (e.g., number of validated reports of elder abuse) and highly visible events, crises, or disasters (e.g., elder abuse resulting in death, or a movie about abuse of residents in nursing homes) can elevate issues to the policy agenda. Kingdon labels these events and the role they play as the problem process or stream.

Policies: The model considers who and what generates proposed solutions to problems. Once a condition is defined as a policy problem, what determines the range of alternative solutions considered? Ideas and research make substantial contributions to the policy stream by expanding and limiting the range of policies considered.

Politics: The political stream includes events (such as changes in administration, lobbying efforts, and public opinion) that determine political climate. In Kingdon's model, the politics stream serves as a gate determining what options become policy. At the convergence of three streams—problem, policy, and politics—concerns about a problem become statements of principle and action.

Kingdon's model provides a framework to explain how a research project was used to redefine a narrowly focused public-policy issue into a broadly focused issue. This chapter describes elder abuse as a policy issue in Texas—as it originated and as it was finally presented to the state legislature.

THE PROBLEM STREAM: ELDER ABUSE CAPTURES HEADLINES

August 1985, front-page stories in the *Austin American Statesman* reported the death of Mrs. Dixon, an elderly woman who had mental and physical health problems. Police discovered her dehydrated body in an apartment she had shared with her son. Authorities arrested the victim's son for murder. Because Texas law does not require a son or daughter to care for a parent, no law had been broken, and the sheriff released the son. The tragic death of an elderly woman along with the state's inability to prosecute was, in Kingdon's terms, a focusing event. With this event, elder abuse became an issue for the Texas Legislature; at this point, the problem was identified as not being able to prosecute individuals who fail to provide care for their infirm parents.

THE POLICY STREAM: STRENGTHEN TEXAS LAWS

Inability to prosecute the victim's son increased publicity about the case and led to promises of action by public officials. Shocked lawmakers vowed to tighten laws on the abuse of elderly. State Representative Terral Smith announced that he would hold hearings on elderly abuse. "There is obviously a vacuum in the law," and, Smith concluded, "we have to fill it" (Vargo, 1985a). Within 3 days, the district attorney had assembled a team of attorneys to draw up legislation to fill the void. "It may be difficult to come up with such a law," the Austin newspaper editorialized, "but it is worth the try" ("Starvation case spurs effort for neglect law," 1985). Local, state, and national attention focused on this case and the inability of Texas to prosecute apparent criminal neglect. How to change Texas laws to allow prosecution of people who neglect their parents, not how to stop neglect and abuse, was the policy problem. The definition of the problem—need to prosecute— limited policy alternatives to legislative, punitive options.

THE POLITICS STREAM: APPEASE CONSTITUENCY

A particularly difficult legislative session was approaching. Several contentious issues—revenue shortfall, budget deficit, and taxes—headed the agenda. These issues would not increase voter satisfaction, but attacking elder abuse would give legislators a positive image with their constituency. There was value in following through with the issue ignited by the Dixon case. Legislating familial responsibility appeared to be a politically sound approach to protecting elderly Texans. It would appease constituents' anger and not result in increased public costs.

Senate Subcommittee Vows to Tighten up the Law

On October 22, 1985, State Senator Gonzalo Barrientos announced the formation of a senate select subcommittee on elder abuse. "Not only will we study the extent of elder abuse, but also crisis intervention measures, emergency shelter availability and especially the effectiveness of current state statutes. We hope to find gaps in current state laws and ways to fill them" (Vargo, 1985b). The select subcommittee was asking how bad the problem was and if Texas could handle the incidents that occur. They initially focused on legislative solutions that emphasized punishing perpetrators.

Gray Panthers Seek Broader Focus

The Austin Gray Panthers lobbied for the formation of a senate subcommittee to provide a more thorough study of elder abuse in Texas. They hoped the subcommittee and the 70th legislature would consider more than criminal justice reform. Active players in the passage of 1981 legislation that established elder abuse reporting requirements and adult protective services (Texas Human Resources Code, Chapter 48), the Gray Panthers had followed the developments on elder abuse during the summer of 1985. They did not want legislation that satisfied the public outcry but did nothing to help abused elderly. Charlotte Flynn, Austin Gray Panther Co-Convener, powerfully stated their fear. "I'm concerned that a war on elder abuse will result in stiffer penalties, fines, imprisonment, and ignore the plight of victims. I fear that a criminal justice approach will lead legislators and the citizens to believe that they solved the problem when they have not" (personal communication, February 5, 1986). The Gray Panthers wanted Texas-based research to counter the rush toward legislating filial responsibility—but neither the subcommittee nor the Gray Panthers could pay for research.

Three public hearings on elder abuse were to form the major components of the subcommittee's investigation. Senator Barrientos, the subcommittee chairman, persisted in seeking background and research data. The Gray Panthers volunteered to raise money and conduct a study. They solicited the authors' help as research designers and managers. The subcommittee asked that the research focus on the subcommittee's charge to assess the existence and extent of elder abuse, the availability of crisis intervention, the availability of emergency shelters, and, especially, the effectiveness of current Texas statutes regarding elder abuse. The subcommittee assignment asked how bad the problem was, if the short-term emergency services could handle current levels of abuse, and if the laws were adequate. It did not ask about prevention; nonemergency, ongoing services for victims and families; nor about appropriations for services.

ANALYZING THE ASSIGNMENT

Research could not provide timely, definitive answers to the subcommittee's questions, and answering just these questions was insufficient to make effective policy decisions. The questions placed emphasis on knowing the frequency of abuse and on being able to punish perpetrators, not on understanding elder abuse and identification of ways to address the problem of elder abuse. Kingdon's model provides a framework for explaining how we analyzed the situation and renegotiated the research questions to examine broader issues.

The Problem

The problem definition had two weaknesses. First, it focused on punishing the abusers, rather than on resolution or prevention of elder abuse. Second, the precipitating event, severe neglect and death of an elderly woman, was treated by many as a typical instance of elder abuse. New information on the Dixon case indicated that it was not a cut-and-dried matter of deliberate neglect. Mrs. Dixon had refused offers of help, and that contributed to her death. The Dixon case was more complex than the media had originally reported. Background research showed, and the senate subcommittee staff agreed, that elder abuse, not just punishment of perpetrators, needed to be the research focus.

The Policies

Initially, the policy alternatives were limited to legislation that would make grown children responsible for their aged parents. Evaluations of this type of legislation revealed several major problems. The potential problems included retired, elderly people being held responsible for their infirm parents, and judicial complications of determining who is responsible for what extent of care for which parents.

Changing the problem from punishing the abusers to prevention and amelioration of elder abuse meant expanding the research to examine ways the state can deal with elder abuse. Filial responsibility legislation became only one of many policy alternatives that needed consideration.

The Politics

As we negotiated the research assignment in February 1986, punishment-oriented legislation, such as a filial responsibility law, still found favor among legislators. Expert opinion that filial responsibility legislation is difficult to apply and is often counterproductive carried little weight in light of political realities. The impending state budget crisis meant that people were looking for inexpensive solutions; money was not available for expanded services.

The political climate elevated the importance of the research. Senator Barrientos, subcommittee chairman, knew that recommendations for more service or funding needed to be based on more than testimony from public hearings. The senator wanted research that provided persuasive evidence attesting to the value of other approaches to stopping elder abuse.

The Research Project

The research needed to provide information about possible ways to deal with elder abuse, employ accepted research methods that counter the limitations of public hearings, and be completed in less than 1 year with no designated funding.

The research questions moved from being ones of how bad the problem was and how effective were current statutes to a broader focus on how Texas could deal with the problem. The information required to evaluate policy options in this broader framework included:

1. What services are most used, most needed but not available, and most crucial to addressing the problem of abuse?
2. What causes abuse?
3. Where in Texas does abuse occur?

We chose to answer those questions through a key-informant survey. A frequently used technique in needs asessment (Attkisson, Hargreaves, Horowitz & Sorensen, 1978), the key-informant technique involves collecting information from informed professionals and community leaders about their understanding of a social or community problem and possible solutions. We surveyed members from 10 professions whose work was likely to bring them into contact with victims of elder abuse and neglect. Because the success of most attempts to prevent or alleviate elder abuse depends in part on the cooperation of professionals such as those surveyed, knowledge about their beliefs and the approaches they support is important.

We selected the key-informant technique because it was feasible, the results would be credible, and the findings would be useful to the subcommittee. Support and cooperation from the 10 professional associations surveyed made the study feasible. They helped select systematic samples, provided mailing labels—and many of the organizations paid for the mailings to their members. Because the study used standard survey-research methods it provided more credible evidence than that collected at the public hearings. The report was based on responses from 1,653 professionals from 5 fields: health, financial, judicial, law enforcement, and social work. They were more likely than the general public to have informed opinions about elder abuse and knowledge about existing ways of dealing with it. Also, they comprised a persuasive data source. We believed that legislators were likely to listen to responses from influential constituencies. Both the methodology and the data sources enhanced the credibility of the findings. Finally, the key-informant survey provided the subcommittee with useful information; information that could be used to judge a broad range of policy alternatives. The information was presented in a straightforward, factual manner, with each finding directly linked to survey questions.

PERSUASIVE FINDING: CRUCIAL SERVICES

The key informants' responses indicated that elder abuse was pervasive and serious throughout Texas. The informants held a broad range of opinions about the causes of elder abuse. A particularly important finding in terms of helping the subcommittee was the identification of crucial services for elderly Texans.

Survey responses showed that community support services constitute a crucial response to elder abuse. The survey asked professionals who had experience with elder abuse about 18 services they might have used with one or more cases of elder abuse and the services that they needed but could not obtain (Table 19-1). Each professional also identified the services that would be most helpful in addressing each of five types of elder abuse—physical abuse, emotional abuse, exploitation, caregiver neglect, and unintentional neglect (Table 19-2).

We used their responses to these three questions to identify the services that are most crucial in addressing the problem of elder abuse and neglect. Crucial services are ones perceived as being most helpful and are either used by a large percentage of the respondents or are needed but not available to a large percentage. Three of the crucial services are frequently used and available, and three are frequently not available. Of the six

**Table 19-1   Services Used or Needed
by Largest Percentage of Professionals**

Most used[a]	%[b]	Most needed not available[c]	%[b]
Long-term care	55	Respite care	24
Home health and personal care	46	Bill paying	22
State and federal welfare	46	Emergency shelter	22
Emergency medical	46	Legal and financial assistance	20
Meals on wheels	43	Protective services	19
Counseling	43		

[a] The six services that the largest number of respondents used at least once.
[b] Percentages out of the 769 professionals who had contact with at least one incident of elder abuse or neglect.
[c] The five services that the largest number of respondents needed but could not obtain on one or more occasion.

services, emergency medical and emergency shelter address immediate crises. The other four services are usually focused on problem resolution and prevention (Table 19-3).

The opinions of professionals who carry weight with legis-

Table 19-2   Services Most Helpful in Addressing Elder Abuse Situations

Type of abuse	Services ranked most helpful	Percent[a]
Physical abuse		
	Protective services for adults	24.0
	Emergency medical treatment	21.2
	Emergency shelter	14.7
Verbal/emotional abuse		
	Social casework/counseling	31.2
	Protective services for adults	13.3
Exploitation		
	Legal advice or assistance	29.5
	Protective services for adults	13.2
	Legal guardianship	11.2
Caregiver neglect		
	Respite care to relieve caregivers	19.0
	Protective services for adults	12.7
	Home health and personal care	11.5
	Social carework/counseling	10.9
Unintentional neglect		
	Social casework/counseling	13.2
	Home health and personal care	12.5
	Friendly visitor	10.7

[a] Percentage out of all professionals who responded.

Table 19-3   Services Identified as Crucial by Key Informants

Crucial services[a]	
Frequently available	Frequently not available
Emergency medical	Respite care
Social casework/counseling	Emergency shelter
Home health/personal	Financial advice

[a] The largest number of professionals identified these services as most helpful, and the services were either used by or not available to the largest number.

lators and a straightforward logical analysis of the survey responses made a case for preserving and developing aspects of existing services to address the problem of elder abuse. The analysis also supports an observation that prevention and amelioration, rather than punishment, is of greater interest to professionals whose roles require them to deal with elder abuse and its complications.

IMPLICATIONS

Every aspect of the total effort, not just the research, was important to ensure that informed decisions were made. The broad base of input provided the research with credibility. Broad distribution ensured that a large number of people were aware of the study and the findings. Distribution to interest groups ensured that legislators would be frequently reminded of the study findings and subcommittee recommendations. And, media publicity for this study and its viewpoint on treatment of elder abuse—rather than reports of sensational incidents—ameliorated the public outcry for punitive solutions. The research was a major part of a policy project, not an isolated research effort reviewed during the policy process.

The most significant and direct consequence of the survey was that it stopped at least one legislator from submitting a filial responsibility law. The survey also provided the subcommittee, concerned legislators, and lobbyists with ammunition to advocate for the development and funding of specific services to assist the elderly and caregivers of elderly people. Charlotte Flynn, Austin Gray Panther Co-Convener, explained: "We took it to one legislator who was about to submit a bill that would, among other things, have punished children who neglect their parents, and he withdrew the bill. The study helped people realize that the problem is very complex and isn't going to be solved by sending people to jail" (Chance, 1987, p. 25).

Many of the recommendations from the subcommittee were not dealt with, but funds for critical services, in particular home health, personal care, social casework, and counseling, were increased. John Willis (personal communication, July 28,

1987), State Ombudsman/Advocacy Coordinator for the Texas Department of Aging, credited the timely publication of the findings and their use by Austin Gray Panthers with increased funding for services. Specifically, in a tight budget session, the legislature approved a 23.8% increase in adult protective service funds and a 15.3% increase in community care funds. These increases were made when budgets for many Texas Department of Human Service programs were being cut. The proposed state budget was cut by about 5%. The Texas Department of Human Services administration was cut by 16.3%, and the state general revenue portion of the agency budget was cut approximately 1% (computed from information in the DHS Proposed Fiscal Year 1988 Operating Budget, August 6, 1987).

Community-based efforts like this, undertaken as policy projects, are a significant opportunity for researchers, interest groups, and citizens to collaborate to ensure that legislators make informed ·if not correct policy decisions. As Paul Chance (1987, p. 25) noted in his review of this policy project, "No one knows for sure whether the new laws will lessen abuse and neglect of the elderly. After all, the information provided by the survey consisted merely of the opinions of experts, and experts can be wrong. But at least the laws that came out of the Texas legislature last spring were based on informed opinion, and not merely anger and good intentions."

Examining the policy context helped to define and design policy research. The value of the elder abuse research was greatly enhanced by careful examination of the policy context —the policy problem, policy alternatives, and the politics—in which the study was conducted. If the elder abuse study had focused on the misidentified problem, punishing the abusers, the research product would not have helped the legislators understand and address the problem of elder abuse. The respecified problem and the wider range of policy alternatives investigated increased the likelihood of identifying options that might help. Circumstances allowed for dealing directly with the problem and policy streams. The political stream was not subject to revision, but had to be considered if the study were to influence policy development. The combination of involving professional associations, reporting the opinion of informed professionals, and broadly distributing a report that included straightforward analyses and clearly stated findings, overcame predicted resistance to policy alternatives that required increased funding.

Acknowledgments

This chapter is based on a study done for the Texas Senate Select Subcommittee on Elder Abuse. The Southwest Long Term Care Gerontology Center at the University of Texas Health Science Center, Dallas, and the Institute of Human Development and Family Studies at the University of Texas, Austin, provided vital support for the research.

Chapter 20

ABUSE OF THE INSTITUTIONALIZED AGED
Recent Policy in California

Arline Cowell

In this chapter, abuse of the institutionalized aged is the focus. Specifically, the growing recognition of the problem in California and recommended solutions are examined. The problems of abuse of the institutionalized aged uncovered in California are not unique (cf., Kimsey, Tarbox, & Bragg, 1981), nor are the solutions, and the obstacles to solutions, likely to be limited to that state. The course of policy development in California in recent years clearly illustrates that the passage of laws alone is inadequate to eradicate abuse of the elderly. Abuse of the institutionalized aged can only be tackled through the collaboration of all involved parties, including residents of institutions and their family members; community, professional, and business organizations; law enforcement agencies; as well as state and federal legislatures. A collaborative effort of this sort will be briefly outlined.

In California, the Little Hoover Commission convened in 1982 to study the causes of abuse and neglect and to develop solutions to these problems in nursing homes. The commission members had received information documenting that the health care standards in nursing homes were not being adequately enforced. In order to obtain firsthand knowledge, the members of the committee visited four nursing homes in Los Angeles and in the San Francisco Bay area. Commission members observed examples of "dirty, understaffed facilities which were providing a demeaning environment for the residents" (Blum & Wadleigh, 1983, p. 1). Following these visits, the commission conducted public hearings in October of 1982, during which it heard testimony from over 20 witnesses who described cases of neglect, physical and sexual abuse, and the frustration of dealing with the state's "bureaucracy of care" (Blum & Wadleigh, 1983).

This was not the first time the commission or the legislature had heard and witnessed such horrors. Since 1970, assembly and senate committees, as well as the Little Hoover Commission, have held extensive hearings on conditions in nursing homes and on the state's licensing and certification activities. Although past efforts had resulted in the enactment of numerous laws to correct problems, the reorganization of the licensing activities, and increased public awareness, these changes had apparently not been sufficient.

The system for licensing of nursing homes and monitoring the conditions in these facilities was found lacking in the authority and resources necessary to eliminate the most severe problems. Many of the problems are quite complex and go beyond new statutes and regulations: Government cannot mandate love and caring.

Nevertheless, the commission believed more could be done to protect the 105,000 frail and elderly individuals living in California's 1,200 nursing homes. At the conclusion of the October 1982 hearing, the commission pledged to go beyond simply writing another report that might only serve to take up space on a bookshelf.

In response to these special problems, the commission appointed the Blue Ribbon Advisory Committee chaired by Lieutenant Governor Leo T. McCarthy, and represented by the assembly and senate policy-committee chairs responsible for aging issues. The Department of Health Services, the legal profession, consumer groups, the state ombudsman, academia, the

California Nurses Association, and the nursing home industry itself participated in the process.

The advisory committee's study reported the following findings (Blum & Wadleigh, 1983):

1. The Department of Health Services Licensing and Certification Division (LCD) has not determined whether its function is best served by a "friendly consultant" role or by an adversarial "strict-enforcement" role. As a result, survey teams appear to operate at either or both extremes.

2. No regular ongoing training program is presented for all LCD staff. LCD relies on "the buddy system" for on-the-job training.

3. LCD does not see facilities at their worst, because the timing of the federally required inspection is too predictable.

4. LCD still fails to focus on matters concerning patient's mental and physical well-being. Its "abbreviated survey" relies on traditional regulatory approaches instead of building upon new patient-oriented screening techniques. LCD does not take full advantage of outcome-oriented measures of quality, and it does not sufficiently seek and use information from patients, facility staff, and others in a consistent and purposeful way.

5. The citation-and-fine system, perhaps more through stigma than through financial impact, does motivate some improvements. But some facilities seem to have ignored the system quite comfortably, and public demand has grown for more and larger fines.

6. The review of available statistics reveal that facilities appeal 60% of A and 35% of B citations. (A citations refer to life-threatening episodes; B citations to those that involve health and safety but are not life threatening). Recent review conferences upheld only 12% of the violations heard, modified 77%, and dismissed 11%; fines were reduced by well over half.

7. Recalcitrant repeat violations do not tend to result in imprisonment. A cited study located only one case

where a jail term was imposed in the past 3 years outside the City and County of Los Angeles. According to LCD, the enforcement sanctions available to them are limited, and other prosecutors are disinterested. Prosecutors, on the other hand, state that LCD seldom or never refers cases to them, and that referred cases are seldom adequately documented.

8. The industry argues that a major direct route to better care is a combination of decreased regulation and increased reimbursement. Given that over 70% of the state's nursing home residents are Medi-Cal patients, the cost and consequences of this argument are significant.

9. Medi-Cal patients are not as desirable to facilities as are private patients, due to the discrepancy between the two payment rates. Consequently, many facilities do not accept them, or have set quotas limiting the number they will accept. Medical discrimination often extends even to patients who are already living in a Medi-Cal participating facility.

10. Most nursing care in nursing homes is provided by nurse aides (72 + %). Few physicians have an interest in geriatrics, fewer still in nursing home visits, and even fewer still in accepting Medi-Cal rates paid to physicians for such visits.

11. Present law and regulation require a (bare) minimum 2.8 nursing hours per patient day in nursing homes. However, in calculating this standard, the hours of an RN or LPN are doubled.

12. LCD is hampered by staff shortages, with significant losses in 1982–1983.

In order to insure that the state fulfilled its moral and legal responsibility for protecting and providing quality care for patients of nursing homes, the advisory committee and the commission recommended the following:

1. Inspection should be broken into segments to be conducted at random times throughout the inspection cycle.

2. LCD should develop a patient-satisfaction index, enhancing the enforceability of patients' rights. Additional information about facilities derived from systematic interviews with patients, family, staff, and ombudsman (or public) hearings, should be sought by LCD, possibly with the aid of volunteers.

3. Statutes should be amended to ensure complainants the right to appeal.

4. Maximum fines should be raised.

5. LCD should file cases involving under $1,500 in small-claims court and obtain rapid, inexpensive decisions. The attorney general could file cases between $1,500 and $15,000 in municipal court.

6. LCD should adopt Los Angeles County's guidelines for referring cases to local prosecutors, and should expand recent efforts to join with those prosecutors in improving communication and training.

7. Statutes should be amended to provide that when LCD finds conditions which threaten health, safety, or welfare of patients, it may declare an immediate moratorium on admissions. Another statute, linked to forthcoming federal regulations, should be enacted to permit withholding of Medi-Cal payments for new admissions under specific conditions.

8. A statewide consumer information system should be created for all persons interested in nursing homes.

9. If eviction of current patients when they convert to Medi-Cal is held to be legal under a pending attorney general's legal opinion, California should join the increasing number of states that are enacting specific legislation to prohibit such treatment of dependent persons who have entrusted themselves to the professional care of a nursing home.

10. Nursing homes should be encouraged to use geriatric nurse practitioners. Facilities with fewer than 50 beds should have a half-time nurse practitioner; those with between 50 and 100 beds, a full-time practitioner.

11. The 2.8 hours nursing standard is not very useful, nor informative of patient needs, and is perhaps

harmfully low. Nevertheless, it should not be eliminated until more accurate and stringent patient-centered standards can be revised and applied.

12.   Funds are needed to replace LCD positions lost due to cutbacks, because if not, the enforcement process will eventually suffer.

The work of the commission and the Nursing Home Study Advisory Committee did not stop with the submission of this report. In fact, it was only the beginning of a very long process involving the governor and the legislature. Legislation had to be introduced, regulations developed, information provided to the public, resources committed, and the cooperative assistance and support of the citizens of the communities enlisted in order to translate the words and ideas of the report into the reality of providing quality of care and protection to nursing home residents. The committee argued, "because people's lives are at risk, this government's responsibility must never be compromised nor its performance be second rate" (Blum, 1987, p. 5).

It is worth noting that the findings of California's commission were mirrored by a nationwide study conducted during the same period. The National Citizens Coalition for Nursing Home Reform conducted a study to measure the quality of care actually being provided in nursing homes and to bring attention to the need for a "people orientation" rather than a "paper orientation" in the regulatory process. The study was conducted by setting up small discussion groups involving a total of 450 nursing home residents representing nursing homes in 15 cities across the United States (Nusberg, 1985). A discussion format was chosen because the residents wanted not only to be heard, but wished others to listen and to respond. An analysis of the viewpoints was then presented at a national symposium on quality of care, held in February 1985 in Florida. This symposium was unique in bringing professionals concerned with long-term care issues together with residents who had participated in the original discussion groups. Residents made it clear that the following factors were critical to feeling that their facility was a home rather than a mere shelter:

1. Respectful and kind treatment by all levels of staff.
2. Prompt response to the needs of residents.
3. The ability to exercise autonomy and choice.
4. An attractive physical site and a variety in the range of services provided.

More specific suggestions were made regarding staffing. They felt that more staff and more adequately trained staff were necessary to provide sensitive care to residents. Residents felt strongly that they should be part of the training process. Residents also recognized that better motivated staff would require higher pay and career opportunities. This would go a long way to reduce staff turnover, which often creates havoc in residents' lives. Residents were also in favor of strong resident councils that could accept and help resolve complaints. Residents felt that they should be included in various staff committees so that their needs would be voiced and responded to. Most importantly, residents felt that inspection teams should take the time to interview patients in order to find out first-hand how the patients felt about the care they were receiving.

Following the 1983 report, in California, the commission and the advisory committee translated more than 75% of the report's recommendations into a package of legislation that was signed into law in March 1985. This package was known as the Nursing Home Patients Protection Act of 1984 (NHPPA). At the time this legislation was enacted, the Little Hoover Commission pledged it would follow up and monitor the implementation of these reforms. To do this, the commission held two public hearings, one in January 1986, and the other in February 1987. In addition, the commission reconvened its Blue Ribbon Advisory Committee in October 1986 to review the impact of the NHPPA on the quality of care in the state's nursing homes.

The study (Blum, 1987) showed that there had been some improvements in nursing home conditions in California since the passage of NHPPA. For example, the Department of Health Services Licensing and Certification Division had better defined and stepped up its role in surveying and enforcing nursing home conditions and enforcing regulations. In addition, the state had taken positive action to crack down on clearly substandard nursing home facilities through its enforcement efforts.

However, the commission also found that not all of their expectations for reforms had been fulfilled. They therefore issued a report titled *New and Continuing Impediments to Improving the Quality of Care in California Nursing Homes* (Blum, 1987). During the course of the study, the commission analyzed a variety of major issue areas including: enforcement of nursing home regulations; theft and loss in nursing homes; admissions contracts; consumer information services; and the training and monitoring of nursing home personnel. The problems revealed during this review indicated that there were still obstacles in ensuring that the residents of nursing homes, whom the commission referred to as society's "forgotten people," were treated with consideration, respect, and full recognition of their dignity and individuality, in a safe and secure environment.

The specific areas where problems persisted were identified in this 1987 report in a study "Nursing Home Abuse and Neglect," conducted by the Bureau of Medical Fraud Advisory Council (Blum, 1987, pp. 3–4). The Advisory Council was made up of experts in the field of patient abuse and neglect, including law enforcement personnel, prosecutors, and long-term care ombudsman. The problem areas identified were:

1.   Insufficient involvement by local law enforcement.
2.   Lack of training and/or expertise in investigation and prosecution techniques needed in the nursing home environment.
3.   Inappropriate statutory language concerning referral of medically oriented complaints to criminal justice agencies.
4.   Lack of clarity regarding reporting procedures at both the local and state level.
5.   Unavailability of statistical data and other information on the nature and scope of nursing home abuse and neglect.

6. Insufficient screening of nursing-home-employee applicants.
7. Inadequate procedures and safeguards at nursing home facilities to prevent theft from patients.

In light of these continuing barriers to eliminating abuse and regulating nursing homes, the commission's report made a series of new recommendations, including:

1. An urgency statute should be enacted to stop the forced eviction of Medi-Cal residents from facilities that are decertifying from the Medi-Cal program. This legislation should also insure that present private-pay residents who may later convert to Medi-Cal are allowed to remain in the facility.
2. The Board of Examiners of Nursing Home Administrators, and the Board of Registered Nurses should be required to track and monitor the performance of facility administrators and directors of nursing, respectively.
3. The Department of Health Services and the Attorney General's Office should more vigorously pursue the collection of assessments for the violation of nursing home regulations. Training to assist law enforcement and prosecutors working in the area of nursing home offenses should be provided.
4. Legislation should be passed to reduce the period of time that facilities have to contest B citations, which now may take up to 5 years.
5. Nursing homes should be required by statute to work actively and cooperatively with the Department of Health Services, local law enforcement agencies, and concerned consumer groups to develop theft- and loss-prevention programs.
6. Fingerprinting should be required of all nursing home employees who provide care or have access to residents.
7. Changes should be made in the content of nursing home admission agreements, and the latter made available to the public.

8. Procedures should be established to collect statewide data on occurrence of nursing home abuse and neglect, to be published in an annual statistical report. Data derived from complaints reported to various regulatory agencies would be used to identify patterns of crime occurring in long-term care facilities and to assist local agencies in current investigations.

The report led directly to legislation, at this writing pending in the state legislature. This landmark legislation will authorize the Office of the Attorney General and the Bureau of Medi-Cal Fraud (BMCF) to review, investigate and prosecute complaints of abuse and neglect in health-care facilities that receive Medi-Cal payments. Additionally, the Bureau of Medi-Cal Fraud would be authorized to collect data about crimes against certain patients in health-care facilities and to coordinate with local law enforcement agencies to ensure that such crimes are appropriately investigated and prosecuted.

Existing California law does not provide for the collection, analysis, and dissemination of information on a statewide basis about crimes committed against elders and dependent adults, nor about the investigation and prosecution of those crimes. By an analysis of data received from various sources such as ombudsman coordinators, police agencies, licensing agencies, and adult protective services, BMCF would be able to determine whether the criminal justice system has responded appropriately to complaints of abuse of the elderly in nursing homes. It is also hoped that by reviewing the published data, agencies will be stimulated to fulfill their reporting responsibilities.

At present, another study is being launched as a result of the Blue Ribbon Commission's recommendations. The study will look at:

1. The doubling of RN and LPN time.
2. Paperwork and its effect on limited time of professional nursing and medical staff.
3. The effect of DRGs and increased illness of patients being received by LTC facilities.
4. Alternative reimbursement mechanisms.

5. Changes in law enforcement for reporting and prose-
    cution of abuse cases in nursing homes.

This overview of policy response in California clearly indicates that the problems of abuse of the institutionalized aged
are multifaceted. They cannot be solved through the efforts of
the legislature exclusively, and laws that are without the collaboration of individuals, families, community agencies, business
organizations, and law enforcement, remain tokens. There is
the need for an increased role of citizens through their local
community-volunteer agencies to provide their services as well
as to participate in fund-raising efforts that would raise additional monies necessary to provide activities, medications, and
prosthetic equipment not paid for by Medicare, Medi-Cal, or
Medicaid funds.

The feasibility of a joint public effort to attain these goals
in the nursing home is exemplified in a voluntary effort with
which I was associated. The Nursing Home Administration,
the author as Director of Nurses, and the legal department of
the corporation that owned the nursing home met with local
community leaders to set up a non-profit charter for the purpose of fund-raising. A board of directors composed of residents, families, community members, staff, and administrators
was developed. We met once a month to plan fund-raising
events, discuss any problems within the institution, legislation,
and so forth. Problem-solving methods were implemented and
reviewed and communication improved.

A vital ingredient of the project was the involvement of
local community organizations such as the local Rotary Club
and the Chamber of Commerce. Not only were they able to
provide credibility to the group, and lend their experience in
fund-raising, but they also led to the involvement of (nonin-
stitutionalized) seniors (who were members of these organizations) in the project. Because of the heterogeneity of the
group, we were able to make a diverse cross-section of the community aware of the financing mechanisms of nursing homes,
and of the severe limitations on programs and services provided under current funding systems. The volunteer group
provided ongoing review of the conditions of the nursing

home, assuring that the problems were visible, yet not sensationalized.

Through the volunteer effort, and with the assistance of a hospital service league, local churches, preschool groups, and the institution's employees, a wide variety of social programs and personal assistance was made available to residents and their families. Succsss was achieved for an improved environment that benefited residents, families, and the community at large. Furthermore, when funds were low, we knew why, and we were able to raise what we needed. We worked together with the nursing home industry and the state legislature to generate the ways and means necessary to provide quality of care for residents of nursing homes in California, always an ongoing project.

Only when the public is aware of the cost of providing quality care can we be successful in obtaining state and federal monies for this care. When the public becomes aware of the problems faced by the professional staff in nursing homes in their efforts to help residents and families deal with the anger and frustration that follow separation and loss of independence (Seligman, 1975), they realize the need for their emotional support and increased resource allocation.

There is evidence that our efforts to bring to light the problems in nursing homes does bring about fruitful ends, despite the fact that each commission study reports new and continuing problems alike. Can we obtain the support of community organizations? Again, to quote the commission's words, "We cannot legislate love and caring." This can only come from the hearts of the people. Respect of our aged members of society is respect for ourselves.

REFERENCES

Ablan, M. (Ed.). (1986). Bills of interest. *Aging Alert, 2* (Special issue), 1–4.

American Public Welfare Association (APWA) and National Association of State Units on Aging (NASUA). (1986a). *A comprehensive analysis of state policy and practice related to elder abuse: A focus on legislation, appropriations, incidence data and special studies.* Washington, DC: APWA.

American Public Welfare Association (APWA) and National Association of State Units on Aging (NASUA). (1986b). *A comprehensive analysis of state policy and practice related to elder abuse: A focus on roles and activities of state-level agencies, interagency coordination efforts and public education/information campaigns.* Washington, DC: APWA.

American Public Welfare Association (APWA) and National Association of State Units on Aging (NASUA). (1986c). *A comprehensive analysis of state policy and practice related to elder abuse: A focus on state reporting systems.* Washington, DC: NASUA.

Anderson, J., Eddy, M., Fendrick, M., Harvey, A., Kelley, S., Mountain, K., & Strong, K. (1984, November). *A survey of abuse of the elderly in Texas.* Paper presented at the meeting of the Gerontological Society of America, San Antonio, TX. (ERIC Document Reproduction Service No. ED 254787)

Anetzberger, G.J. (1986). *The etiology of elder abuse by adult offspring: An exploratory study.* Unpublished doctoral dissertation, Case Western Reserve University, Cleveland, OH.

Anetzberger, G.J. (1987). *The etiology of elder abuse by adult offspring.* Springfield, IL: Charles C. Thomas.

Attkison, C.C., Hargreaves, W.A., Horowitz, M.J., & Sorensen, J.E. (Eds.). (1978). *Evaluation of human service programs.* New York: Academic Press.

Becker, H. (1963). *The outsiders: Studies in the sociology of deviance.* New York: Free Press.

Bergman, J. (Ed.). (1981). *Abuse of older persons: Report of the first national conference on abuse of older persons.* Boston, MA: Legal Research and Services for the Elderly.

Bergman, J. (1982). *Elder abuse reporting laws: Protection or paternalism?* Unpublished manuscript.

Bergman, J.A. (1984). *Advocacy for the elderly: A practical approach manual.* Fall River, MA: Bristol County Home Care for Elderly, Inc.

Block, M.R., & Sinnott, J.D. (1979). *The battered elder syndrome: An exploratory study.* College Park: University of Maryland, Center on Aging.

Blum, S. (1987). *New and continuing impediments to improving the quality of care in California's nursing homes* State of California Commission on California State Government Organization and Economy Report. Sacramento, CA: Little Hoover Commission.

Blum, S., & Wadleigh, E. (1983). *The bureaucracy of care.* State of California Commission on California State Government Organization and Economy, and The Nursing Home Study Advisory Committee. Sacramento, CA: Little Hoover Commission.

Bookin, D., & Dunkle, R.E. (1985). Elder abuse: Issues for the practitioner. *Social Casework, 66,* 3–12.

Bookin, D., & Dunkle, R.E. (1987). *Exploratory survey of protective service workers in an urban area.* Unpublished manuscript.

Brody, E.M. (1981). "Women in the middle" and family help to older people. *The Gerontologist, 21,* 471–480.

Butler, R.N., & Lewis, M.I. (1976). *Sex after sixty—A guide for men and women for their later years.* New York: Harper & Row.

Callahan, J. (1982). Elder abuse programming: Will it help the elderly? *Urban and Social Change Review, 15,* 15–16.

Callahan, J.J. (1986, November). In R.S. Wolf (Chair), *Elder abuse and public policy: are we on the right track?* Symposium conducted at the meeting of the Gerontological Society of America, Chicago, IL.

Cazenave, N.A. (1981). *Elder abuse and black Americans: Incidence, correlates, treatment and prevention.* Paper presented at the meeting of the National Council on Family Relations, Milwaukee, WI. (ERIC Document Reproduction Service No. ED 217367)

Chance, P. (1987). Attacking elderly abuse. *Psychology Today, 21*(9), 24–25.

Chen, P.N., Bell, S.L., Dolinsky, D.L., Doyle, J., & Dunn, M. (1982). Elderly abuse in domestic settings. *Journal of Gerontological Social Work, 4,* 3–17.

Collins, M., & LaFrance, A.B. (1982). *Improving protective services for older Americans: social worker role.* Portland, ME: Human Services Development Institute, Center for Research and Advanced Study, University of Southern Maine.

Congressional Record. (1985, June 20). *E2926, Daily Editions.* Washington, DC: U.S. Government Printing Office.

Costa, J. (1984). *Abuse of the elderly: A guide of resources and services.* Lexington, MA: Heath.

Cronin, R., & Allen, B. (1982). *The uses of research sponsored by the Administration on Aging (AoA). Case Study No. 5. Maltreatment and abuse of the elderly.* Washington, DC: American Institute for Research in the Behavioral Sciences/Gerontological Research Institute. (ERIC Document Reproduction Service No. ED 226100)

Crouse, J., Cobbs, D., Harris, B., Kopecky, F., & Poertner, J. (1981). *Abuse and neglect of the elderly in Illinois: Incidence and characteristics, legislation and policy recommendations.* Springfield, IL: Illinois Department of Aging.

Crystal, S. (1987). Elder abuse: The latest "crisis." *The Public Interest, 88,* 56–66.

Department of Health and Human Services. (1986). *State of N.H. Welfare Laws, 1985.* Orford, NH: Equity Publishing Corporation.

Department of Health and Rehabilitative Services. (1982). *Adult services program* (HRS Manual). Tallahassee, FL: Author.

Diamond, L.M., & Berman, D.E. (1981). The social/health maintenance organization: A single entry, prepaid, long term care delivery system. In J.J. Callahan, Jr. & S.S. Wallack (Eds.), *Reforming the long term care system* (pp. 185–213). Lexington, MA: Lexington Books, Heath.

Dluhy, M.J. (1987). *Michigan needs assessment of the 60 and over population—1985 statewide survey of needs*. Unpublished manuscript. Lansing, MI: Michigan Office of Services to the Elderly.

Douglass, R. (1979). *A study of neglect and abuse of the elderly in Michigan*. Presented at the annual meting of the Gerontological Society of America, Washington, DC.

Douglass, R. L. (1983). Domestic neglect and abuse of the elderly: Implications for research and service. *Family Relations, 32,* 395–402.

Douglass, R.L., & Hickey, T. (1983). Domestic neglect and abuse of the elderly: Research findings and a systems perspective for service delivery planning. In J.I. Kosberg (Ed.), *Abuse and maltreatment of the elderly: Causes and interventions* (pp. 115–133). Littleton, MA: John Wright PSG.

Douglass, R.L., Hickey, T., & Noel, C. (1980). *A study of maltreatment of the elderly and other vulnerable adults*. Final report to the United States Administration on Aging and the Michigan Department of Social Services, The Institute of Gerontology, The University of Michigan. Ann Arbor: MI: University of Michigan, Institute of Gerontology.

Eggers, J.E. (1985). Elder abuse identified as nursing challenge. *New Jersey Nurse, 15,* 20.

Estes, C.L. (1987, February 26). *Medicare hospital diagnosis related group (DRG) margins*. Testimony before the U.S. House of Representatives, Committee on Ways and Means, Subcommittee on Health. Congressional Record (2/26/87).

Family Research Laboratory. (1986). *Elderly abuse and neglect: Recommendations from the research conference on elder abuse and neglect*. Durham, NH: University of New Hampshire.

Faulkner, L.R. (1982). Mandating the reporting of suspected cases of elder abuse: an inappropriate, ineffective and ageist response to the abuse of older adults. *Family Law Quarterly, 16,* 69–91.

Ferguson, D., & Beck, C. (1983). H.A.L.F.–A tool to assess elder abuse within the family. *Geriatric Nursing, 4,* 301–304.

Finkelhor, D., & Pillemer, K. (1984, August). *Elder abuse: Its relationship to other forms of family violence*. Paper presented at the Second National Conference on Family Violence Research, Durham, NH.

Floyd, J. (1984). Collecting data on abuse of the elderly. *Journal of Gerontological Nursing, 10*(12), 11–15.

Freeman, H.E., & Sherwood, C.C. (1970). *Social research and social policy*. Englewood Cliffs, NJ: Prentice-Hall.

Fulmer, T., & Ashley, J. (1986). Neglect: What part of abuse? *Pride Institute Journal, 5*(4), 18–24.

Fulmer, T., & O'Malley, T. (1987). *Inadequate care of the elderly: A health care perspective on abuse and neglect*. New York: Springer.

Galbraith, M.W. (1984). *Profile of elder abuse of reported cases from the Oklahoma Coalition on Domestic Violence and Sexual Assault*. Unpublished doctoral dissertation, Oklahoma State University, Stillwater, OK.

Galbraith, M.W. (ed.) (1986a). *Elder abuse: Perspectives on an emerging crisis*. Kansas City, MO: Mid-America Congress on Aging.

Galbraith, M.W. (1986b). Elder abuse: An overview. In M.W. Galbraith (Ed.), *Elder abuse: Perspectives on an emerging crisis* (pp. 5–27). Kansas City, MO: Mid-America Congress on Aging.

Galbraith, M.W., & Davison, D. (1985). Stress and elder abuse. *Focus on Learning, 11*(1), 87–92.

Galbraith, M.W., & Zdorkowski, R.T. (1984a). Teaching the investigation of elder abuse. *Journal of Gerontological Nursing, 10*(12), 21–25.

Galbraith, M.W., & Zdorkowski, R.T. (1984b). Heuristic models of elder abuse: Implications for the practitioner. *Lifelong Learning: An Omnibus of Practice and Research, 7*(8), 16–21.

Galbraith, M.W., & Zdorkowski, R.T. (1985). A preliminary model of elder abuse. *Free Inquiry to Creative Sociology, 13*, 10–14.

Galbraith, M.W., & Zdorkowski, R.T. (1986). Systemizing the elder abuse research. In M.W. Galbraith (Ed.), *Elder abuse: Perspectives on an emerging crisis* (pp. 168–176). Kansas City, MO: Mid-America Congress on Aging.

Gelles, R.J., & Cornell, C.P. (1985). *Intimate violence in families*. Beverly Hills, CA: Sage.

Gelles, R.J., & Straus, M.A. (1979). Determinants of violence in the family: Toward a theoretical integration. In W. Burr, R. Hill, F.I. Nye, & I. Reiss (Eds.), *Contemporary theories about the family* (pp. 549–581). New York: Free Press.

Ghent, W.R., DaSylva, N.P., & Farren, M.E. (1985). Family violence: guidelines for recognition and management. *Canadian Medical Association Journal, 132*, 541–553.

Gil, D.G. (1974). *A holistic perspective on child abuse and its prevention*.

Paper presented for the National Institute of Child Health and Human Development, Washington, DC.

Gioglio, G., & Blakemore, P. (1983). *Elder abuse in New Jersey: The knowledge and experience of abuse among older New Jerseyans.* Trenton, NJ: New Jersey Division on Aging.

Giordano, N.H. (1982) Individual and family correlates of elder abuse. Unpublished doctoral dissertation. University of Georgia.

Hammel, E.A. (1984). On the *** of studying household form and function. In R. McNetting, R.R. Wilk, & E.J. Arnould (Eds.), *Households* (pp. 29–43). Berkeley, CA: University of California Press.

Henton, J., Cate, R. & Emery, B. (1984). The dependent elderly: Targets for abuse. In W.H. Quinn & G.A. Hughston (Eds.), *Independent aging: Family and social systems perspectives* (pp. 149–162). Rockville, MD: Aspen Systems Corporation.

Hickey, T., & Douglass, R. (1981a). Mistreatment of the elderly in the domestic setting: An exploratory study. *American Journal of Public Health, 71,* 500–507.

Hickey, T., & Douglass, R.L. (1981b). Neglect and abuse of older family members: Professionals' perspectives and case experiences. *The Gerontologist, 21,* 171–176.

Homans, G.C. (1961). *Social behavior: Its elementary forms.* New York: Harcourt, Brace & World.

Hudson, M.F. (1986). Elder mistreatment: Current research. In K.A. Pillemer & R.S. Wolf (Eds.), *Elder abuse: Conflict in the family* (pp. 125–166). Dover, MA: Auburn House.

Hwalek, M. (1986). *Evaluation of four elder abuse demonstration projects: Year Two final report.* Detroit: SPEC Associates.

Hwalek, M.A., & Sengstock, M.C. (1986). Assessing the probability of abuse of the elderly: Toward development of a clinical screening instrument. *Journal of Applied Gerontology, 5,* 153–173.

Hwalek, M., Sengstock, M.C., & Lawrence, R. (1984, November). *Assessing the probability of abuse of the elderly.* Paper presented at the meeting of the Gerontological Society of America, San Antonio, TX. (ERIC Document Reproduction Service No. ED 257016)

Iris, M.A. (1987). *Final research report: North Suburban Cook County Elder Abuse Project.* Metropolitan Chicago Coalition on Aging.

Janis, I.L., & Mann, L. (1973). *Decision-making: A psychological analysis of conflict, choice, and commitment.* New York: Free Press.

Johnson, T. (1986). Critical issues in the definition of elder mistreatment. In K.A. Pillemer & R.S. Wolf (Eds.), *Elder abuse: Conflict in the family* (pp. 167–196). Dover, MA: Auburn House.

Johnson, T., O'Brien, J., & Hudson, M. (Eds.) (1985). *Elder neglect and abuse: An annotated bibliography*. Westport, CT: Greenwood.

Kapp, M., & Bigot, A. (1985). *Geriatrics and the law*. New York: Springer.

Katz, K. (1980). Elder abuse. *Journal of Family Law, 18*, 695–722.

Katz, S., Branch, L.G., Branson, H.H., Papsidero, J.A., Beck, J.C., & Green, D.S. (1983). Active life expectancy. *The New England Journal of Medicine*, 309, 1218–1223.

Kerness, J. (1984). *Preventing abuse and neglect Vol. II: An analysis of state law and proposed model legislation*. Miami Shores, FL: Barry University School of Social Work.

Kimsey, L.R., Tarbox, A.R., & Bragg, D.F. (1981). Abuse of the elderly: The hidden agenda. I: The caretakers and the categories of abuse. *Journal of the American Geriatrics Society, 29*, 465–472.

Kingdon, J.W. (1984). *Agendas, alternatives, and public policies*. Boston: Little, Brown.

Korbin, J.E., Eckert, J.K., Anetzberger, G.J., Whittemore, E., Mitchell, L., & Vargo, E. (1987). *Elder abuse and child abuse: Commonalities and differences*. Paper presented at the Third National Family Violence Research Conference, Durham, NH.

Kosberg, J. (Ed.). (1983). *Abuse and maltreatment of the elderly: Causes and interventions*. Littleton, MA: John Wright PSG.

Kuhn, T.S. (1970). *The structure of scientific revolutions*. Chicago, IL: University of Chicago Press.

Langley, A. (1981). *Abuse of the elderly* (Human Services Monograph No. 27, pp. 1–29). Washington, DC: U.S. Department of Health and Human Service, Project SHARE.

Lau, E.E., & Kosberg, J.I. (1978, November). *Abuse of the elderly by informal care providers: Practice and research issues*. A paper presented at the annual meeting of the Gerontological Society of America, Dallas, TX.

Lau, E.E., & Kosberg, J. (1979). Abuse of the elderly by informal care providers. *Aging, 299*, 10–15.

May, W.F. (1982, December). Who Cares for the Elderly? *The Hastings Center Report*, pp. 31–37.

McCall, G., & Simmons, J. (1966). *Identities and interactions*. New York: Free Press.

Minuchin, S. (1974). *Families and family therapy*. Cambridge, MA: Harvard University Press.

Newcomer, R., Wood, J., & Sankar, A. (1985). Medicare prospective payment: Anticipated effect on hospitals, other community agencies and families. *Journal of Health Politics, Policy and Law, 10*, 275–282.

Nusberg, C. (1985). Consumer perspective on quality of institutional care in the U.S. *Ageing International, 12*(3), 16–17.

O'Brien, J.G., & Greenblatt, B.A. (1985, November). *Family mediated elder abuse: The role of the primary care physician*. Paper presented at the annual meeting of the Gerontological Society of America, New Orleans, LA.

O'Malley, T.A., Everitt, D.E., O'Malley, H.C., & Campion, W. (1983). Identifying and preventing family-mediated abuse and neglect of elderly persons. *Annals of Internal Medicine, 98*, 998–1005.

O'Malley, T.A., O'Malley, H.C., Everitt, D.E., & Sarson, D. (1984). Categories of family-mediated abuse and neglect of elderly persons. *Journal of the American Geriatrics Society, 32*, 362–369.

O'Malley, H., Segars, H., Perez, R., Mitchell, V., & Knuepfel, G. (1979). *Elder abuse in Massachusetts: A survey of professionals and paraprofessionals*. Boston: Legal Research and Services for the Elderly.

Pedrick-Cornell, C., & Gelles, R.J. (1982). Elder abuse: The status of current knowledge. *Family Relations, 31*, 457–465.

Phillips, L.R. (1983a). Abuse and neglect of the frail elderly at home: An exploration of theoretical relationships. *Journal of Advanced Nursing, 8*, 379–392.

Phillips, L.R. (1983b May/June). Elder abuse-what is it? Who says so? *Geriatric Nursing*, pp. 167–170.

Phillips, L. (1986). Theoretical explanations of elder abuse: Competing hypotheses and unresolved issues. In K.A. Pillemer & R.S. Wolf (Eds.), *Elder abuse: Conflict in the family* (pp. 197–217). Dover, MA: Auburn House.

Phillips, L.R., & Rempusheski, V.F. (1985). Diagnosing and intervening for elder abuse and neglect: An empirically generated decision-making model, *Nursing Research, 34*, 134–139.

Phillips, L.R., & Rempusheski, V.F. (1986a). Caring for the frail elderly at home: Toward a theoretical explanation for the dynamics of poor family caregiving. *Advances in Nursing Science, 8*(4), 62–84.

Phillips, L.R., & Rempusheski, V.F. (1986b). Making decisions about elder abuse. *Social Casework, 67,* 131–140.

Pillemer, K.A. (1985). The dangers of dependency: New findings on domestic violence against the elderly. *Social Problems, 33,* 146–158.

Pillemer, K.A. (1986). Risk factors in elder abuse: Results from a case-control study. In K.A. Pillemer & R.W. Wolf (Eds.), *Elder abuse: Conflict in the family* (pp. 239–263). Dover, MA: Auburn House.

Pillemer, K., & Finkelhor, D. (1986, November). *The prevalence of elder abuse: A random sample survey.* Durham, NH: Family Violence Research Program, University of New Hampshire, Family Research Laboratory (Also, paper presented at the annual meeting of the Gerontological Society of America, Chicago, IL)

Pillemer, K., & Finkelhor, D. (1988). The prevalence of elder abuse: a random sample survey. *The Gerontologist, 28,* 51–57.

Pillemer, K.A. & Wolf, R.S. (Eds.) (1986). *Elder abuse: Conflict in the family.* Dover, MA: Auburn House.

Pynoos, J., Hade-Kaplan, B., & Fleisher, D. (1984). Intergenerational neighborhood networks: a basis for aiding the frail elderly. *The Gerontologist, 24,* 233–237.

Quinn, M.J., & Tomita, S.K. (1986). *Elder abuse and neglect—Causes, diagnoses, and intervention strategies.* New York: Springer.

Rathbone-McCuan, E. (1978). *Intergenerational family violence and neglect: The aged as victims of reaction and reverse neglect.* Paper presented at the International Congress of Gerontology, Tokyo, Japan.

Rathbone-McCuan, E. (1980). Elderly victims of family violence and neglect. *Social Casework, 61,* 296–304.

Rathbone-McCuan, E., Travis, A., & Voyles, B. (1983). Family intervention: applying the task-centered approach. In J.I. Kosberg (Ed.), *Abuse and maltreatment of the elderly* (pp. 355–375). Littleton, MA: John Wright PSG Inc.

Regan, J. (1981). Protecting the elderly: the new paternalism. *The Hastings Law Journal, 32,* 1111–1132.

Regan, J.J. (July, 1985). *The discovery of elder abuse: Learning to live in the brave new world of mandatory reporting, protective service and public guardianship.* Paper presented at the Elder Abuse Prevention and Intervention Policy: A Working Conference, Chicago, IL.

Reiter, E. (1987, January). *Missouri's computerized response to elder abuse.*

Paper presented at the National Conference on Elder Abuse, Washington, DC.

Rudner, R.S. (1966). *Philosophy of social science*. Englewood Cliffs, NJ: Prentice-Hall.

Salend, E., Kane, R., Satz, M., & Pynoos, J. (1984). Elder abuse reporting: limitations of statutes. *The Gerontologist, 24*, 61–69.

Seligman, M.E.P. (1975). *Helplessness*. San Francisco: Freeman.

Sengstock, M., Hwalek, M., & Moshier, S. (1986). A comprehensive index for assessing abuse and neglect of the elderly. In M.W. Galbraith (Ed.), *Elder abuse: Perspectives on an emerging crisis* (pp. 41–64). Kansas City, MO: Mid-America Congress on Aging.

Sengstock, M.C., & Liang, J. (1982). *Identifying and characterizing elder abuse*. Detroit, MI: Wayne State University, Institute of Gerontology. (ERIC Document Reproduction Service No. ED 217368)

Silverstein, N.M. (1984). Informing the elderly about public services: The relationship between source of knowledge and service utilization. *The Gerontologist, 24*, 37–40.

Stark, E., & Flitcraft, A. (1983). Social knowledge, social policy, and the abuse of women: The case against patriarchal benevolence. In D. Finkelhor, R. J. Gelles, G.T. Hotaling, & M.A. Straus (Eds.), *The dark side of families: Current family violence research* (pp. 330–348). Beverly Hills, CA: Sage.

Starvation case spurs effort for neglect law. (1985, August 23). *Austin American-Statesman*, p. A14.

Steinmetz, S. (1978). Battered parents. *Society, 15*(5), 54–55.

Steinmetz, S. (1981). Elder abuse. *Aging*, Jan.–Feb., *315–316*, 6–10.

Steinmetz, S. (1983). Dependency, stress and violence between middle-aged caregivers and their elderly parents. In J. Kosberg (Ed.), *Abuse and maltreatment of the elderly: Causes and interventions* (pp. 134–149). Boston, MA: Wright.

Steinmetz, S.K., & Amsden, D.J. (1983). Dependent elders, family stress, and abuse. In T.H. Brubaker (Ed.), *Family relationships in later life* (pp. 173–192). Beverly Hills: Sage.

Straus, M.A., Gelles, R.J., & Steinmetz, S.K. (1980). *Behind closed doors: Violence in the American family*. Garden City, NY: Anchor.

Tamme, P. (1985). Abuse of the adult client in home care. *Family and Community Health, 8*, 54–65.

Thobaben, M., & Anderson, L. (1985). Reporting elder abuse: It's the law. *The American Journal of Nursing, 85*, 371–374.

Traxler, A. (1986). Elder abuse laws: A survey of state statutes. In M.W. Galbraith (Ed.), *Elder abuse: Perspectives on an emerging crisis* (pp. 139–167). Kansas City, MO: Mid-America Congress on Aging.

U.S. Bureau of the Census. (1980a). *Census of the population. Chapter C: General social and economic characteristics. Part 45: Texas.* Washington, DC: U.S. Government Printing Office.

U.S. Bureau of the Census. (1980b). *Current population report* (Series 25, Number 930 [Florida]). Washington, DC: U.S. Government Printing Office.

U.S. Department of Health, Education and Welfare. (1974). *An annotated bibliography: Violence at home.* Washington, DC: Author.

U.S. Department of Health and Human Services (1980) USDHEW *Publication OHDS 79-3021,* pp. 47–48. Washington DC: USDHEW

U.S. House of Representatives, Select Committee on Aging. (1979). *Elder abuse: The hidden problem.* Hearing held June 23, in Boston, MA.

U.S. House of Representatives, Select Committee on Aging. (1980). *Elder abuse* (Report No. 96-261). Joint hearing before the Senate Special Committee on Aging and House Select Committee on Aging. Second Session, 96th Congress, June 11. (ERIC Document Reproduction Service No. ED 204663)

U.S. House of Representatives, Select Committee on Aging. (1981a). *Abuse of older persons* (Comm. Pub. No. 97-289). Hearing before the Subcommittee on Human Services of the Select Committee on Aging, First Session, 97th Congress, March 23.

U.S. House of Representatives, Select Committee on Aging. (1981b). *Elder abuse: An examination of a hidden problem* (Comm. Pub. No. 97-277). A report by the Select Committee on Aging, First Session, 97th Congress, April 3. (ERIC Document Reproduction Service No. ED 190979)

U.S. House of Representatives, Select Committee on Aging. (1981c). *Physical and financial abuse of the elderly.* Hearing before the Subcommittee on Retirement Income and Employment (ERIC document Reproduction Service No. ED 216295)

U.S. House of Representatives, Select Committee on Aging. (1985a). *Elder abuse: A national disgrace* (Comm. Pub. No. 99-502). A report of the Subcommittee on Health and Long Term Care of the Select Committee on Aging, First Session, 99th Congress, May 10. Washington, DC: U.S. Government Printing Office.

U.S. House of Representatives, Select Committee on Aging. (1985b). *The rights of America's institutionalized aged: Lost in confinement* (Comm. Pub. No. 99-543). Hearing before the Subcommittee on Health and Long Term Care of the Select Committee on Aging, First Session, 99th Congress, September 18.

Vargo, J. (1985a, August 22). Austin starvation case brings call to tighten elderly abuse law. *Austin American-Statesman*, p. B2.

Vargo, J. (1985b, October 22). Study set on abuse of elderly. *Austin American-Statesman*, p. B1.

Villmoare, E., & Bergman, J. (Eds.). (1981). *Elder abuse and neglect: A guide for practitioners and policy makers.* Appendix to U.S. House of Representatives Select Committee on Aging (1981c) *Physical and financial abuse of the elderly.* San Francisco, CA: U.S. Printing Office. (Also published by the Oregon Office of Elderly Affairs)

Walker, J.C. (1983). Protective services for the elderly: Connecticut's experience. In J.I. Kosberg (Ed.), *Abuse and maltreatment of the elderly: Causes and Interventions* (pp. 292–301). Littleton, MA: John Wright PSG.

Wardell, L., Gillespie, D.L., & Leffler, A. (1983). Science and violence against wives. In D. Finkelhor, R.J. Gelles, G.T. Hotaling, & M.A. Straus (Eds.), *The dark side of families: Current family violence research* (pp. 69–84). Beverly Hills, CA: Sage.

Wilcox, D. (1983). Abuse of the elderly and children–The physician's role in detection and prevention. *Texas Medicine, 79,* 74.

Wolf, R.S. (1986). Major findings from three model projects on elderly abuse. In K. Pillemer & R. Wolf (Eds.), *Elder abuse: Conflict in the family* (pp. 218–234). Dover, MA: Auburn House.

Wolf, R.S., Godkin, M.K., & Pillemer, K.A. (1984). *Elder abuse and neglect: Final report from three model projects and Appendixes 1 and 2.* Worcester: University of Massachusetts, Medical Center and University Center on Aging. (ERIC Document Reproduction Service No. ED 254796)

Wolf, R.S., & Pillemer, K.A. (1984). *Working with abused elders: Assessment, advocacy, and intervention.* Worcester, MA: University of Massachusetts Medical Center.

Zawadski, R.T., & Ansak, M. (1983). Consolidating community-based long term care: early returns from the On Lok demonstration. *The Gerontologist, 23*, 364–369.

Zdorkowski, R.T. & Galbraith, M.W. (1985). An inductive approach to the investigation of elder abuse. *Ageing and Society, 5*, 413–429.

INDEX